教育部首批国家级职业教育教师教学创新团队电子商务专业领域实践课题
（跨境电子商务核心课程新形态教材和教学资源建设，项目编号：SJ2020110102）建设成果

国家级“跨境电子商务综合服务应用技术协同创新中心”建设成果

浙江金融职业学院电子商务与新消费研究院建设成果

中国特色高水平高职专业群（国际贸易实务）建设成果

浙江金融职业学院课程思政领航专业建设成果

新编21世纪高等职业教育精品教材·电子商务类

跨境电商客服（双语）

主　编　张　敏　茹　宝

副主编　杨　莹　刘东光　秦诗雨
　　　　卓佳妮　吕方伊

中国人民大学出版社
·北京·

首批国家级职业教育跨境电子商务教师教学创新团队
跨境电子商务系列新形态教材建设委员会

顾　问：陆春阳　全国电子商务职业教育教学指导委员会副主任

张　红　浙江经贸职业技术学院副校长

主　任：郑亚莉　浙江金融职业学院校长

副主任：戴小红　首批国家级职业教育电子商务专业（跨境电子商务方向）教师教学创新团队负责人

章安平　中国特色高水平高职专业群（国际贸易实务）负责人

委　员（按汉语拼音排序）：

陈越波	韩　斌	韩梦凡*	韩香馨*	侯维田*	胡张胜
黄　萍	黄一奇*	蒋想想*	来　昊*	吕　希	马天有
牟群月	倪华芬*	史　浩	王枞桎*	王　舵	王恩江*
王　婧	王晴岚	王　琼	王　薇*	韦昌鑫	肖　旭
徐雪鹏	易成林*	占星星*	张　帆	张　敏	周蜀成*

注：带*者为行业企业专家。

前言
Preface

中国共产党二十大报告要求加快发展数字经济，促进数字经济和实体经济深度融合，同时还要努力培养一流高技能人才。数字经济时代的跨境电商新业态强势突起，已然成为我国传统外贸企业竞争能力扩展和运营模式转换的重要途径。跨境电商行业对人才的综合性需求较强，人才缺口较大。其中，跨境电商客服岗位的从业人员必须具备扎实的英语语言基础和较强的跨文化沟通能力，同时通晓跨境电商售前、售中、售后环节的相关技能和知识，成为对外连接客户、对内协调运营和物流的枢纽。基于此，我们结合多年与多家跨境电商企业合作的经验以及扎实的实地调研，组织优秀的一线教师和行业专家共同编写了本书，让学习者习得跨境电商客服技能和知识的同时，提高英语语言能力和跨文化沟通能力，为高效率培养跨境电商优质客服人员服务。

本书的主要特色有：

1. 中英双语编写填补国内空白

以“基于内容的教学”（Content-Based Instruction）理论为依据，教材使用汉语和英语两种语言编写，开国内同类教材的先河。中英双语一方面有利于学习者在学习跨境电商客服技能和知识的同时，大量接触英语语言，使英语语言水平也同步提升；另一方面有利于本教材的国际化推广，让在中国学习的留学生和国外合作院校的学生更轻松地习得教材的内容。

2. 思政元素高度凝练、自然融入

积极响应国家“三全”育人的号召，结合跨境电商客服岗位特点，深入挖掘教材应有的思政元素，凝练为“坚忍力、共情力、合作力、辨析力”，并设计微视频、微案例、微游戏、微辩论等思政课堂载体，使课程思政的可操作性大大增强。本书构建了完整的课程思政实施框架，在教学中实现德行修养和专业技能齐头并进的目标。在课程的微观系统内，最大可能地实现全员育人、全程育人、全方位育人。

3. 双元主编确保内容新颖实用

本书采用的是专任教师和行业专家双元主编模式，专任教师了解中国学生的学习习惯、规律和需求，具有很强的理论总结能力和教学设计能力。行业专家保证教材选取案

例、相关技能和语料的新颖、实用和地道。双元编者通过研讨会、企业挂职锻炼、共同授课等形式，扬长避短，使本教材的质量最优化。

4. 活页装订凸显立体化新形态

教材的五个项目灵活封装，具有可拆解、可组合的特点，有利于教师根据学情和工作过程，随时重组教学内容和结构，开展模块化、项目化教学。教材的数字资源与相对应课程的在线开放平台一体化，课件、微视频等富媒体资源拓展了教材维度，实现课程与教材的“互联网＋”互动，助力学习者实现线上线下混合式学习，也有助于使用教材的老师进行课程建设。

本书适用于高职高专的商务英语专业、跨境电商专业、国际经济与贸易专业学生使用，也可供留学生作为教材使用。同时，本书也适用于对外贸易、跨境电商等在职人员业务培训或自学使用。本书由浙江金融职业学院张敏、杭州司腾网络技术有限公司茹宝担任主编，浙江金融职业学院刘东光、秦诗雨、卓佳妮、吕方伊，浙江大田国际货运有限公司总经理杨莹担任副主编，杭州衣来科技有限公司倪卫青、杭州嘉珩电子商务有限公司总经理殷超群，也对本书的编写提供了宝贵建议和资料。在编写过程中，编者参阅了大量资料及网络信息，有的资料无法找到原作者，未能一一列出，在此一并表示诚挚的谢意。

本书的编写力求严谨、科学，但书中难免有不尽如人意之处，恳请专家同行和读者惠予批评和指正。

主编

2022 年 6 月

目 录

Contents

导　论

知识目标

1. 掌握跨境电商客服的定义、特点和作用；
2. 熟悉跨境电商客服的工作流程、沟通技巧和岗位要求；
3. 了解课程的学习目标和内容。

能力目标

1. 能说出跨境电商客服的特点和作用；
2. 能说出跨境电商客服的基本工作流程。

素质目标

认识跨境电商客服的四大核心能力。

知识点索引

- 导论
  - 一、跨境电商客服理论描述
    - （一）跨境电商客服的定义
    - （二）跨境电商客服的特点
      - 1.服务两大客户群体
      - 2.注重人本化服务
      - 3.参与企业的整体运营
    - （三）跨境电商客服的作用
      - 1.开发潜在客户
      - 2.提升购物体验
      - 3.挖掘流量效益
      - 4.聚拢忠实粉丝
      - 5.获得平台推荐
      - 6.避免交易纠纷
  - 二、跨境电商客服实操认知
    - （一）跨境电商客服的工作流程
    - （二）跨境电商客服的沟通技巧
      - 1.建立客户档案
      - 2.学会倾听
      - 3.书面沟通
      - 4.建立常用表达和禁忌表达表
    - （三）跨境电商客服的岗位要求
  - 三、跨境电商客服课程总论
    - （一）课程学习成效
      - 1.具备岗位业务能力
      - 2.提升跨文化沟通能力
      - 3.强化学习能力
      - 4.提升文化素养
    - （二）课程学习内容
    - （三）课程学习活动
    - （四）课程考核方法

一、跨境电商客服理论描述

跨境电商是新近发展起来的新兴业态，跨境电商客服也是一个崭新的领域。它在原有客户服务理论的基础上融合了更多技术手段，并在更加复杂的跨文化、多语种的背景下不断探索。

（一）跨境电商客服的定义

跨境电商客服是指跨境电商企业为客户所做的任何能够增强客户体验的事情，具体是指通过网络技术，解答咨询、处理订单、解决售后问题等服务。顾客满意是客服要达到的根本目标。

（二）跨境电商客服的特点

对于跨境电商客服的理解，有人认为与淘宝客服的岗位职责大同小异，也有人说这个岗位就是导购。这些岗位与跨境电商客服有哪些区别呢？

● 跨境电商客服与淘宝客服

两者虽然都是服务客户，但是淘宝客服的服务对象更多是中国人，双方思维模式类似，易于沟通。而跨境电商客服服务对象是全球客户，不仅沟通语言是非母语，而且与客户在思维模式、价值观以及宗教信仰方面存在着巨大差异。

● 跨境电商客服与实体店导购

除了服务对象和语言，差别还体现在以下两方面：首先，从沟通媒介方面，导购多是面对面交流，用实物展示；而跨境电商客服必须借助网上即时通信软件和邮件，通过文字、图片、视频等形式与客户交流。其次，在工作内容上，导购主要负责迎客与推销产品，其他环节基本不涉及；而跨境电商客服会参与交易的全过程，包括售前、售中和售后。

从以上比较可以看出，与电子商务行业和传统外贸行业的客户服务相比，跨境电商客服有其自身的特点，具体表现在以下几个方面：

1. 服务两大客户群体

跨境电商客服商务沟通对象有两类人群：境外批发商和境外终端消费者。与批发商的交易属于企业与企业之间的贸易（Business to Business，B2B）；与终端消费者的交易属于企业与消费者之间的贸易（Business to Customer，B2C）。

2. 注重人本化服务

跨境电商客服的服务质量直接影响顾客的购物体验，进而影响顾客忠诚度及店铺形象等。因此，客户服务强调以人为本，以满足客户需求为最高宗旨。因此，客服专员要能够与各种状态下的客户沟通，特别是处于愤怒、烦躁、失望、沮丧等消极情绪中的客户。因此，共情、合作、坚韧是客服专员必备的素质。此外，跨境电商客服人员还要了解相关市场的政治经济、文化习俗、宗教信仰、消费偏好等，并能以英语为中介驾驭多种语言，以完成与客户高质量的沟通。

3. 参与企业的整体运营

作为直接和客户交流的岗位，跨境电商客服是店铺形象的主要塑造者。客户的要求需要客服专员及时与企业相关部门，如财务、物流、仓储、网店的美工、文案、选品、营销等沟通，从而促进整个企业的有序运行。

（三）跨境电商客服的作用

跨境电商客服是跨境电商企业的直接对外窗口，对企业的生存和发展起着重要作用。

优质的客服是最经济有效的营销手段之一，对于产品的销售、网店的推广、客户的维护等方面均有较大的促进作用。具体体现在：

1. 开发潜在客户

跨境电商客服通过多种渠道，包括展会网站、黄页、即时通信工具、社交网站等，收集国外潜在客户资源，撰写符合客户文化背景和特点的开发信，拓展客户资源。

2. 提升购物体验

良好的购物体验来自优秀的产品质量和完美的客户服务。提升购物体验不仅有助于增加产品的销量，还可以在买家心中树立良好的店铺形象。

3. 挖掘流量效益

流量是网店的生命之源。在商业竞争日趋激烈的今天，每一个流量都有较高的引流成本。网店不仅需要利用优质客服来增加订单成交的概率，而且还需要使买家重复购买，并将店铺宣传出去，尽可能使每一个流量都产生额外的效益。

4. 聚拢忠实粉丝

优秀的客服能为网店培养一批忠实的粉丝，也就是熟客或老客户。当客服的服务细致贴心，产品也令人满意，买家为了节省搜索时间和规避购物风险，一般不会轻易更换店铺。

5. 获得平台推荐

网购平台会根据买家对店铺评分，计算搜索排名，确定参加平台相关推荐活动的资质。优质的客服可以保证店铺服务类评分达到或者超过同行业平均值。

6. 避免交易纠纷

客服对市场、产品熟悉，做精准推荐，能有效地控制退换货、退款，尽量避免交易纠纷；熟悉平台交易规则，就能正确处理买家投诉，大大降低店铺遭受平台处罚的风险。

二、跨境电商客服实操认知

（一）跨境电商客服的工作流程

跨境电商客服工作与网购交易的大部分流程同步，按照交易的完成度，可以依次划分为售前、售中和售后三个阶段。售前与售中的阶段节点为订单付款，售中与售后的阶段节点为买家签收包裹。具体来说，工作任务包括：收集潜在客户资源，发送客户开发信，处理客户询盘，解答咨询处理订单，处理差评、纠纷、投诉，维护客户信息库，维护客户关系等。

（二）跨境电商客服的沟通技巧

1. 建立客户档案

更深入地了解客户的方法是建立客户档案，即收集客户信息，建立历时性客户数据库，以了解当前、潜在和失效的客户。建立客户档案能更好地服务于客户群体。

2. 学会倾听

倾听客户的意见就是向他们表明你关心并理解他们的问题和顾虑。做一个好的倾听者并不容易；提高你的听力技巧需要练习和奉献精神。

3. 书面沟通

跨境电商客服工作以书面形式为主要沟通方式，尽量避免与境外客户进行语音对话。因为书面形式沟通，不仅能使双方的交流更加清晰、准确，也能够留下交流的证据，有利于后期纠纷处理。

4. 建立常用表达和禁忌表达表（见表0-1）

表0-1 常用表达和禁忌表达表

常用表达	禁忌表达
请	不能
是的	绝不
……可以吗？	不
考虑到……	你必须……
我们协商一下……	难道不能……？
谢谢	我们没有规定……
我们	……不是我的职责
感激	脏话
你愿意……	我们会试着做……
机会	我还没有时间……
遗憾	我不知道……

（三）跨境电商客服的岗位要求

作为一名跨境电商客服人员，需要满足以下要求：

熟悉公司的产品业务；

熟悉主营跨境电商平台的规则、订单处理流程、相关即时通信工具和常用翻译软件；

了解目标市场客户的文化背景，具备跨文化沟通的能力；

能够为B类客户和C类客户解决售前、售中和售后的各种问题并提供服务。

三、跨境电商客服课程总论

（一）课程学习成效

学完本课程，学习者将达成以下目标：

1. 具备岗位业务能力

能够利用搜索引擎、社交网站、展会网站等寻找潜在的海外客户；

能够结合具体的平台，完成业务操作。

2. 提升跨文化沟通能力

能够针对某一国家或地区的文化背景，撰写营销邮件；

能够通过客户询盘，分析客户购买意向及交际风格，并给出有效回复；

能够积极引导客户达成交易；

能够妥善解决售后问题。

3. 强化学习能力

能够在实践中提出问题；

能够在集体智慧中激发信心、获取思路、修正方向。

4. 提升文化素养

具有文化自信与自觉；

理解、尊重多元文化；

具备团队沟通协作能力。

（二）课程学习内容

本课程包括六个部分：导论和五个项目，五个项目即跨境电商客服工作准备、跨境电商售前客服、跨境电商售中客服、跨境电商售后客服及跨境电商客服技巧进阶。

导论部分首先从理论上介绍跨境电商客服工作的定义、特点及对整个跨境电商企业运营的作用；其次明确在工作实践中跨境电商岗位的工作流程、沟通技巧及岗位要求；再次介绍跨境电商课程学习能达到的目标、学习内容、方法及考核方式；最后阐述课程培养的四大核心素养：共情力、坚忍力、合作力和辨析力。

项目一为跨境电商客服工作准备。主要介绍即时通信工具的应用、电子邮件的撰写、以英语为中介的常用翻译软件的使用技巧以及跨境电商工作中其他通信工具的使用方法等。另外还包括主要市场的介绍，如美国、欧洲、拉丁美洲、非洲等市场的经济、文化、习俗、消费偏好等。这些内容有利于学习者认识并跨越文化的差异，在客户服务中建立高质量的沟通，让客户获得良好的购物体验。

项目二为跨境电商售前客服。该部分介绍了利用搜索引擎、展会网站、黄页、Facebook 等社交媒体寻找客户资源的方法，还探讨了如何通过设计新颖的标题、展开条理清晰的表达来撰写开发信。此外，此部分提供了基于售前客服典型问题的开发信模板，有助于学习者快速完成高质量的邮件。

项目三为跨境电商售中客服。该部分主要涉及订单处理，客户下单未付款时如何催款、完成订单，以及客户付款后如何同步出单产品的库存信息、跟踪物流信息，做好异常包裹处理及关联产品推介。

项目四为跨境电商售后客服。该部分主要包括如何对客户收到货物后出现的各种问题及时做出响应。具体包括如何运用平台售后规则处理纠纷，并介绍了如何提升店铺的留评率，如何修改评价，如何进行客户维护。

项目五为跨境电商客服技巧进阶。该部分主要针对跨境电商客服能力的进一步提升展开，重点培养客服的职业素养、较强的持续学习能力，并初步具备一定的创新及管理意识。

（三）课程学习活动

针对每一个项目，课程提供一个具体的场景，设定一个具体的项目任务。对于这项工作任务，老师会用问题的形式启发学习者逐步将任务分解，从而厘清解决问题的具体步骤。接下来，学习者将组建学习小组，探究讨论、分工合作，尝试解决问题。在此过程中，学习者可能需要到图书馆或网上查阅相关资料，可能需要利用课余时间走访调研，也可能需要和小组同学一起组成工作坊模拟演练，甚至需要与老师探讨或咨询行业专家。总之，经过大家的共同努力，学习成果以小组为单位按时在线上或线下提交。之后，教师会引导大家梳理解决相关任务的知识要点，并通过习题测验强化知识巩固。最后，凭借所学习的知识和技能，学习者就可以在能力实训活动中一试身手了。

（四）课程考核方法

本课程的考核包括过程性评价和终结性评价两部分。终结性评价以期末笔试成绩为主要参考指标，着重考查学习者对知识的理解和掌握，以及对于工作意义的理解。过程性评价包括学习态度评价、平台作业成绩、书面作业成绩、能力实训活动评价等。其中，能力实训活动评价会由多方进行评定，比如学习者本人、学习同伴、其他同学、专业教师、行业教师、相关社会人士等。学习者能从这些反馈中更加全面准确地认识自己，并在此基础上不断前进。

本课程的学习，除了要训练跨境电商客服岗位所需的知识和能力外，还要培养以下四大核心素养：共情力、坚忍力、合作力和辨析力。

共情力。在经济合作与发展组织（OECD）的“教育 2030：未来的教育与技能”项目中，共情力作为“学习框架 2030”中的核心价值观被提出。共情力被认为是个体尊重他人和参与社会事务的重要因素。在跨境电商客服人员岗位上，共情力也是一项核心职业能力，是与客户高质量沟通的基础。跨境电商客服人员主要是根据客户需求推荐产品，并针对客户付款后出现的物流、产品质量等问题与客户进行积极的沟通，因此需要理解和认同客户的境遇及困难，并积极给予帮助。特别是在面对处于消极情绪，如愤怒、急躁、不耐烦、沮丧、失望等情绪中的客户，客服专员应能够使客户尽快平静下来，并积极配合后续工作，快速解决问题，因此共情力是高质量客服工作的基石。在本教材中，共情力将在跨境电商客服工作准备中详细阐述，并在跨境电商售中客服和售后客服部分集中体现。

坚忍力。坚忍力由习近平总书记在 2021 年中青年干部培训班开班式上提出，指顶住压力、克服困难、勇敢前进的勇气和信心，它也是客服专员的核心职业能力之一。在 B2B 商业模式中，利用撰写开发信、黄页、社交媒体等渠道开发新客户是客服专员的业务范围。在此过程中，对于那些石沉大海的邮件或客户的冷言冷语，客服专员需要有极大的忍耐力和顽强的进取心。在售中客服中，客服专员同样需要有极大的坚忍力去面对愤怒与焦虑的客户及复杂棘手的问题。在本教材中，坚忍力主要体现在跨境电商售前客服和售中客服部分内容中。

合作力。习近平总书记在 2018 年出席二十国集团（G20）领导人峰会的重要讲话中提出了携手合作、互利共赢的伙伴精神。合作力是客服专员核心职业能力之一，客服岗位是客户和商家沟通的纽带，客户需求的满足需要客服专员与企业的其他职能部门如产品技术支持、物流、财务、新产品开发、运营等及时衔接沟通。只有通过与这些部门的有效合作才能解决客户的问题，提升客户的购物体验。在本教材中，合作力主要体现在跨境电商售后客服部分和跨境电商客服技巧进阶部分。

辨析力。辨析力主要是指风险识别能力和防范化解各种风险的能力。在工作中，客服专员会收到各种各样的询盘，如果不能准确辨析其真伪，将面临商业机密泄露的风险。对于新老客户的订单，客服专员应敏锐地辨析其购买意图及喜好，为二次营销及客户关系维护奠定基础。辨析力在本教材中主要体现在跨境电商售前客服和跨境电商客服技巧进阶部分的内容中。

本教材以微案例、微故事、微问卷、微辩论为载体，将以上四个思政元素与五个项目的教学内容融合，前者旨在德行修养塑造，后者着眼于专业技能培养，两者并行发力，在知识维度、能力维度和素质维度都获得了良好的教学成效，能最终实现学习者的德技并修。具体如图 0－1 所示：

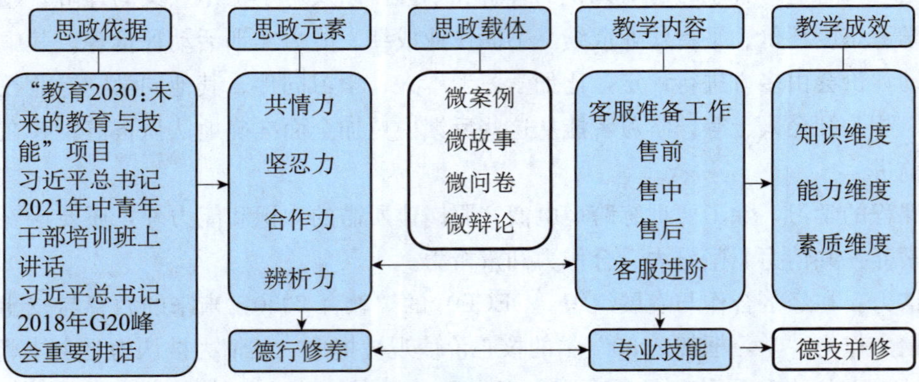

图 0－1 《跨境电商客服》课程思政实施设计图

思考题

1. 根据对跨境电商客服工作内容的了解，谈谈你对跨境电商客服工作意义的理解。

2. 2～3 人一组，回忆最让你气愤的一次与客服沟通的经历，分析你为什么会生气，对方是怎么处理的。结合导论所介绍的跨境电商客服的沟通技巧，说说如果你是客服，你会怎么做。

参考答案

Introduction

Knowledge Objectives

1. To understand the definition, characteristics and functions of customer service in cross-border e-commerce (abbreviated as CBEC in the following text);

2. To be familiar with the workflow, communication skills and job requirements of CBEC customer service;

3. To understand the objectives and contents of the course.

Competency Objectives

1. Be able to articulate the characteristics and functions of customer service in CBEC;

2. Be able to describe the basic workflow of CBEC customer service.

Quality Objectives

To recognize the four core qualities of CBEC customer service.

Key Points Index

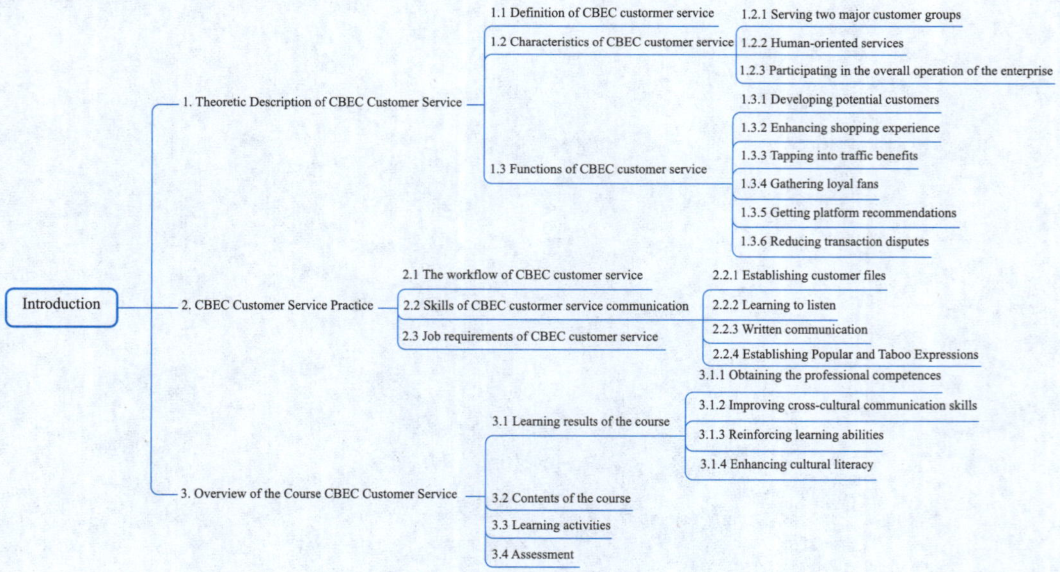

1. Theoretic Description of CBEC Customer Service

CBEC is a newly emerging industry, and CBEC customer service is also a brand-new field. It incorporates more technological tools based on the original customer service theory and continues to be explored in a more complex cross-cultural and multilingual context.

1.1 Definition of CBEC customer service

CBEC customer service refers to anything that CBEC firms do for their customers to enhance customer experience. Specifically, it refers to services such as answering inquiries, processing orders, and resolving after-sales issues through online technology. Customer satisfaction is the fundamental goal of customer service.

1.2 Characteristics of CBEC customer service

Speaking of CBEC customer service specialists, some people think it's not unlike Taobao customer service personnel; some people compare them to the salesmen or saleswomen in physical shops. What are the differences of these positions from CBEC customer service specialists?

- CBEC customer service specialists Vs Taobao customer service specialists

Although they also aim to serve customers, Taobao is mainly for Chinese people, so it is easier to communicate with each other since they share the similar mindset. In contrast, CBEC customer service personnel have to face global customers. Thus, not only should they communicate in non-native languages, but they also have to cope with vast difference in terms of thinking patterns, values, and religions and beliefs.

- CBEC customer service personnel and salespeople in physical stores

In addition to the target customers and working languages, the differences also lie in the following two aspects: the first is communication medium. Salesmen mostly talk face-to-face by means of physical displays; while CBEC customer service personnel have to communicate with customers through texts, images and videos with the help of instant messaging tools and emails. The second difference lies in duties of the position. Salespeople in a physical store are only in charge of welcoming customers and marketing products. However, CBEC customer service will be involved in the whole process of a transaction, including pre-sales, in-sales and after-sales.

From the above comparison, it can be seen that, compared with the traditional foreign trade industry, CBEC customer service has its own characteristics, specifically in the following aspects:

1.2.1 Serving two major customer groups

CBEC customer service personnel serve two types of people: overseas wholesalers and overseas end consumers. Transactions with wholesalers are business-to-business (B2B), while transactions with end consumers are business-to-consumer (B2C).

1.2.2 Human-oriented services

The quality of CBEC customer service directly affects the shopping experience of customers, which in turn influences customer loyalty and the store image. Therefore, customer service is human-oriented, and satisfying customers' needs is the ultimate mission.

Therefore, customer service specialists should be able to serve customers especially in such negative moods as anger, irritation, disappointment and frustration. Therefore, empathy, cooperation and resilience are essential qualities for customer service specialists. In addition, CBEC customer service specialists must understand the politics, economy, culture, customs, religions, beliefs, and consumer preferences of the relevant markets, and be able to apply multiple languages facilitated by English to complete high-quality communication with customers.

1.2.3 Participating in the overall operation of the enterprise

As a position that communicates directly with customers, CBEC customer service is the main shaper of the store's image. Customer satisfaction is achieved by customer service specialists cooperating timely with other relevant departments of the enterprise, such as finance, logistics, warehousing, online store's artwork, copywriting, product selection, marketing, etc. Therefore, it facilitates the orderly operation of the entire enterprise.

1.3 Functions of CBEC customer service

CBEC customer service is a window of the enterprises, and plays an important role in the survival and development of enterprises. Quality customer service is one of the most cost-effective marketing tools for product sales, online store promotion, customer maintenance and other aspects. Details are as follows:

1.3.1 Developing potential customers

CBEC customer service obtains foreign potential customer resources through various channels, such as exhibition websites, yellow pages, instant messaging tools, social networking sites, etc., and then writes development letters that match the cultural background and characteristics of customers to expand business relations.

1.3.2 Enhancing shopping experience

A good shopping experience comes from excellent product quality and perfect customer service. Improving the shopping experience is not only helpful to increase the sales of products, but it also contributes the establishment of a good store image.

1.3.3 Tapping into traffic benefits

Traffic is the source of life of an online store. In today's increasingly competitive business world, every traffic costs more than before. Online stores need quality customer service to increase closed orders, and it's also needed to guide buyers to repeat purchases and advertise the store so that every bit of traffic generates additional benefits whenever possible.

1.3.4 Gathering loyal fans

Excellent customer service personnel can cultivate a group of loyal fans and regular customers for online stores. If customer service specialists are considerate and attentive, and the products are satisfactory, buyers will stick to the stores in order to reduce searching time and avoid shopping risks.

1.3.5 Getting platform recommendations

The online shopping platform will calculate the search ranking based on the buyer's rating of the store and determine the qualification to participate in the relevant recommended activities of the platform. Quality customer service will ensure that the store's service scores meet or exceed the industry average.

1.3.6 Reducing transaction disputes

If customer service personnel are familiar enough with the relevant markets and products to make accurate recommendations for consumers, returns, exchanges and refunds can be reduced. Being familiar with the platform trading rules, customer service personnel are able to cope with buyer complaints legitimately, thus greatly reducing the risk of store suffering from platform penalties.

2. CBEC Customer Service Practice

2.1 The workflow of CBEC customer service

CBEC customer service routine is similar to the processes of online shopping transactions, including three stages: pre-sales, in-sales and after-sales. Pre-sales and in-sales are divided by the time of order payment, and in-sale and after-sale by buyer receiving the package. Specifically, the work tasks include collecting potential customer data, sending customer development letters, handling customer inquiries, processing orders, handling bad reviews, disputes and complaints, managing customer database, and maintaining customer relationships.

2.2 Skills of CBEC customer service communication

2.2.1 Establishing customer files

A way to get a clearer picture of customers is to build customer profiles. That is to collect customer information and create and update a customer database to understand current, potential and lapsed customers. Creating a customer profile guarantees higher-quality customer service.

2.2.2 Learning to listen

Listening to your customers is showing them that you care for and understand their problems and concerns. Being a good listener is not easy. Improving your listening skills takes practice and dedication.

2.2.3 Written communication

CBEC customer service takes written communication as the main form. Try to avoid voice conversation with overseas customers, because the written communication enjoys higher clarity and accuracy. And what's more, it's easier to remain evidence for justification in disputes if needed.

2.2.4 Establishing Popular and Taboo Expressions

Table 0-1 Popular and Taboo Expressions

Popular Expressions	Taboo Expressions
Please...	Can not
Yes	Never
Is...okay?	No
Considering...	You are supposed to do...
Let's talk about...	Can't you...?
Thank you	We have no such stipulation about...
We	...is not my responsibility
Appreciate	F-words
Would you like...	We will try to do...
Opportunities	I don't have time to...
Regretful	I don't know...

2.3 Job requirements of CBEC customer service

A CBEC customer service specialist needs to meet the following requirements:

Be familiar with the company's products and business;

Be familiar with the rules of the main CBEC platforms, order processing process, instant messaging software and common translation software;

Understand the cultural background of the target markets and having the ability to communicate across cultures;

Be able to solve frequently asked problems for business and individual customers before, during and after sales.

3. Overview of the Course CBEC Customer Service

3.1 Learning results of the course

Upon completion of this course, learners will be equipped to:

3.1.1 Obtaining the professional competences

- Able to use search engines, social networking sites, trade show sites, etc. to find potential overseas clients;
- Able to complete business operations legitimately on main platforms.

3.1.2 Improving cross-cultural communication skills

- Able to write marketing emails tailored to the cultural context of a particular country or region;

- Able to analyze customers' purchase intentions and communication style through inquiries and make effective responses;
- Able to actively guide customers to complete a transaction;
- Able to properly resolve after-sales problems.

3. 1. 3 Reinforcing learning abilities

- Able to identify questions from practice;
- Able to generate confidence, gain inspiration and correct direction from the collective wisdom.

3. 1. 4 Enhancing cultural literacy

- Able to have cultural confidence and self-awareness;
- Able to understand and respect multiculturalism;
- Able to communicate and work in a team.

3. 2 Contents of the course

This course includes six parts: introduction and five projects, namely, Preparation for CBEC Customer Service, CBEC Pre-sales Customer Service, CBEC In-sales Customer Service, CBEC After-sales Customer Service and Advanced Skills of Customer Service for CBEC.

The introduction firstly presents the definition, characteristics and the functions of CBEC customer service from a theoretical perspective; secondly, it clarifies the workflow, communication skills and job requirements of CBEC customer service in practice; After that, the objectives, contents, teaching approaches and assessment methods are introduced; Finally, the four core qualities of CBEC customer service are described: empathy, resilience, cooperation, and discernment.

Project 1 is preparation for CBEC Customer Service. It covers the application of instant messengers, some translation software, and communication software and email writing. Also included is an introduction to major markets, including the economy, cultures, customs, and consumer preferences of the United States, Europe, Latin America, Africa, and other markets. Acquisition of these knowledge and skills facilitates learners to recognize cultural differences, establish quality communication, and bring customers good shopping experience.

Project 2 is CBEC Pre-sales Customer Service. This section explains how to find potential customers by means of search engines, trade show websites, yellow pages, Facebook and other social media. This section also explores how to write a development letter by designing an innovative headline and developing a logical and organized presentation. Finally, this section provides development letter templates based on typical questions, which helps learners to quickly complete high-quality emails.

Project 3 is CBEC In-sales Customer Service. This part is mainly related to order processing, such as how to call for payment when customers place orders without payment, and how to register and update the inventory information of products, track logistics information, and handle problematic packages and make related product recommendations.

Project 4 is CBEC After-sales Customer Service, which is mainly about dealing with various problems arising after customers receive their goods. Specifically, it involves how to handle customer complaints according to the platform's after-sales rules. And it also discusses the approaches to increase the positive reviews, modify the negative reviews, and maintain customers.

Project 5 includes Advanced Skills of Customer Service for CBEC, focusing on cultivating professional literacy, continuous learning ability, and skills of innovation and management.

3.3 Learning activities

For each project, the course provides a specific scenario and a related project task. For this task, the teacher will raise questions to inspire learners to break down the task step by step so that they can sort out the specific steps to solve the problem. Next, learners will form learning groups with delegated roles to achieve tasks together. In this process, learners may need to consult relevant materials in the library or online, conduct research, form a workshop for practice, or even discuss and consult with industry experts. Next, the learning results were submitted on or offline as teamwork through joint efforts. After that, the instructor will guide learners to sort out the main points of knowledge and skills related to the tasks and reinforce the knowledge through exercises and quizzes. Finally, with the knowledge and skills learned, learners are ready to try their hand at training activities.

3.4 Assessment

The assessment of this course includes both process evaluation and summative evaluation. The summative evaluation takes the final exam scores as the main reference indicator and mainly checking the learner's understanding of knowledge. The process evaluation includes the evaluation of learning attitude, platform assignment grades, written assignment grades, and evaluation of training activities. Among them, the evaluation of training activities will be assessed by multiple agencies, such as oneself, peers, teachers, industry experts, other relevant people etc. Thus, learners are able to get a more comprehensive and accurate picture of themselves from this feedback and make progresses on base of it.

In addition to training the knowledge and abilities required for CBEC customer service, this course is designed to develop the following four core values: empathy, resilience, cooperation, and discernment.

● Empathy. In the project the Future of Education and Skills 2030 launched by the Organization for Economic Co-operation and Development (OECD), empathy is presented as a core value for individuals to respect others and participate in social affairs. In CBEC customer service, as a core professional quality, empathy is critical for quality communication with customers. CBEC customer service mainly covers recommendation of products, and active communication with customers to resolve the problems related to logistics, product quality and other issues. Therefore, the job requires people to show sympathy and understanding to customers, and actively offer help. Especially in the face of customers in negative emotions, customer service specialists should be good at comforting customers timely, and get cooperation from customers until the problems get settled down. All of this is based on empathy—the cornerstone of quality customer service. In this textbook, empathy will be elaborated in Preparation for CBEC Customer Service, and concentrated in CBEC In-sales Customer Service and CBEC After-sales Customer Service.

● Resilience. Resilience was proposed by China's General Secretary Xi Jinping at the opening ceremony of 2021 training course for young and middle-aged cadres, referring to the courage and confidence to withstand pressure, overcome difficulties and carry on firmly. It is also one of the core professional qualities of customer service specialists. For instance, when developing new customers, CBEC customer service personnel have to face tons of unanswered emails or cold words from customers, which require great patience and impetus to get out of the trouble. During the transaction, customer service specialists also need great resilience when facing angry and anxious customers to cope with complex problems. In this textbook, resilience is mainly reflected in the contents of CBEC Pre-sales and In-sales Customer Service.

● Cooperation. General Secretary Xi Jinping put forward the spirit of partnership for joint cooperation and mutual benefit in his important speech at G20 Leaders' Summit 2018. Cooperation serves as one of the core professional qualities of customer service specialists. Customer service personnel are the link between customers and business, and satisfied customers needs customer service specialists timely and fully communicating with other functional departments of an enterprise such as technical support, logistics, finance, R&D, online operations etc... It is only through effective collaboration with these departments that customers' problems can be resolved efficiently and customers' shopping experience enhanced. In this textbook cooperation is mainly reflected in CBEC After-sales Customer Service and Advanced Skills of Customer Service for CBEC.

● Discernment. Discernment mainly refers to the ability to identify risks and the ability to avoid and manage risks. In practice, customer service specialists will receive a variety of inquiries. And if they cannot accurately identify their authenticity, they will face the risk of leaking business secrets. For new and existing customers' orders, customer service specialists should be keen to identify their purchase intentions and preferences to lay the foundation for secondary marketing and customer relationship maintenance. Discernment is reflected in this textbook mainly in CBEC Pre-sales Customer Service and Advanced Skills of Customer Service for CBEC.

This textbook employs micro-cases, micro-stories, micro-questionnaires and micro-debates etc. as carriers, and integrates them into the teaching contents of five chapters, namely Preparation for CBEC Customer Service, CBEC Pre-sales Customer Service, CBEC In-sales Customer Service, CBEC After-Sales Customer Service and Advanced Skills of Customer Service for CBEC. The former aims at moral cultivation, while the latter focuses on professional skill training, both working in parallel to obtain improvement in the knowledge, ability and quality. Finally, it's expected to achieve the integration of learners in both morality and professional competencies. This relationship is shown in the following figure 0 - 1.

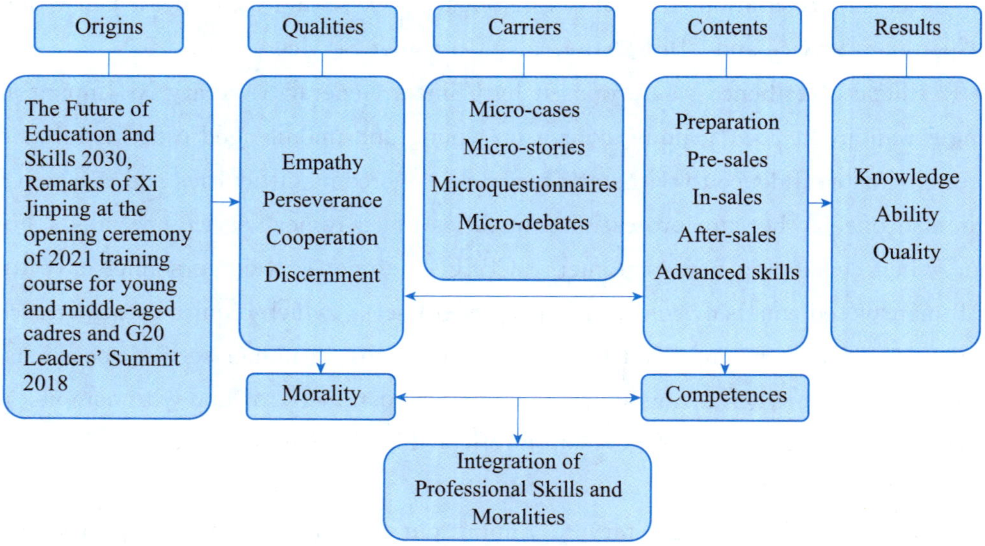

Figure 0 - 1 CBEC Customer Service Moral Education Design

Reflection questions

1. According to what you have learnt about CBEC customer service, please talk about your understanding of the meaning of it.

2. In groups of 2 - 3 people, recall the most depressing experience of communication with customer service personnel. Please describe how the situation was going and analyze why you were upset. Combining with the communication skills of CBEC customer service introduced in this chapter, could you tell your partners what you would do as a customer specialist on such occasion?

Reference answer

项目一

跨境电商客服工作准备

知识目标

1. 了解主要跨境电商对象国常用即时通信软件的特点；
2. 掌握常用在线翻译工具的用法；
3. 了解主要跨境电商市场的特点。

能力目标

1. 能熟练收发邮件和使用常用即时通信软件；
2. 能熟练使用翻译工具，得到较准确的译文。

素质目标

能够具备跨文化沟通和共情意识。

知识点索引

- 项目一　跨境电商客服工作准备
  - 项目背景
  - 任务分解
  - 任务完成
  - 知识要点
    - 一、即时通信工具
      - （一）Messenger　（二）Skype
      - （三）WhatsApp　（四）LINE
      - （五）Viber
    - 二、电子邮件
      - （一）延时互动
      - （二）内容清晰
      - （三）存档安全
      - （四）自由统一
    - 三、常用翻译工具
      - （一）ImTranslator
      - （二）Nice Translator
      - （三）知网学术翻译
    - 四、主要跨境电商市场特点
      - （一）北美市场　（二）南美市场
      - （三）德国市场　（四）俄罗斯市场
      - （五）东南亚市场　（六）非洲市场

项目背景

小艾从一所职业学院毕业后，应聘杭州奇迹电子商务公司的跨境电商客服岗位。小艾已经通过了大学英语等级六级考试，在学校学习了“商务英语读写”“跨境电商英语”“跨文化交际”等专业课程，平时也比较注重英语口头和笔头能力的锻炼。小艾对跨境电商工作十分感兴趣，成功通过了杭州奇迹电子商务公司的笔试和面试。小艾对这份工作胸有成竹，信心满满。

任务分解

今天是小艾正式上岗的第一天，让她略感意外的是，部门主管 Alice 并没有直接分配给她具体的工作任务，而是带她熟悉产品，了解公司主要业务对象国情况，并向她提出了以下问题：

1. 常用的跨境电商通信和翻译工具有哪些？
2. 你了解公司潜在客户国的消费文化和特点吗？

任务完成

中国常用的跨境电商即时通信工具是 WeChat，韩国是 KakaoTalk，泰国用 LINE，英国、巴西、南非、印度尼西亚和印度使用 WhatsApp 较多，美国最普及的即时通信工具是 Facebook。除了即时通信工具外，还可以使用邮箱发送电子邮件跟客户沟通。

小贴士

表 1-1　不同类型邮箱的优缺点

电子邮箱	优点	缺点
企业邮箱	正式、可信度高	域名易被屏蔽
国内个人邮箱	国内用户多、邮件收发速度快	国外用户少、认可度不高
国外个人邮箱	国外用户多、界面简洁	大邮件速度较慢、登录困难

跨境电商面对的是国外消费者，是否能够了解这些消费者的消费心理、消费习惯、消费取向对于中国卖家卖好产品、开发产品有着至关重要的意义。北美洲、南美洲、欧洲、东南亚、俄罗斯、非洲的买家都有各自的特点，这些国家和地区之间的市场状况和差异也比较大，作为一名客服人员，对此应该有较为详细的了解。

知识要点

一、即时通信工具

运用即时通信工具与客户交流具有时效性强、成本低廉、亲切直接等优点，不少平台拥有内置的即时通信工具，比如阿里巴巴国际站提供的聊天工具 Trademanager，如同国际版的淘宝旺旺。也有平台允许运营商自行下载聊天工具，比如 Wordpress 和 Shopify 等 B2C 商店中被多数运营商使用的 Tidio Live Chat，这是一款设计极为简约的实时聊天软件，目前被广泛应用。但是更多的平台是没有聊天工具的，这就需要客服人员根据每款即时通信工具的特点和主要使用国家和地区分布选择合适高效的一款或者几款。下面介绍最常用的几款即时通信工具。

（一）Messenger

Messenger 是 Facebook 自主研发的全球排名第二的即时通信工具，月活跃用户达到 10 亿，主要集中于欧洲和美国。使用者无须拥有 Facebook 账号，可以直接下载使用，十分快捷方便，使用者还可以发送各种表情和私密图片、进行群组聊天、语音聊天、在线支付。据悉 Messenger 的打开率比普通邮件高 8～10 倍，因此是企业做营销效果较好的一款工具。

（二）Skype

Skype 拥有 6.63 亿注册用户，同时在线人数超过 3000 万。Skype 作为老牌的免费网络电话，拥有大量私人用户及企业级用户，使用 Skype 可以拨打全球的座机或者手机，是比较清晰的网络电话，特别是工作场合用 Skype 的频率较高。当然，除此之外，用户同样可以用语音、文字留言。这款软件澳大利亚和欧洲国家使用较多。

（三）WhatsApp

这款应用程序在欧美、东南亚和南美等地区备受欢迎，除了发送视频、图片和语音信息等一般性功能外，它的最大特点在于可以像手机短信一样直接关联手机号码，并和现有的手机通信录实现结合。因此本应用程序可利用手机通信录中的信息，自动实现使用者与其联络人之间的连接，省去了添加好友这个步骤，因此更加便捷高效。

（四）LINE

LINE 是韩国互联网集团 NHN 的日本子公司 NHN Japan 推出的一款即时通信工具，在日本、泰国和中国台湾地区大受欢迎。LINE 可随时随地免费通话，最吸引人的是 LINE 拥有 250 多种更能表达心情的贴图和表情。

（五）Viber

Viber 是一种智能手机用的跨平台网络电话即时通信工具，能在 3G 和 WiFi 网络上运作。Viber 用户无须注册或付款，只要双方都安装了这套软件就能彼此免费通信。用户可以通过无线网络或 UMTS，与其他用户免费通话及传送短信、图片、视频和音频，其中网络电话这个功能与 Skype 十分相似。目前 Viber 支持包括中文在内的多种语言。东欧、中亚地区注册人数较多。

二、电子邮件

即时通信工具越来越普及，但是有些国家仅仅把即时沟通软件用于日常生活的交流，涉及商务方面的沟通，他们更习惯于使用邮箱，因为邮箱有其独特的优点：

（一）延时互动

邮件是一种延时的互动，因此可以实现全天候的交流。不管对方是否在线，我们并不介意，只管表达自己想要传达的信息或者观点，因为我们确认对方会定时检查邮件。

（二）内容清晰

邮件的接收和回复是交流内容的记录，清晰易追踪。而即时沟通的信息都是实时的文本流，不同的内容没有任何组织，不容易回溯核心内容和信息。

（三）存档安全

邮件的交流通常建立在认真阅读所收邮件和深入理解邮件的基础上，无论收件还是发件以及附件都会自动保存，方便后期翻阅参考和查阅。

（四）自由统一

电子邮件具有全世界通用的协议，所以我们可以使用任何一种邮件的客户端，以任何一种方式去查看邮件和发送邮件，不管对方使用的邮箱与我们自己的邮箱是不是同一家公司的。这就真正实现了"邮箱在手，接发自由"，统一的通信协议保障了这种自由。

三、常用翻译工具

一名跨境电商客服人员的英语水平再好，也可能碰到翻译难题，所以翻译工具是很常用的。有道词典、金山词霸、谷歌翻译等是比较常见的翻译软件。除此之外，还有一些比较专业的在线翻译网站也是很好的选择：

（一）ImTranslator（https://imtranslator. net/translate-and-speak/）

ImTranslator 提供了一个自然发声的文本和语音系统，具有翻译功能，只需单击一下按钮，即可快速翻译文本并被大声朗读出来。

（二）Nice Translator（https://nicetranslator. com/）

Nice Translator 是一个在线翻译网站，界面十分简洁，使用方便，翻译质量较好，最大的特点是所有的翻译文本均不会被服务器保存，最大限度地保护使用者的隐私。

（三）知网学术翻译（https://dict. cnki. net/index#）

知网学术翻译的准确性很高，适合正式文本的翻译。

翻译工具具有大容量的专业词库、交互翻译功能、记忆功能，可使人们在翻译时省时、省力。但是目前的翻译工具只能按照事先预制的词库进行翻译，翻译的质量好坏在很大程度上取决于翻译工具原有词汇量的大小。但由于一个词语在特定的行业内会有不同的含义，甚至有时会千差万别，机器翻译在现有的技术条件下几乎是无法实现有针对性的翻译的。此外，由于在特定的环境下，语言所表述的意义会因人们所赋予的感情色彩不同而有天壤之别，因此如果我们单方面要求翻译工具在语言翻译时做到"忠实和通顺"，只能是一厢情愿。因此，我们要采取一些策略，尽可能提高翻译工具产出的译文的质量。

首先，将复杂句转化成简单句。例如图 1－1 和图 1－2 中，在没有转化成简单句之前，译文显得头重脚轻，很容易出现语法错误。而转化后译文变得流畅，逻辑更清晰，客户读起来也更轻松。

其次，将意合文字转换为形合文字。从图 1－3 和图 1－4 中不难看出，汉语是意合文字，译成英语后时态、逻辑产生了混乱。而当我们加上"因为"这个表示因果关系的连词后，句子具有了形合的特点，相应的译文也更容易被目的语读者明白。

图 1－1　原文为复杂句的译文

图 1－2　原文为简单句的译文

图 1－3　原文为意合文字的译文

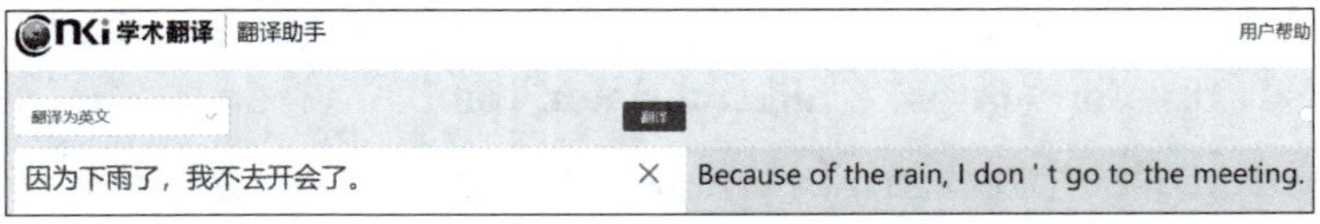

图 1－4　原文为形合文字的译文

小贴士

形合与意合

形合和意合是语言学句法中两个最基本的概念。形合是指借助语言形式手段（包括词汇手段和形态手段）实现词语或句子的连接；意合是指不借助语言形式手段而借助词语或句子的意义和逻辑关系实现它们的连接。前者注重语言形式上的接应，后者注重行文意义上的连贯。汉语意合和英语形合和两种语言所处的文化背景存在密切关系。中国传统文化讲究整体性以及天人合一，说话存在模糊性特征。而英语注重理性思维和逻辑思维，强调外在形式结构完整严谨，词法句法清晰详细，各种逻辑和动态意思的表达是通过词语的形态和时态变化表达出来的。总之，在具体翻译实践过程中，我们要特别注重两种语言在形合和意合两方面的差异。

再次，将英语作为中转语言。由于语系间差异大小不同，有些语言由汉语直接翻译，译文会比较生硬或者准确度欠佳。如果使用英语作为中转语言，得到的译文会较为准确。例如图 1－5 和图 1－6 中的例句，由中文直接译为西班牙语和由英语译为西班牙语相比，后者得到的译文更流畅准确。

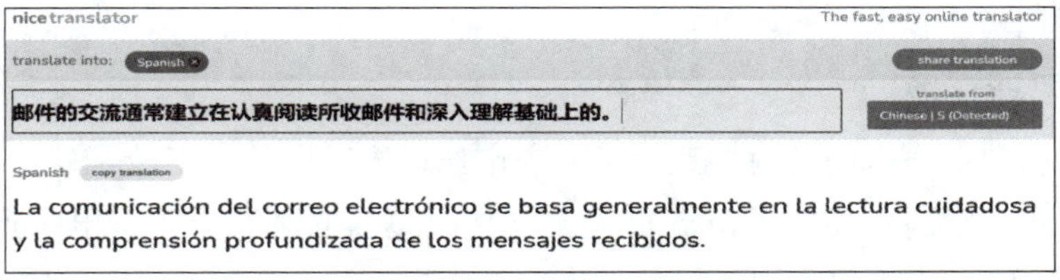

图 1－5　原文为中文的译文

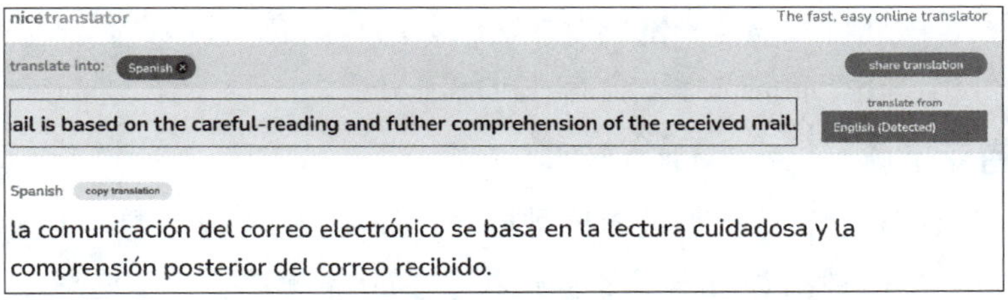

图 1－6　原文转化为英语后的译文

最后，人工反复检查。即使使用以上翻译工具和技巧，所得的译文也未必是准确、流畅的，所以人工检查的步骤必不可少。我们要反复检查语法、用词、感情色彩等方面，有时候还要进一步考虑文化因素对于语言表达的影响，争取用最恰当的语言给客户留下值得信赖的印象，为后续的业务开展打下良好的基础。

四、主要跨境电商市场特点

（一）北美市场

北美市场是中国跨境出口的主要市场，其中美国是世界上最大的电子商务市场之一，在线买家数量众多，消费能力极强。由于移民众多、文化多元，美国对商品的接受度很强。美国十分重视商标和专利，关注环保和劳工方面的问题。美国电商的销售旺季集中在下半年，比如黑色星期五、网购星期一等网购季和圣诞节、感恩节等传统节日引发一年一度的网络消费热潮，销售额占全年的 30％以上。

（二）南美市场

南美是跨境电商的一个新兴市场，互联网普及程度、跨境消费群体、移动化购物的人群比例都在不断增长，南美人不注重资金储蓄，这给中国的跨境卖家带来了一定的商机。目前的数据调查显示，巴西人对手机和平板电脑的需求量相对较大。但是南美的物流相对落后，即便是南美洲最大的国家巴西，也只是主干物流通路比较完善，枝干物流通路非常差。各国的海关手续烦琐，官僚主义严重，通关周期很长，导致卖家库存增加、成本上升，买家收货周期拉长。

（三）德国市场

德国人对商品品质精益求精，同时德国人的退货率很高，将近 50％，他们经常会购买多个颜色或者尺码的产品，在试用过后将不满意的那部分退掉。德国人的消费观念相比其他国家更为理性，基本上不会冲动消费，购买奢侈品的人比较少。此外，德国人很看重节日，每当重大节日时都会跟朋友互赠礼物，借此联络和增强感情。德国的物流基础设施高度发达，因此企业开展电商业务很轻松。

（四）俄罗斯市场

俄罗斯市场和中国市场是两个高度互补的市场，俄罗斯的重工业和轻工业比例严重失衡，俄罗斯人对日常消费品的进口需求很大，其中包括服装、鞋子、电子产品、配饰等，这给中国的跨境卖家带来了机遇和挑战。俄罗斯人对网络支付的安全性持有怀疑态度，所以很少有人使用电子支付，仍以现金支付方式为主。俄罗斯小包的时效在20～30天，其物流体系的不完善由此可见一斑。俄罗斯网购人数约占其总人口数的2%。俄罗斯人比较关注产品的性价比，在产品的选择上会有一定的滞后性。

（五）东南亚市场

东南亚人口众多，是一个典型的多语种区域，语种有10种左右，中国跨境卖家想要开拓东南亚市场，多语种的跨境电子商务运作就变得非常重要。东南亚本土电商发展较好，比如Lazada就很受欢迎，目前Lazada已被阿里巴巴集团收购。东南亚的互联网买家大部分都是基于移动端，其移动端的交易比例在62%以上，因此进军东南亚市场，适应当地的移动消费群体的习惯和需求是很重要的。当前东南亚还是一个非常具有前景和吸引力的消费市场，进入壁垒略高，未来的增长空间值得期待。

（六）非洲市场

非洲有54个独立国家，其中南非和尼日利亚的网络零售的发展速度居于非洲的领先位置，当地越来越多的居民都已经参与了跨境购物，尤其日益增长的中产阶级越来越青睐跨境购物。但非洲国家在基础设施和物流网络等方面的建设还不完善，可供选择的物流方式非常有限。另外，非洲消费者和俄罗斯人一样，对互联网支付的安全性持有不信任的态度，因此货到付款是非常普遍的支付方式。

习题测验

（一）选择题

1. 如果主要客户是泰国人，那么选用（　　）作为沟通工具比较高效。

A. WeChat　　B. Kakao Talk

C. LINE　　D. WhatsApp

2.（　　）可以像手机短信一样直接关联手机号码，与手机通信录中的信息实现结合。

A. Kakao Talk　　B. Skype

C. LINE　　D. WhatsApp

3. 除了延时互动的优点外，邮箱还具备以下优点。（　　）

A. 内容清晰　　B. 存档安全
C. 自由统一　　D. 以上皆是

4. 以下哪个在线翻译网站在提供译文的同时还能提供语音系统？（　　）
A. ImTranslator　　B. Nice Translator
C. 知网学术翻译　　D. 有道词典

5. 保质期较短的产品，可以作为（　　）跨境电商市场的选品。
A. 巴西　　B. 德国
C. 法国　　D. 俄罗斯

（二）判断题

1. 国外个人邮箱的域名容易被屏蔽。（　　）
2. Messenger 和 WeChat 两款即时通信工具都具有支付功能。（　　）
3. 邮箱的自由性是指同一通信协议使用者不必考虑对方邮箱是哪家公司的，自由发送和接收邮件。（　　）
4. 售前客户开发信以及商品介绍选用 Nice Translator 翻译会比较准确。（　　）
5. Lazada 电商平台是南非的本土电商平台。（　　）

能力实训

一、除了教材中所列的五种常用即时通信软件外，请通过网上查询，列出其他三种常用软件，并分析其特点。

软件名称	使用国家	主要特点

二、通过网上查询，写出以下邮箱后缀对应的国家名称。

1. @yandex. ru（　　）
2. @westnet. com. au（　　）
3. @sinaos. net（　　）
4. @webmail. co. za（　　）
5. @club-internet. fr（　　）
6. @aol. com（　　）
7. @t-online. de（　　）
8. @vsnl. com（　　）

三、使用 Nice Translator 在线翻译工具将下文翻译成英文，然后进行修改完善。

文化是一个国家经过历史沉淀形成的诸如知识、风俗、艺术信仰等的总和，中国和其他国家历史的差异导致文化的极大差异。中国文化深受儒家思想的影响，强调世界上的万事万物都存在联系。在看待问题时，中国人习惯综合考虑，把握整体。这就使得中国人更注重形象思维、综合思维、整体思维。而其他国家则不是这样，甚至恰恰相反。如英、美等国更注重个体思维习惯，先从个体出发，仔细考虑，以求掌握整体。文化差异还体现在等级制度上，一些国家存在严重的等级制度，比如印度等。

Culture is the sum of knowledge，customs，artistic beliefs and so on formed by the historical precipitation of a country，and the historical differences between China and other countries lead to great differences in culture. Chinese culture is deeply influenced by Confucianism，emphasizing that everything in the world is connected，in the view of the problem，the habit of comprehensive consideration，from the overall point of view，grasp the whole，which makes Chinese pay more attention to image thinking，comprehensive thinking，overall thinking. While other countries are not，or even on the contrary，such as Britain and the United States and other countries pay more attention to individual thinking habits，starting from the individual，careful consideration，so as to master the whole. Cultural differences are also reflected in hierarchies，which exist in some countries，such as India.

修改后的译文：

参考答案

思政微问卷

跨境电商打破了时间和空间的限制，让商家直接面对来自不同文化背景的企业批发商或个体消费者。不同文化差异是影响消费心理、消费偏好的重要隐性因素，也是跨境电商企业在经营过程中的一大困扰。跨境电商客服中常见的文化差异主要体现在语言障碍和沟通方式的差异、审美观及习俗的差异、价值观和消费观的差异三个方面。跨境电商客服人员想要为客户提供优质、贴心、高效的服务，必须提升跨文化沟通意识，可以通过扩充本国和他国文化知识的储备、增强对本国文化的自信和增强对他国文化的尊重三个途径，不断积累，不断学习，逐步提升跨文化沟通能力。

以下是几个有助于提升跨文化沟通能力的小技巧：

1. 开放的思维

如果你不能对别人的观点抱有开放宽容的态度，你就很难理解并接受别人的观点。不管你的信仰或习俗是什么，接受别人可能会以不同的方式处理同样的事情的事实，并对此表示尊重。

2. 学习的心态

双方之间缺乏理解往往会导致关系紧张，这就是为什么我们要不断地教育自己，这很重要。互联网提供了一个巨大的资源库，在这里有各种各样的文化实践，同时也有许多传统的方式可以让我们学习了解多样的文化，比如通过读书、看电影——或者更实际的方式——旅行。

3. 互动的意识

虽然书籍和电影可能会给你提供许多实用的信息，但你会从实际与人接触中学到最多的东西。你和不同的人交流得越多，你就越能学会从不同的角度看待问题，增强你与他人共情的能力，并在更深的层次上理解他们。

4. 自我反思

认真反思一下你与对方的相处方式、你说话的方式和你的整体态度：你认为你给对方留下了什么印象？你的行为会不会被误解，或者你的言语会不会冒犯别人？调整自己的沟通方式是与他人建立积极关系的一个重要因素。

5. 不先入为主

当你基于刻板印象或用先入为主的观点来判断一个人时，你实质上是完全忽略了他们的个性；你不考虑他们的真实情况就给他们贴了标签。尽可能地去了解和理解对方，平等地对待每个人。

其中第 4 个技巧中提到要“增强你与他人共情的能力”，也就是提升共情力。共情力，指的是能够躬身入局，设身处地地理解他人处境的一种能力，其形成基于共同的价值观和感受，超越文化差异的壁垒达成信任，从而保障成功的沟通。共情是跨境电商客服岗位十分需要的，但也是较难获得的一种能力。下面先请大家完成以下《多伦多共情力问卷》(The Toronto Empathy Questionnaire，TEQ)，测试一下自己目前的共情力水平。

说明：请仔细阅读每个句子，并评估你以上述方式思考或行动的频度。在表格上勾出你的答案，答案没有正确或错误之分，请尽可能诚实地回答每个问题。

表 1-2 多伦多共情力问卷

问题	从不	很少	有时	经常	总是
1. 当有人感到开心时，我也会感到开心。					
2. 别人的不幸对我没有多少影响。					
3. 看到有人受到不尊重时，我很不高兴。					
4. 与我亲近的人感到快乐的时候，我无动于衷。					
5. 我喜欢做让别人感到舒服的事。					

续表

问题	从不	很少	有时	经常	总是
6. 我对那些不如我幸运的人怀有温柔、关心的感情。					
7. 当一个朋友开始谈论他/她的问题时，我会试着改变话题。					
8. 别人难过的时候我能看出来，即使他们什么都没说。					
9. 我发现我能够和别人的心情“合拍”。					
10. 我不同情那些因自己原因而生重病的人。					
11. 当有人哭的时候，我会变得很烦躁。					
12. 我对别人的感受并不感兴趣。					
13. 当我看到有人难过时，我就会有强烈的冲动去帮助他。					
14. 当我看到有人受到不公平的对待时，我并不感到同情他们。					
15. 我觉得人们喜极而泣是愚蠢的。					
16. 当我看到有人被利用时，我有一种要保护他/她的感觉。					
得分说明： 得分越高，表明自我报告的共情力水平越高。男性的综合得分在43.46～44.45，而女性倾向于在44.62～48.93，根据这份调查问卷所测量的性别差异被认为是适度的。	第1、3、5、6、8、9、13、16项： 从不＝0，很少＝1，有时＝2，经常＝3，总是＝4 第2、4、7、10、11、12、14、15项： 从不＝4，很少＝3，有时＝2，经常＝1，总是＝0				

Project 1
Preparation for CBEC Customer Service

Knowledge Objectives

1. To understand the characteristics of instant messaging software commonly used in major CBEC target countries;
2. To master the usage of commonly used online translation tools;
3. To understand the characteristics of major CBEC markets.

Competency Objectives

1. Be able to send and receive emails and use commoninstant messaging software;
2. Be able to skillfully employ translation tools and obtain accurate translation.

Quality Objectives

Be able to have the awareness of cross-cultural communication and empathy.

Key Points Index

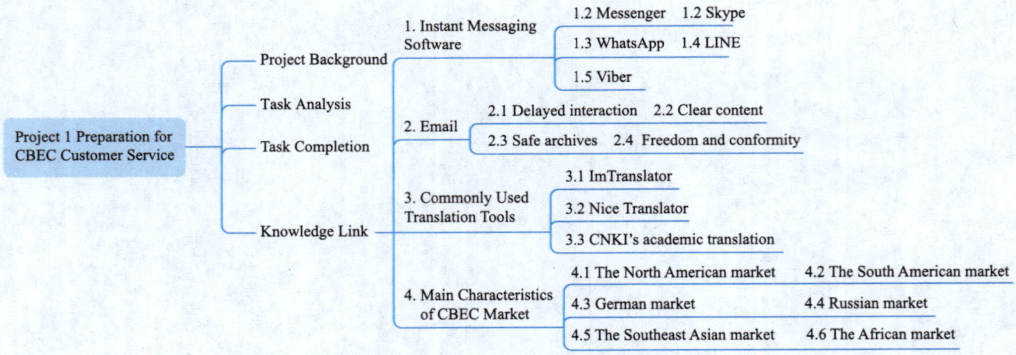

Project Background

After graduated from a vocational college, Eyre applied for the customer service position of Hangzhou Miracle E-Commerce Co., Ltd. Eyre has passed Band 6 of College English Test and studied professional courses such as "Business English Reading and Writing", "CBEC English" and "Intercultural Communication" at college. Meanwhile, she pays more attention to the practice of oral and written English. She is very interested in CBEC work and successfully passed the written test and interview of Hangzhou Miracle E-Commerce Co., Ltd. She is confident in this job.

Task Analysis

Today was Eyre's first day in office. She was slightly surprised that Alice, head of department, did not assign her specific tasks directly, but rather familiarized her with the products, the company's main business target countries and asked her the following questions:

- What are the commonly used CBEC communication and translation tools?
- Do you know the consumption culture and characteristics of customers in some potential trade target countries?

Task Completion

The most popular CBEC instant messaging software in China is WeChat, Kakao Talk in Korea, LINE in Thailand, WhatsApp in Britain, Brazil, South Africa, Indonesia and India, and Facebook in the United States. In addition to instant communication, you can also use email to communicate with customers.

Tips

Table 1-1 Advantages and disadvantages of different types of mailboxes

Email	Advantages	Disadvantages
Enterprise mailbox	Formal; High credibility	Domain names are easily blocked
Domestic personal mailbox	Large number of domestic users; Quick mail delivery	Few foreign users; Lower credibility
Foreign personal mailbox	Large number of foreign users; Simple interface	Slow delivery of large mail; Difficult login

CBEC largely targets foreign consumers. Whether they can understand their consumption psychology, consumption habits and consumption orientation is of great significance for Chinese sellers to sell products and develop products. Buyers in North America, South America, Europe, Southeast Asia, Russia and Africa have their own characteristics. The market conditions and differences between these countries and regions are also relatively large, which a customer service specialist should have a detailed understanding of.

Knowledge Link

1. Instant Messaging Software

Using instant messaging software to communicate with customers has the advantages of timeliness, low cost, friendliness and directness. Many platforms have built-in instant messaging software, such as the chat tool Trademanager provided by Alibaba. com, which is like the international version of Aliwangwang. There are also platforms that allow operators to download chat tools themselves, such as Tidio Live Chat used by most operators in B2C stores such as Wordpress and Shopify. This is a real-time chat software with extremely simple design and is currently widely used. But more platforms don't have a chat tool, which requires customer service specialists to choose one or more of the most efficient ones based on the characteristics of each instant messaging software and the country and region distribution. Here are some of the most commonly used instant messaging software.

1.1 Messenger

Messenger is the second global instant messaging software developed by Facebook. Its monthly active users reach 1 billion, mainly in Europe and the United States. Users do not need to have Facebook accounts, and they can download and use software directly, which is very fast and convenient. Users can also send various emoticons and private pictures, group chat, audio chat and make online payment. It is reported that Messenger's opening rate is 8—10 times higher than that of ordinary mails, so it is a good tool for enterprises to improve their marketing.

1.2 Skype

Skype has 663 million registered users, with more than 30 million simultaneous online users. Skype, as an old-fashioned free network phone, has a large number of private and enterprise users. Skype users can dial the world's landline or mobile phones, and Skype is a very clear network phone and widely used in workplaces. Of course, in addition, users can also use audio chatting and text messages. This software is more popular in Australia and European countries.

1.3 WhatsApp

WhatsApp is popular in Europe, America, Southeast Asia and South America. In addition to general features such as sending video, pictures and audio message, its biggest feature is that it can associate phone numbers directly like text messages and combine with mobile phone contacts. Therefore, this application can use the information in the mobile phone contacts to automatically realize the connection between the user and the contacts, skipping the step of adding friends, so it is more convenient and efficient.

1.4 LINE

LINE is an instant messaging software launched by NHN Japan, a Japanese subsidiary of South Korean Internet group NHN, which is popular in Japan, Thailand and Taiwan of China. LINE can be used anytime, anywhere, free of charge. The most attractive is that LINE has more than 250 kinds of stickers and emotions that can express feelings.

1.5 Viber

Viber is a cross-platform network phone and instant communication software for smartphones, which can operate on 3G and WiFi networks. Viber users do not need to register or pay and they can communicate with each other free as long as both sides have installed this software. Users can use wireless networks or UMTS to make free calls and send text messages, pictures, videos and audio message to other users. The feature of network phones is very similar to Skype's. At present, Viber supports multinational languages including Chinese. Eastern Europe and Central Asia have more registrations.

2. Email

Instant messaging software is becoming more and more popular, but some countries only use instant messaging software for daily communication. They are more accustomed to using mailboxes in business communication because email has its unique advantages.

2.1 Delayed interaction

Email is a delayed interaction, so it can become an around-clock communication. We do not mind whether or not the other party is online and just express the information or opinions that we want to convey, because we are sure that the other party will regularly check the mail.

2.2 Clear content

The receipt and response of an email is a record of the content of the communication, which is clear and easy to track. Instant communication information is real-time text flow and involves different contents without any organization, so it is not easy to trace the core information.

2.3 Safe archives

The communication of emails is usually based on careful reading of the received mails and in-depth understanding. All the outgoing mail and incoming mail as well as accessories will be automatically saved, which is convenient for later reference and inspection.

2.4 Freedom and conformity

Email has universal protocols all over the world, so we can use any kind of mail client software to view and send mails in any way, regardless of whether the mailbox used by the other party is the same as our own mailbox. The unified communication protocol really guarantees the freedom of sending and receiving.

3. Commonly Used Translation Tools

A CBEC customer service specialist may have a good command of English but he or she is very likely to encounter translation problems, so translation tools are very commonly used. Youdao dictionary, Jinshan Ciba, Google translation are common translation software. In addition, some more professional online translation sites are also good choices:

3.1 ImTranslator (https://imtranslator.net/translate-and-speak/)

ImTranslator features a natural sounding text and speech system with translation capabilities that allow text to be quickly translated and read aloud with the click of a button.

3.2 Nice Translator (https://nicetranslator.com/)

Nice Translator is an online translation site with a simple interface. It is easy to use and has good translation quality. All translated text is not saved by the server, protecting users' privacy to the greatest degree.

3.3 CNKI's academic translation (https://dict.cnki.net/index#)

The accuracy of CNKI's academic translation is very high, which is suitable for the translation of formal texts.

Translation tools have large professional lexicons, interactive translation functions and memory functions, which make translation tools save people time and effort in specific applications. However, the current translation tools can only do translation according to the preset lexicon. The quality of this translation is good or not largely depends on the size of the original vocabulary translation tools. However, because the meaning of a word varies in different industries, and sometimes with tremendous difference, this is almost impossible for machine translation under the existing technical conditions. On the other hand, in a specific context, the meaning expressed by language will be different because of the different emotional colors given by people. If we unilaterally require translation tools to be "faithful and smooth" in language translation, it will be a wish. Therefore, we should adopt some strategies to improve the quality of translations produced by translation tools as much as possible.

Figure 1-1 The Translation When the Original Sentence is Complex

First, turn complex sentences into simple ones. For example, before the following sentence is turned into simple sentence, the translation is top-heavy and prone to grammatical mistakes. The translation is smoother, more logical and easier for customers to read after it is turned into simple sentence.

Figure 1 - 2 The Translation When the Original Sentence is Simple

Secondly, convert the paratactic text into the hypotactic text. From the following example, it is not difficult to see that Chinese is paratactic, and the tenses and logic are confusing after being translated into English. When we add the conjunction "because", which indicates causality, the sentence has the characteristic of hypotaxis, and the corresponding translation is easier to be understood by the target language readers.

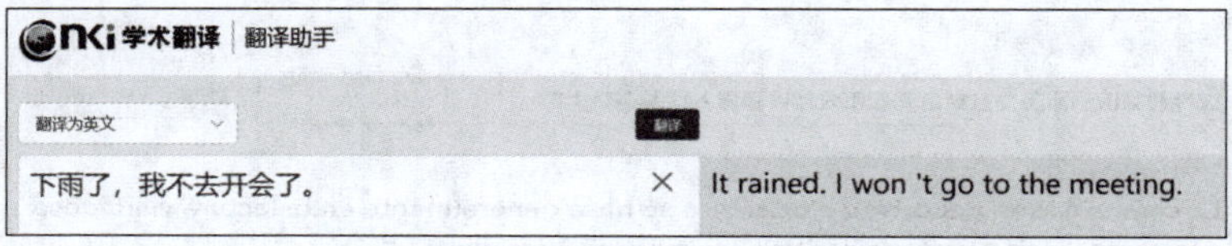

Figure 1 - 3 The Translation When the Original Text is Parataxis

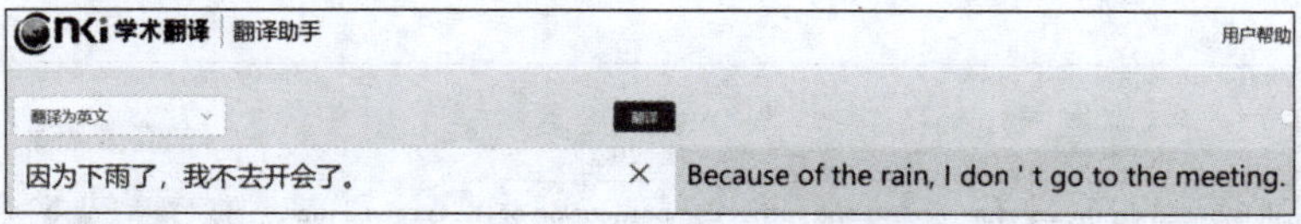

Figure 1 - 4 The Translation When the Original Text is Hypotaxis

Tips

Hypotaxis and Parataxis

Hypotaxis and parataxis are two basic concepts in linguistic syntax. Hypotaxis refers to the connection of words or sentences by means of linguistic forms (including lexical and morphological means); parataxis refers to the realization of their connection by means of the meaning and logical relationship of words or sentences without resorting to linguistic forms. The former pays attention to the formal correspondence of language, while the latter stresses the coherence of the text. Chinese parataxis and English hypotaxis are closely related to the cultural background of the two languages. Chinese traditional culture lay emphasis on the integrity and unity of man and nature and there are fuzzy characteristics in speech. English focuses on rational and logical thinking, emphasizing that the external form structure is complete and rigorous, the syntax is clear and detailed, and the expression of various logic and dynamic meaning is expressed through the morphological and temporal changes of words. In short, in the English-Chinese translation practice, we should pay special attention to the differences in hypotaxis and parataxis between the two languages.

Thirdly, use English as an intermediate transit language. Due to the differences between different languages, the translation done by translation tools will be relatively stiff or inaccurate if some languages are directly translated from or into Chinese. If you use English as an intermediate transit language, the translation will be relatively accurate. In the following example, the translation from English to Spanish is more fluent and accurate than that from Chinese to Spanish.

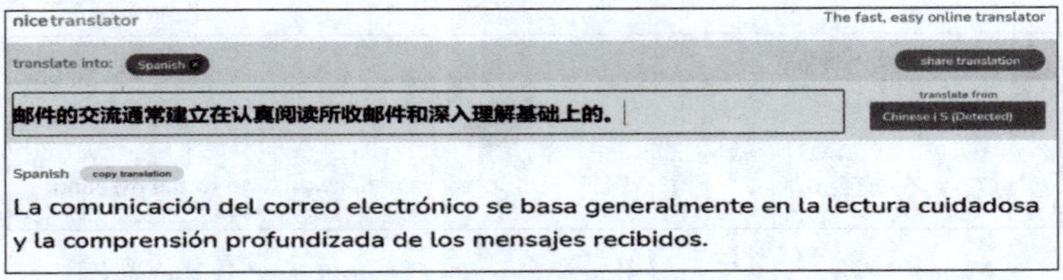

Figure 1 - 5 The Translation When the Original in Chinese

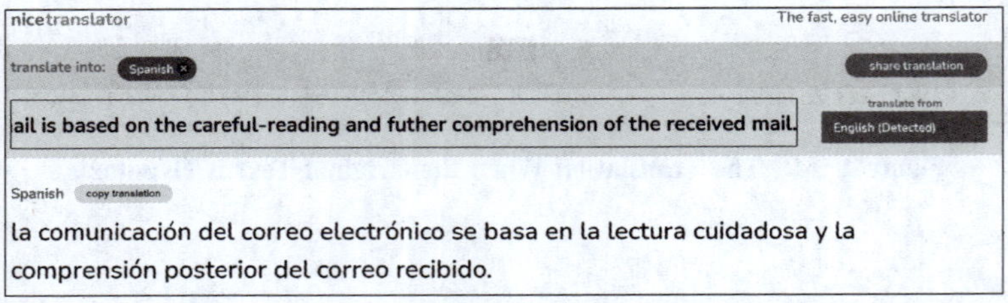

Figure 1 - 6 The Translation When the Original in English

Finally, check the translation carefully. Even with the above translation tools and techniques, the translation is not necessarily accurate and fluent, so human checking is essential. We should repeatedly check the grammar, wording, emotional color and other aspects, sometimes need to further consider the influence of cultural factors on language expressions. We should try to use the most appropriate language to leave a trustworthy impression on customers, and lay a good foundation for the follow-up business.

4. Main Characteristics of CBEC Market

4.1 The North American market

The North American market is the main market for China's cross-border exports, among which the United States is one of the largest e-commerce markets in the world, with a large number of online buyers and strong online consumption capacity. Due to the large number of immigrants and cultural diversity, the United states has very strong acceptance of goods. The United States attaches great importance to trademarks and patents, and stresses environmental protection and labor issues. The peak sales season of American e-commerce is concentrated around the second half of the year. Online shopping season such as Black Friday and online shopping Monday, and traditional festivals such as Christmas and Thanksgiving have triggered an annual online consumption boom, with sales accounting for more than 30% of the year.

4.2 The South American market

South America is an emerging market for CBEC, with growth in internet penetration, cross-border consumer groups and mobile shopping. South Americans do not focus on saving money, which gives Chinese cross-border sellers some business opportunities. Brazilians are in relatively large demand for mobile phones and tablets, according to current surveys. However, South America's logistics is relatively backward. Even Brazil, the largest country in South America, is only relatively complete in the main logistics pathway, and the branch logistics pathway is very poor. Customs procedures in various countries are cumbersome, bureaucratic and with long customs clearance cycles, resulting in increased vendor inventories, higher costs and longer delivery.

4.3 German market

Germans are keen on the good quality of the goods, so Germany has a high return rate of nearly 50 percent. They often buy products of multiple colors or sizes and return the unsatisfied ones after trial. Compared with other countries, Germans' consumption concept is relatively rational, basically not impulsive, and there are fewer people buying luxury goods. In addition, the German people attach great importance to festivals. In major festivals, they will give gifts to friends to enhance mutual relationships. The logistics infrastructure in Germany is highly developed, so it is very easy for enterprises to carry out e-commerce business.

4.4 Russian market

Russian market and Chinese market are highly complementary markets. The proportion of heavy industry and light industry in Russia is seriously unbalanced. They have great import demand for daily consumer goods, including clothing, shoes, electronic products, accessories and so on, which brings opportunities and challenges to Chinese cross-border sellers. Russians are skeptical about the security of online payment, so few people use electronic payment and cash payment is more acceptable. The delivery period of Russian small bag is about 20-30 days, and the imperfection of its logistics system can be seen from this. The number of online shoppers in Russia accounts for about 2% of its total population. The Russian online shoppers pay more attention to the cost effectiveness of products, and their product selection cannot keep up with market trend.

4.5 The Southeast Asian market

Southeast Asia has a large population and is a typical multi-lingual region with about 10 languages. If Chinese cross-border sellers want to explore the Southeast Asian market, multi-lingual CBEC operation becomes very important. In Southeast Asia, local e-commerce companies are doing well, such as Lazada, which is now owned by Alibaba Group. Most of the Internet buyers in Southeast Asia are based on mobile terminals, which account for more than 62% of transactions. Therefore, it is important to adapt to the habits and needs of local mobile consumer groups. At present, Southeast Asia is still a very promising and attractive consumer market. In spite of the slightly higher barriers to entry, it has a promising growth space in the future.

4.6 The African market

There are 54 independent countries in Africa, with South Africa and Nigeria taking the lead in online retail development, and an increasing number of local residents have been involved in cross-border shopping groups, particularly the growing middle class. However, the construction of infrastructure and logistics network in African countries is not sufficient, and the available logistics modes are very limited. In addition, African consumers, like some Russians, are distrustful of the security of Internet payment. Therefore, payment by delivery is a very common payment method.

Exercises

1. Multiple Choices

(1) If main customers are Thai, ____________ should be selected as a more efficient communication tool.

A. WeChat　　B. Kakao Talk

C. LINE　　D. WhatsApp

(2) ____________ can directly associate mobile phone number with mobile phone text messages, and realize the combination with information in mobile phone address book.

A. Kakao Talk　　B. Skype

C. LINE　　D. WhatsApp

(3) In addition to the advantages of delayed interaction, mailboxes have the following advantages: ____________.

A. Clear content　　B. Safe archives

C. Freedom and conformity　　D. All the above

(4) What online translation website can provide translation and pronunciation sys-

tem? ________

A. ImTranslator　　B. Nice Translator

C. CNKI's academic translation　　D. Youdao dictionary

(5) Products with shorter shelf life can be selected for CBEC market in ________.

A. Brazil　　B. Germany

C. France　　D. Russia

2. True or False

(1) The domain name of foreign personal email is easy to be blocked. (　　)

(2) Messenger and WeChat both have payment capabilities. (　　)

(3) The freedom of mailbox means that the users of the same communication protocols are able to send and receive mails freely without considering the company of the other party's mailbox. (　　)

(4) Nice Translator translation is a good choice for pre-sales customer development letters and product introductions. (　　)

(5) Lazada is South Africa's indigenous e-commerce platform. (　　)

Skills&Drills

(1) In addition to the five kinds of commonly used instant communication software listed in the textbook, please list the other three commonly used software through online search and analyze their characteristics.

Software Brand	Countries Using the Software	Main Characteristics

(2) Please do an online search and write the country name for each of the email suffixes below.

@yandex. ru (　　)　　@club-internet. fr (　　)

@westnet. com. au (　　)　　@aol. com (　　)

@sinaos. net (　　)　　@t-online. de (　　)

@webmail. co. za (　　)　　@vsnl. com (　　)

(3) Use Nice Translator to translate this text into English, then revise it.

文化是一个国家经过历史沉淀形成的诸如知识、风俗、艺术信仰等的总和，中国和其他国家历史的差异导致文化的极大差异。中国文化深受儒家思想的影响，强调世界上的万事万物都存在联系。在看待问题时，中国人习惯综合考虑，把握整体。这就使得中国人更注重形象思维、综合思维、整体思维。而其他国家则不是这样，甚至恰恰相反。如英、美等国更注重个体思维习惯，先从个体出发，仔细考虑，以求掌握整体。文化差异还体现在等级制度上，一些国家存在严重的等级制度，比如印度等。

Culture is the sum of knowledge，customs，artistic beliefs and so on formed by the historical precipitation of a country，and the historical differences between China and other countries lead to great differences in culture. Chinese culture is deeply influenced by Confucianism，emphasizing that everything in the world is connected，in the view of the problem，the habit of comprehensive consideration，from the overall point of view，grasp the whole，which makes Chinese pay more attention to image thinking，comprehensive thinking，overall thinking. While other countries are not，or even on the contrary，such as Britain and the United States and other countries pay more attention to individual thinking habits，starting from the individual，careful consideration，so as to master the whole. Cultural differences are also reflected in hierarchies，which exist in some countries，such as India.

Rerised translation：

Reference answer

Questionnaire in Moral Education

CBEC breaks the limitation of time and space，allowing businesses to directly face business whole salers or individual consumers from different cultural backgrounds. Cultural differences are an important implicit factor affecting consumer psychology and consumer preference，and also a big problem for CBEC enterprises in the process of operation. The common cultural differences in CBEC customer service are mainly reflected in three aspects: language barriers and differences in communication modes, differences in aesthetics and customs, and differences in values and consumption views. If CBEC customer service personnel want to provide customers with high-quality, attentive and efficient services, they must improve their awareness of cross-cultural communication. They can gradually improve their cross-cultural communication ability by expanding the reserves of cultural knowledge in their own country and other countries, enhancing their self-confidence in their own culture and improving their respect for other cultures.

Here are a few tips to improve your intercultural communication skills:

1. Be open-minded

It's hard to understand someone else's perspective if you don't allow yourself to be open to their point of view. Whatever your convictions or customs are, accept that others might do things differently and show respect for this.

2. Learn

A lack of understanding between two parties will often lead to a strained relationship, which is why it's important to educate yourself. The internet represents a vast repository of knowledge about different cultural practices, while there are also more old-school options: reading a book, watching a film or, for a more hands-on approach, travelling.

3. Interact

While books and films may provide you with useful practical information, you'll learn more from actually engaging with people. The more you talk to different people, the more you'll learn to see things from a whole range of different perspectives, increasing your ability to empathise with others and connect with them on a deeper level.

4. Be self-aware

Think about how you present yourself, the way you talk and your overall attitude: what impression do you think you're making on those around you? Could your behaviour be misinterpreted or is there any way your actions might cause offence? Adjusting your own way of communicating is an important element in building positive relationships with others.

5. Don't make assumptions

When you judge someone based on stereotypes or assumptions you're essentially stripping them of their individuality, you're putting a label on them without considering who they really are. Take time to get to know and understand the people around you and treat everyone equally.

The fourth tip is to "increase your ability to empathize with others", which is to increase empathy. Empathy refers to the ability to put oneself in the situation of others and to understand their feelings. An empathic approach, based on shared values and feelings, builds trust across cultural boundaries and ensures a successful cohesive exchange. Empathy is a skill very needed by CBEC customer service personnel, but it is also difficult to acquire. This textbook will explain it in succession. Now, please complete the following questionnaire to test your current empathy level.

Directions: Please read each of the statement carefully and rate how frequently you feel or act in the manner described. Tick your answer on the response form. There are no right or wrong answers. Please answer each question as honestly as you can.

Table 1 - 2 The Toronto Empathy Questionnaire

Questions	Never	Rarely	Sometimes	Often	Always
1. When someone else is feeling excited, I tend to get excited too.					
2. Other people's misfortunes do not disturb me a great deal.					
3. It upsets me to see someone being treated disrespectfully.					
4. I remain unaffected when someone close to me is happy.					
5. I enjoy making other people feel better.					
6. I have tender, concerned feelings for people less fortunate than me.					
7. When a friend starts to talk about his/her problems, I try to steer the conversation towards something else.					
8. I can tell when others are sad even when they do not say anything.					
9. I find that I am "in tune" with other people's moods.					
10. I do not feel sympathy for people who cause their own serious illnesses.					
11. I become irritated when someone cries.					
12. I am not really interested in how other people feel.					
13. I get a strong urge to help when I see someone who is upset.					
14. When I see someone being treated unfairly, I do not feel very much pity for him/her.					
15. I find it silly for people to cry out of happiness.					
16. When I see someone being taken advantage of, I feel kind of protective towards him/her.					
Interpretation Higher scores indicate high levels of self-reported empathy. Males' general score for this measure ranges from 43.46 to 44.45, while females tend to score within the range of 44.62 to 48.93. Gender differences, as measured by this questionnaire are reported as being moderate.	Items 1, 3, 5, 6, 8, 9, 13, 16: Scoring Never=0, Rarely=1, Sometimes=2, Often=3, Always=4 Items 2, 4, 7, 10, 11, 12, 14, 15 are reverse-scored. Total score=Total items 1 to 16				

项目二

跨境电商售前客服

知识目标

1. 列举寻找客户资源的主要方式及使用技巧；
2. 撰写有吸引力的客户开发信；
3. 掌握跨境电商售前客服遇到的典型问题及对策。

能力目标

1. 能通过多种渠道及方法寻找潜在客户资源；
2. 能根据客户特点撰写具有针对性的、成功率较高的客户开发信；
3. 能及时处理类似询价、商品细节、运费等常见售前服务问题。

素质目标

具备一定的坚忍力和辨析力。

知识点索引

- 项目二　跨境电商售前客服
  - 项目背景
  - 任务分解
  - 任务完成
    - （一）寻找客户资源的渠道及方法
    - （二）撰写和发送开发信的技巧
    - （三）跨境电子商务售前客户服务典型问题
  - 知识要点
    - 一、寻找客户资源
      - （一）利用搜索引擎寻找客户
        - 1.选择搜索引擎
        - 2.优化关键词
      - （二）利用展会网站寻找客户
      - （三）利用黄页寻找客户
      - （四）利用社交平台寻找客户
    - 二、撰写开发信
      - （一）发送多封电子邮件
      - （二）凸显邮件标题，长短适宜
      - （三）邮件正文要简洁
    - 三、跨境电商售前客服典型问题及对策
      - （一）关于询价
      - （二）关于商品细节
      - （三）关于支付方式
      - （四）关于运费
      - （五）关于关税

项目背景

杭州奇迹电子商务有限公司于2019年在全球速卖通平台建立店铺，主营生活家居用品，产品类目包括床上用品、厨卫用具、室内配饰及其他常见日用品。由于选品得当、服务贴心，2019年年销售额破60万美元，店铺流量稳步上升。公司安排新员工小艾参加了为期两周的培训，目前先从售前服务做起。小艾积极学习了公司的企业文化，了解了公司的产品以及与售前客服相关的职责内容和职业素养等知识。售前客服的工作十分关键，影响客户对卖家的第一印象和后续购买行为。

任务分解

为了进一步让小艾掌握各种客服辅助工具的使用、熟悉跨境电商海外主流市场客户的特点，店铺经理安排小艾开发海外客户，包括收集和整理潜在客户信息并发送客户开发信、掌握售前客户服务中典型的问题处理办法。因此，目前小艾需依次解决以下问题：

1. 可以通过哪些渠道及方法寻找客户资源？
2. 针对不同国家客户撰写和发送开发信的技巧有哪些？
3. 跨境商务售前客户服务典型问题主要涉及哪些方面？

任务完成

（一）寻找客户资源的渠道及方法

1. 利用搜索引擎寻找客户；
2. 利用展会网站寻找客户；
3. 利用黄页寻找客户；
4. 利用社交平台寻找客户。

（二）撰写和发送开发信的技巧

1. 设计有吸引力的标题；
2. 撰写有效开发信正文；
3. 利用客户开发信模板提高工作效率。

（三）跨境电子商务售前客户服务典型的问题

主要涉及询价、商品细节、支付方式、运费与关税等。

知识要点

跨境电商的客户服务工作所面临的环节多、情况复杂，涉及多种跨境运输渠道，以及不同国别在语言、文化、产品标规上的各种差异。非专业化的客服工作方式已经不能适应行业的发展与客户的需求，客户服务人员的从业队伍不断壮大、分工日趋专业化。在整个客户服务的工作流程中，售前客户服务主要涉及开发潜在客户、接待客户、推荐产品、回复咨询、引导下单等。

一、寻找客户资源

（一）利用搜索引擎寻找客户

搜索引擎是根据用户需求与一定算法，运用特定策略从互联网检索出指定信息反馈给用户的一门检索技术。搜索结果通常包括网页、图像以及其他文件。它的主要特点为：信息抓取迅速、深入开展信息挖掘、检索内容的多样化和广泛性。跨境电商客服人员在进行客户开发时应该掌握搜索引擎这一有效工具，并学会使用搜索引擎排除不相关信息，快速锁定相关企业信息。

1. 选择搜索引擎

搜索引擎伴随互联网的发展而产生和发展。为了更好地借助搜索引擎为我们服务，我们需要了解国内外常用的搜索引擎。国内常用的搜索引擎有百度、360 搜索等，而国外常用的搜索引擎有谷歌、必应，但谷歌已于 2010 年退出中国大陆市场。

2. 优化关键词

首先，我们需要明确跨境电商客服人员在搜索目标国家客户时，应尽量使用目标国家语言关键词。其次，应充分展开联想，尽量扩展关键词范围，充分利用周边属性，如产品的功能、颜色、使用环境、特色、材质等。除了大词，可以将功能词、长尾词和同义词结合。如搜索耳机买家时，核心关键词是 headphone，功能词可以是 bluetooth headphone、headphone wireless 等，长尾词可以是 white headphone for iphone、red headphone for kids 等，而同义词可以是 earphones、headsets 等。

在选择好关键词之后，需要对关键词进行精准优化。要优先考虑买家的搜索习惯，并且根据不同地域人们的语言习惯进行搜索。搜索关键词时就算是同类产品也会有不同的说法。比如钢化膜，有些中国卖家会用 tempered glass，但是更加地道的说法应该是 screen protector。

（二）利用展会网站寻找客户

作为外贸企业跨境电商客服人员，应了解本行业国内外展会。每一行业的国内外大型进出口商品展览会都有官方网站，里面有大量参展商名录等信息，在这些展会的网站上搜索到的潜在客户信息更有针对性。例如：中国会展门户（http://www.cnena.com/）全面囊括了中国会展产业各延伸类别和项目，全国约 80%的会展活动主办方驻站招商，每年约有百万家企业从这里走向各个展会现场。另外，中国行业会展网（http://www.31expo.com/）是一个集会展信息发布、会展资讯发布、多家网站转载并搜索排名靠前于一体的平台。现已收录超过 8 000 家全球展览公司的信息。

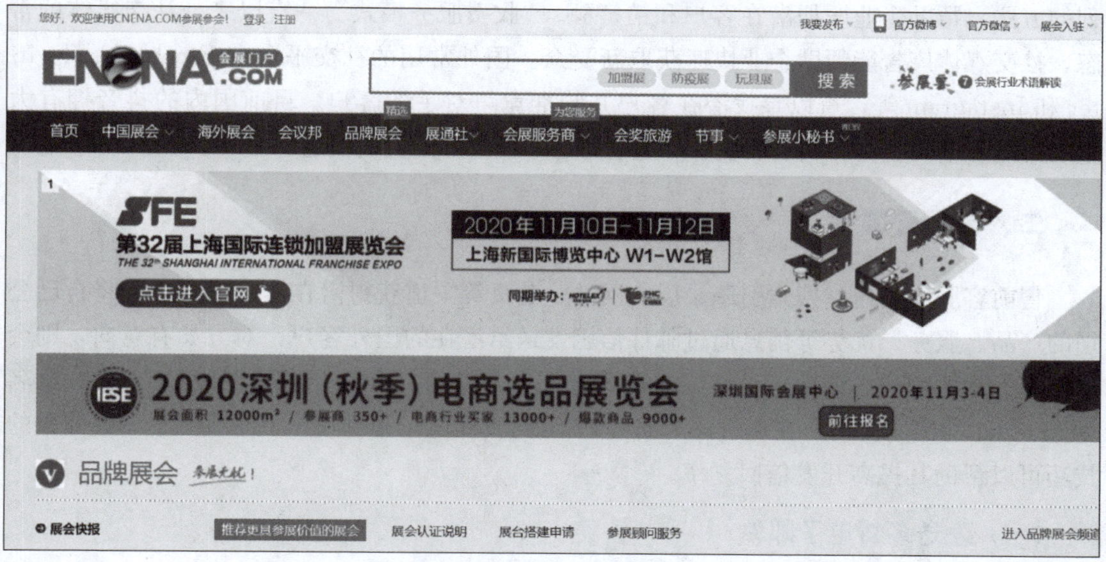

图 2-1　中国会展门户

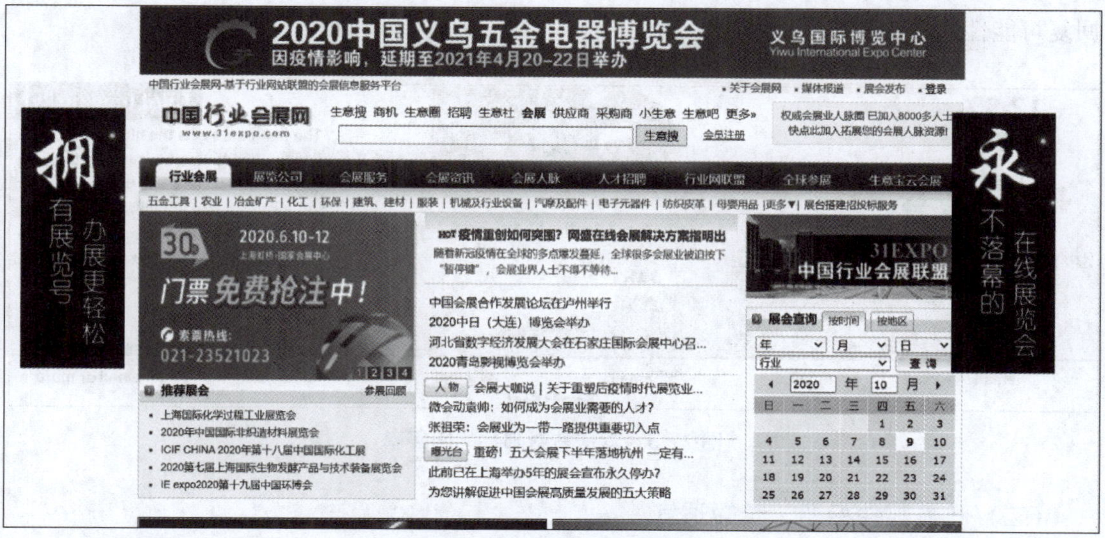

图 2-2　中国行业会展网

（三）利用黄页寻找客户

黄页是国际通用的按企业性质和产品类别编排的工商企业电话号码簿，以刊登企业名称、地址、电话号码为主体内容。国际惯例用黄色纸张印制，故称黄页。互联网上流行的免费中国黄页、企业名录、工商指南、消费指南等，也可以算是黄页的各种表现形式；黄页可以印刷品、光盘、互联网等多种形式向公众发布及出版。但是，黄页更新速度慢、企业数据容量有限。

（四）利用社交平台寻找客户

近几年来，从社交媒体渠道获取客户变得越来越简单。一方面，企业在社交媒体上有曝光率，有利于品牌塑造和客户服务；另一方面，社交媒体渠道也提供了更多走在市场前列的方法，帮助企业增加潜在客户和销售额。“收费服务模式”一直以来是社交媒体的常态，社交媒体广告能帮助企业快速获取新受众。国外常用的社交平台有 Facebook、Twitter 和 Instagram 等，可以寻找潜在客户并瞄准竞争对手的客户。目前国内的抖音拥有大量的用户和消费群体，抖音带货+跨境电商是一个大好的发展机遇。

二、撰写开发信

售前客服人员通过搜索引擎、展会网站、黄页等渠道获得潜在客户信息后，将自己公司的产品、服务、优势等信息通过邮件信函发送给潜在的国外客户，对方如有意向，则会进行进一步的沟通、谈判，最终确立购买合同。开发信是客户开发的“敲门砖”，一家名为 Implisit 的美国公司，在通过深入研究 25 万封真实电子邮件后，从中找到了一些简单的技巧可以帮助其提高开发信回复率。

（一）发送多封电子邮件

售前客服人员向潜在客户发送邮件时，第一封邮件的回复率最高，达 12.5%，第二封和第三封电子邮件的回复率也很高，分别为 8.6% 和 3.1%。但在第三封电子邮件之后，回复可能性几乎为零。

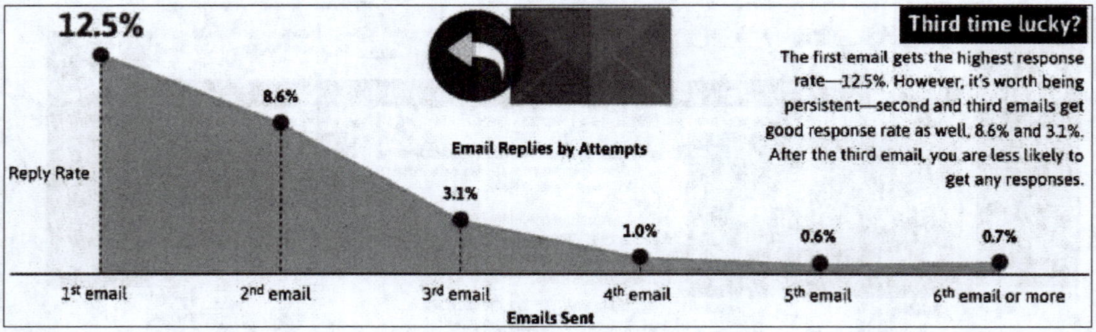

图 2-3　发送多封邮件的回复率

（二）凸显邮件标题，长短适宜

很多资料都建议邮件的标题应该简短，但该研究发现，适当长度的标题获得的回复率更高。与标题较短的邮件相比，标题超过 10 个单词的邮件明显有更高的回复率（46%）。然而，这在第一封邮件中是最有效和最常见的。在第二封邮件及之后，标题字数的重要性下降。

（三）邮件正文要简洁

从内容看，开发信正文内容以三段式居多，一般包括公司实力、产品及价值、服务及特点、从业经验等信息，忌长篇大论，可简单描述公司的优势。在语言文字来看，开发信正文以短句为主，可适当使用口语。另外，全文字数不宜过多（正文不超过 100 个单词），通常第一封和第二封邮件获得的回复率更高。

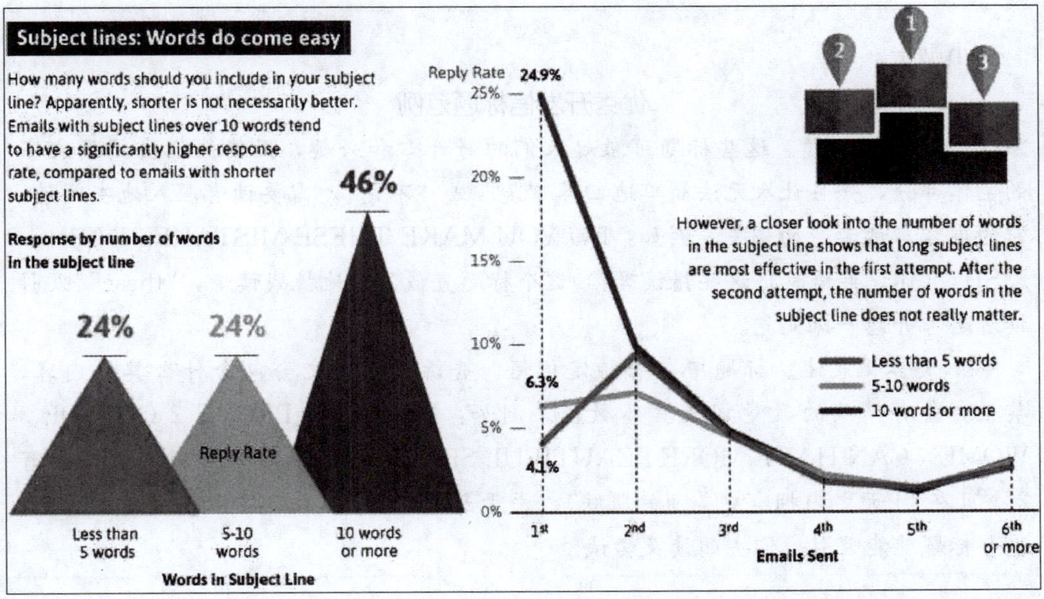

图 2-4　不同字数标题的邮件回复率

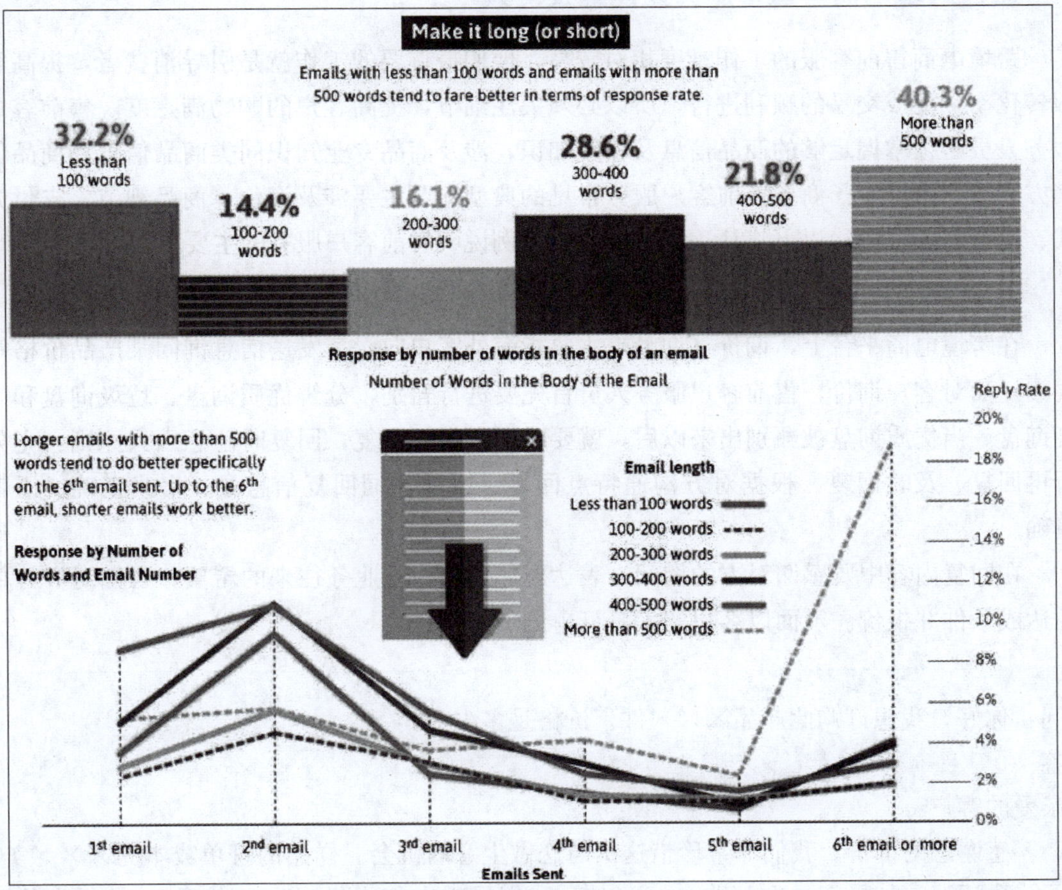

图 2-5　不同长度的邮件回复率

小贴士

优秀开发信标题范例

1. 询问式标题。这些标题可激起人们的好奇心和兴趣，促使他们去阅读文字的主体部分，并且让人无法简单地回答“是”或“不是”，需要读者深入地去阅读，它的内容与读者密切相关。例如：DO YOU MAKE THESE MISTAKES IN ENGLISH?（你说英语时犯这些错误吗?）这个标题直截了当地挑战读者，“these”吸引读者思考并想一探究竟。

2. 具体化表述。标题中包含特定词语，告诉读者正文会包含什么具体内容，甚至会含有精确的数量词及具体数值。例如：DOCTORS PROVE 2 OUT OF 3 WOMEN CAN HAVE MORE BEAUTIFUL SKIN（医生证实，每 3 个女性中就有 2 个可在 14 天之内拥有更美丽的肌肤）。由于女性天性爱美并渴望拥有美丽的肌肤，这个标题就能吸引她们去阅读及尝试。

三、跨境电商售前客服典型问题及对策

跨境电商售前客服的工作难度相对较高，他们最首要的工作就是引导消费者，提高客服转化率，促成交易的顺利进行，所以必须关注细节，提高客户的购物满意度。售前客户服务人员必须掌握足够的商品信息及相关知识，涉及商品专业知识同类商品信息和商品促销方案等。跨境电子商务售前客户服务常见的典型问题主要涉及询价、商品细节、支付方式、运费与关税等，以下将从这五个类别来举例说明售前客户服务的主要工作内容。

（一）关于询价

在跨境电商平台上，询价（询盘）主要指海外客户向卖家发送信息询问某产品价格等要素。面对客户询价，售前客户服务人员首先要进行甄别，分辨优质询盘、垃圾询盘和可疑询盘。当优质询盘被甄别出来以后，就要对询盘进行回复，回复时注意六大原则：先分析再回复、及时回复、根据对方沟通特点回复、增加单词回复信息量、格式正确、语言正确。

在回复内容中要感谢对方的询问，表达想与对方建立业务往来的希望，告知对方订单的达成条件并报价。下面以客户的大量订单询价为例：

问：你好，我想订购此产品×××件，价格是多少呢？

答：

亲爱的客户：

感谢您的询价。我们非常珍惜这次与您做生意的机会。样品的订单成本为×××美元，含运费。如果您一次订购×××件，我们可以向您提供×××美元/件的批发价，并免运费。期待您的答复。祝好！

（你的名字）

Q：Hello，I want to order ×××pieces for this item，how about the price?

A：

Dear buyer：

Thanks for your inquiry. We cherish this chance to do business with you very much. The order of a single sample product costs ×××USD with shipping fees included. If you order ××× pieces in one order ，we can offer you the bulk price of ××× USD/piece with free shipping. I look forward to your reply. Regards!

（Your name）

（二）关于商品细节

售前客服人员与客户的对话内容大部分是围绕商品本身进行的，清晰明了的产品描述能让客户快速获取所需要的信息。售前客服熟悉产品知识是与客户交流谈判的基础，售前客服对商品细节掌握得越多，越能让客户信赖。

例如：跨境电商行业中服装类尺码引起的退货和差评很多，因为服装的尺寸没有统一标准的尺码，需在国际码、中国码、欧洲码和美国码间互相转换，因此售前客服需给客户提供明确的尺码推荐，必要时可以向客户提供尺寸图。

问：你好，卖家，我平时穿美国码 8 号，我该从你这儿买什么尺寸的？

答：您好，亲爱的客户，M 号的连衣裙对您会很合适。如果您有任何其他问题，请随时与我们联系。谢谢！

Q：Hi，seller，I usually wear an American size 8 dress. What size should I buy?

A：Hello，dear customer，our suggestion is that size M suits you well. If you have any questions，please contact us. Thanks!

（三）关于支付方式

订单转化率对店铺十分重要，而支付系统又是提高订单转化率的关键之一。跨境收款支付是运营中要考虑的重要因素，一个好的收款支付方式，能减少很大一笔支出。一般来说，针对没有 PayPal 账号的客户咨询支付方式，客服人员可参考以下例子进行回复，并推荐客户尽量使用 PayPal 进行付款。

问：你们接受支票或银行转账吗？我没有贝宝账户。

答：感谢您的咨询。

为了简化流程，我建议您通过贝宝支付。正如您所知，兑现一张国际支票至少需要2～3个月，那么交易和运输上势必花费太多的时间。

贝宝是一种更快、更便捷、更安全的支付方式。它广泛应用于国际在线业务。即使您不想注册贝宝账户，您仍然可以使用信用卡进行结账，无须任何额外的步骤。

希望我的回答对您有帮助。

Q：Do you accept check or bank transfer? I do not have a PayPal account.

A：We shall be glad to answer your inquiry as to the price of the goods.

For the sake of simplifying the process，I suggest that you pay through PayPal. As you know，it always takes at least 2-3 months to clear international check so that the dealing and shipping time will cost too much time.

PayPal is a faster，easier and saferpayment method. It is widely used in international online business. Even if you do not want to register a PayPal account，you can still use your credit card to go through checkout process without any extra steps.

I hope my answer was helpful to you.

（四）关于运费

客户一次性购买多件商品时，可能会提出合并运费的要求。这个时候，客服可通过修改并发送发货单，对客户购买的多件商品只收取一次运费。在发货单发送成功后，可及时告知客户运费已合并，并让客户直接通过电子发票进行支付。

问：你好，卖家，我从你那儿买了好几样东西，能一起付运费吗？麻烦打包成一个包裹，谢谢！

答：您好，亲爱的客户，谢谢惠顾！

我们已经合并运费，只收取一次费用。请检查一下我刚发给您的发货单。请直接依发货单付款。如果您有任何其他问题，请随时与我们联系。谢谢！

Q：Hello，seller，can the shipping fee be paid together as I've bought several items from you? Please send me just in one package，thanks!

A：Hello，dear customer，thanks for your business!

We have combined the shipping already and only charge you the shipping fee once. You can check the invoice I've just sent to you and please make the payment through the invoice directly. Please feel free to contact us if you have any other questions. Thanks!

（五）关于关税

关税是客户购物时十分关注的问题，在下面例子里，客户服务人员就客户所担心的税费问题给予了耐心、细致的解答，明确告知客户一般情况下购买小额的货品不会产生额外费用，如遇特殊情况，需要向当地海关部门咨询。

问：你好，我想购买这个商品并发往美国纽约，是否需要缴纳进口税或关税？
答：感谢您垂询本店！我非常理解您关于本次购物可能产生其他费用的担忧。根据我以往的经验，大部分地区，像您所购买的类似小件或低价商品不会给您带来任何关税费用，不用太担心。

但是，在某些特殊情况下，客户还是要为自己所购买的哪怕是小件商品缴纳进口关税或消费税。至于具体的税率，请您去咨询您所在地区的海关部门。

非常感谢您的理解！

Q：Hi, I want to buy this and ship it to New York in the United States. What are the import duties or customs charges?

A：Thank you for your inquiry. I understand that you are worrying about any possible extra expense for this item. According to past experience, it did not involve any extra expense at buyer side for similar small or low-cost items. Please do not worry about it too much.

However, in some individual cases, buyer might need to take some import taxes or customs charges in import countries. As to specific rates, please consult your local custom office.

Appreciate your understanding.

习题测验

（一）选择题

1. 目前国内外常用的主流搜索引擎包括（　　）。

A. 百度　　B. 谷歌

C. 必应　　D. 以上都是

2. 在使用搜索引擎搜索胶带买家时，我们可以搜索（　　）。

A. adhesive tape　　B. pressure-sensitive tape

C. PVC adhesive tape　　D. 以上都是

3. 以下哪一个不是利用传统黄页寻找客户的缺点？（　　）

A. 更新速度慢　　B. 查找不方便

C. 收费较高　　D. 沟通方式单一

4. 撰写有效开发信正文不建议（　　）。

A. 插入超链接或图片　　B. 用白色的邮件背景

C. 口语化表达　　D. 使用三段式结构

5. 以下属于售前客户服务工作内容的是（　　）。

A. 通知客户已收到货款　　B. 处理客户纠纷

C. 回答客户咨询并进行导购　　D. 进行退换货处理

（二）判断题

1. 售前客户服务人员的工作内容主要是从事引导性的服务，如推荐产品、回复客户咨询等。（ ）

2. 跨境电商客服就是国际版的淘宝客服。（ ）

3. 按照询盘质量，常见的询盘可分为优质询盘、垃圾询盘和可疑询盘。（ ）

4. 开发信的标题建议越短越好。（ ）

5. 跨境电商客服人员需要掌握不同搜索引擎的操作。（ ）

能力实训

请按照以下提示回函一封。

杭州奇迹电子商务有限公司于2019年在全球速卖通平台建立店铺，主营生活家居用品，产品类目包括床上用品、厨卫用具、室内配饰及其他常见日用品。Mr. John 向小艾咨询了一款新款床单，作为售前客服的小艾，该如何向 Mr. John 推荐产品？

■ 简要列出该产品特点；

■ 对产品的价格、运费、支付等进行说明。

参考答案

思政微短剧

在“互联网+外贸”背景下，跨境电商客服岗位越发成为跨境电子商务体系中重要的一环，被细分为售前、售中和售后客服。其中，售前客户服务主要涉及发掘潜在客户、接待客户、推荐产品、回复咨询、引导下单等。由于工作性质和环境，售前客服除了需要具备基本的职业道德如爱岗敬业、诚信守法之外，还需要具备特定的素质能力，如坚忍力和辨析力。一方面，售前客服需要不断开发客户，屡次面对开发信石沉大海的情况，需要面对形形色色的客户去解答产品细节、支付方式、运费、关税等问题，这就要求售前客服有坚定不移的毅力和热情；另一方面，售前客服会收到很多客户发来的客户询盘，有的是真正有采购需求的客户，有的是套取你账户或者其他信息的询盘，因此售前客服需要有辨析力来区分优质询盘、垃圾询盘和可疑询盘。

坚忍力，往往呈现于遇到困难和挫折之时，衡量着对理想、目标的坚持程度，体现出抗压、抗挫的精神状态。为提取青蒿素，我国诺贝尔奖获得者屠呦呦曾经历190次失败，在科学界，这是普遍的现象。而售前客服也一样，或许会发送无数次的开发信、解答无数纷繁复杂的问题，才能成功建立一次客户关系。

1. 抗压能力小测试

心理测试题——看看你的抗压能力有多大	
问题	也许你很久没骑自行车了，但不妨想一想你喜欢或者正使用的自行车应该是哪一款： A. 轻便型自行车 B. 电动自行车 C. 变速越野自行车
解析	选择 A：压力承受能力 50%。轻便型自行车最大的特点就是无论什么路面，骑起来都比较轻便轻巧。对于骑车的人来说自然省力不少。选择这项的人，通常来说无法忍受自己承受过大的压力。也正因为如此，你选择了轻便型自行车，可以让自己省力不少。不过这并不代表你丝毫不能承受压力。有时候压力反而能够成为你的动力。让你发奋达到你心目中的目标。这样的人不占少数。 选择 B：压力承受能力 20%。把它归类于自行车的行列是因为它还有两个踏板。只要有足够的电力，骑车的人可以毫不费力地行驶在马路上。选择这个选项的人对于压力可以说是非常敏感的。在现实生活中，你绝对不允许也不会让自己承受过大的压力。一旦超过自己的承受范围，立即放弃是你不二的选择。不过，有时压力可以帮助你完成不少事情。不妨试一试，让压力变成自己的动力。 选择 C：压力承受能力 80%。相信很多人都喜欢它能够随时随地变速的特点。骑车的人可以在不同的路面选择不同的方式让自己轻松度过。正如这款车的特点一样，你对于压力有着良好的调节能力。你会非常理智地判断出何种程度的压力对于自己是有利的。而当压力过大时，你优秀的调节能力就体现出来了。你会调整自己的心态或是做些事情使外来的压力立即减轻不少。有时，压力对你来说反倒是一种表现自我的途径。

辨析即辨别分析，自主辨析就是由自己对事物或事件的性质与意义独立做出思考和判断。具备自主辨析能力是一个人思想较为成熟、具有独立抽象思维能力的象征，也是能顺利融入社会生活的基本素质要求。售前客服人员在面对各种询盘的情况下，提升甄别能力至关重要。

2. 辨析力短剧

学生 A 扮演售前客服人员，学生 B 和学生 C 扮演竞争公司工作人员冒充客户向售前客服询价并索要样品，售前客服人员并不知道两位“客户”的真实身份。在实际表演过程中，两位“客户”临场发挥，提出需要店铺中多个产品的样品，并坚持不想付样品费也不付运费。思考：面对学生 B 和学生 C 的“临场发挥”，学生 A 会做何反应？怎么处理？如何帮助学生 A 分辨询盘的真假？

解析：

（1）是否寄样。仅说对贵司的产品很感兴趣，且订量很大，要求寄样，而不具体指某个产品，这种客户基本无效，建议不寄样。能说出具体要求规格、数量的客户，可能是有效客户，但仍要去搜索他的公司名和网址，看是不是有效客户。163、Gmail、Hotmail、

Foxmail、Outlook、Yahoo 等免费邮箱的客户大部分是无效客户。邮箱是付费的企业邮箱，@后面是以公司域名为后缀的，才是有效客户，一定要寄样品。

（2）样品收费问题。分辨客户实力，如果客户是大客户，有网站、品牌，可免费寄样。

（3）寄样运费问题。一般来说，样品免费的话，运费由客户承担。如果客户是大客户，运费又不贵的话，可以考虑向老板申请公司付运费。

Project 2

CBEC Pre-sales Customer Service

Knowledge Objectives

1. List the main ways and tips to develop customers;

2. Write an attractive customer development letter;

3. Master the typical problems and counter measures encountered in pre-sales customer service.

Competency Objectives

1. Able to find potential customers with multiple channels and methods;

2. Able to write targeted customer development letters with high successful rate according to customer characteristics;

3. Able to timely deal with common pre-sales service issues such as inquiry, product details, freight, etc.

Quality Objectives

Possess the capacity of resilience and discernment.

Key Points Index

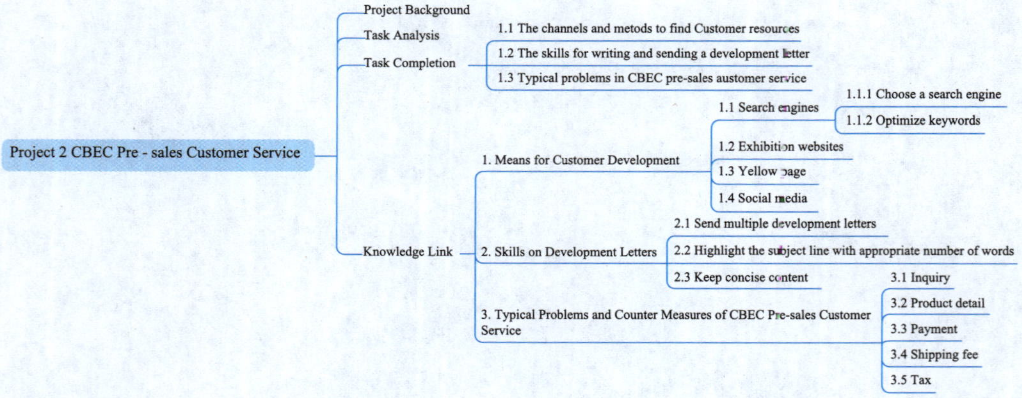

Project Background

In 2019, Hangzhou Miracle E-Commerce Co., Ltd. opened a store on AliExpress to sell daily household products. The product categories include bedding, kitchen and bathroom appliances, indoor accessories and other common daily necessities. Due to the proper selection of products and superior service, the annual sales in 2019 exceeded \$600,000, and the store's customer flow increased steadily. The company has arranged a two-week training program for Eyre, a new employee, who will start her job with pre-sales services. Currently, she has actively studied the company's corporate culture and products, as well as the basic duties and professional quality of pre-sales customer service. Pre-sales customer service is very critical, greatly affecting customers' first impression on the seller and their subsequent purchasing behavior.

Task Analysis

To further enable Eyre to master various customer service assistance tools and to be familiar with the characteristics of CBEC customers in the mainstream overseas market, the store manager placed Eyre to develop overseas customers, including collecting and sorting out potential customer information, sending customer development letters, and mastering the countermeasures of typical problems encountered in pre-sales customer service. Therefore, step by step, Eyre needs to solve the following problems:

■ What channels and methods can be used to find customer resources?

■ What are the skills for writing and sending development letters to customers in different countries?

■ What are the typical problems in CBEC pre-sales customer service?

Task Completion

1.1 The channels and methods to find customer resources

■ Search engines;

■ Exhibition websites;

■ Yellow pages;

■ Social media.

1.2 The skills for writing and sending a development letter

■ Design attractive titles;

■ Write effective development letters;

■ Employ customer development letter templates to improve work efficiency.

1.3 Typical problems in CBEC pre-sales customer service

■ Mainly involving inquiry, product details, payment methods, freight and tariffs, etc.

Knowledge Link

CBEC customer service is a complicated process that involves multiple cross-border transportation channels, and various differences in language, culture, and product standards in different countries. An amateur can no longer adapt to the development of the industry and the needs of customers. The team of customer service personnel continues to grow with the increasingly professional division of labor. In the entire customer service workflow, pre-sales customer service mainly involves discovering potential customers, receiving customers, recommending products, replying to inquiries, and guiding orders, etc.

1. Means for Customer Development

1.1 Search engines

A search engine is a retrieval technology that uses specific strategies to retrieve information from the Internet and give feedback to users based on user needs and certain algorithms. Search results usually include web pages, images, and other files. Its main characteristics are rapid information capture, in-depth information mining, and diversified and extensive retrieval content. CBEC customer service personnel should master search engines as an effective tool when developing customers, and learn to use them to exclude irrelevant information and quickly lock relevant corporate information.

1.1.1 Choose a search engine

Search engines have emerged and developed with the development of the Internet. In order to make better use of search engines, we need to get a general knowledge of the search engines commonly used at home and abroad. In China, people use search engines include Baidu and 360 search, while in other countries (In 2010, Google China has withdrawn from the Chinese mainland market).

1.1.2 Optimize keywords

First of all, we need to make it clear that CBEC customer service personnel should try to use keywords in the language of the target country when searching for customers. Secondly, we should fully associate and expand the scope of keywords as far as possible, and make full use of the features of the products, such as the product's function, color, service environment, features, materials and so on. In addition to big words, we can combine functional description words, long tail words, and synonyms. For example, when searching for buyers of headphones, the keyword is *headphone*, and the functional description words can be *bluetooth headphone*, *headphone wireless*, etc. Long tail words can be *white headphone for iPhone*, *red headphone for kids*, etc., while synonyms can be *earphones*, *headsets*, etc.

After determining a keyword, it is necessary to optimize the keyword accurately. Buyers' search habits should be given as a priority, and generally there will be different words when searching keywords even for similar products because of the different language habits of people in various regions. For example, some Chinese sellers will use *tempered* glass to express "钢化膜", but a more authentic term is *screen protector*.

1.2 Exhibition websites

As CBEC customer service personnel in a foreign trade company, we should understand the domestic and foreign exhibitions in this industry. Domestic and foreign large-scale import and export commodity exhibitions in any industry have official websites which include lots of exhibitor lists and other information. The information of potential customers searched on the websites of these exhibitions is more targeted. For example, the China Exhibition Portal (http://www.cnena.com/) comprehensively covers all extension categories and projects of China's exhibition industry. About 80% of exhibition organizers around whole country are stationed to attract investment, and about one million companies enter various exhibition sites by virtue of this platform every year. In addition, China Industry Exhibition (http://www.31expo.com/) isan integrated exhibition platform that can release and disseminate information, which is reprinted by many websites and ranked top in search. Information of more than 8,000 global exhibition companies has now been included.

Figure 2-1 China Exhibition Portal

1.3 Yellow page

Yellow page is an international telephone directory with names, addresses and telephone numbers for industrial and commercial enterprises, organized according to the nature of enterprises and product categories. This telephone directory is printed on yellow paper according to international practice, so it is called yellow page. The free China yellow pages, business directories, business guides and consumer guides that are popular on the Internet can also be regarded as various manifestations of the yellow pages. The yellow pages can be distributed and published to the public by print, CD-ROM, internet and other formats. However, it is slow in updates and the enterprise data capacity is limited.

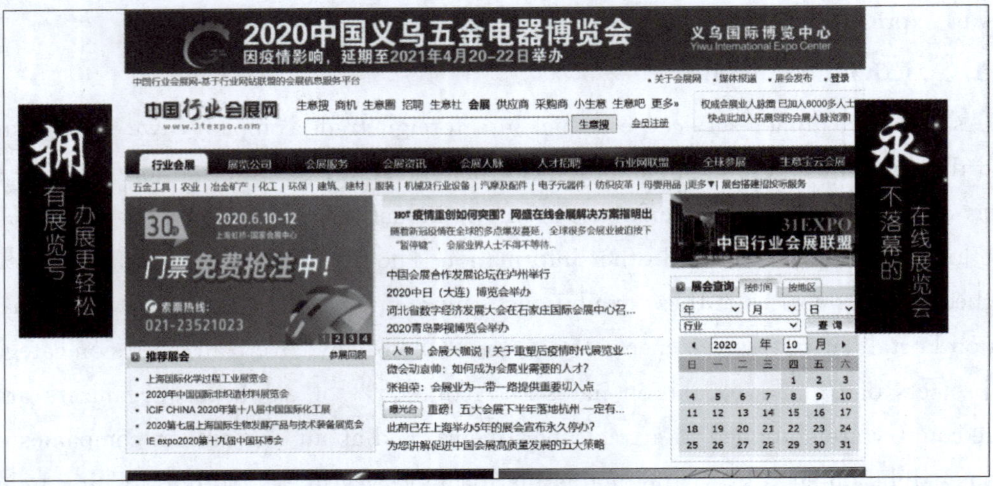

Figure 2-2 China Industry Exhibition

1.4 Social media

Developing customers from social media channels has become easier in recent years. First, companies need exposure on social media, which is good for brand building and customer service. At the same time, social media channels offer more ways to help companies stay ahead of the market, increase potential customers and sales. "Pay to play" has been a norm in social media for a long time, helping companies get access to new customers by advertisements. Popular social platforms in foreign countries include Facebook, Twitter and Instagram, they can be used to develop potential customers or target competitors' customers. In China, Tik Tok has a large number of users and consumer groups, consequently "Tik Tok+CBEC" is a great development opportunity.

2. Skills on Development Letters

After obtaining potential customers' information through search engines, exhibition websites, yellow pages and other channels, pre-sales customer service personnel can send information of products, services and advantages to customers through letters. If they are interested, they will implement an integrated exhibition platform that can release and disseminate information, which can be reprinted, and ultimately establish a purchase contract. *Implisit*, has found some simple tips to help improve the response rate of development letters after digging into 250,000 real emails.

2.1 Send multiple development letters

When pre-sales customer service personnel send email to potential customers, the first email gets the highest response rate—12.5%. However, it's worth being persistent. The second and third emails get good response rate as well (8.6% and 3.1% respectively). After the third email, it's less likely to get any responses.

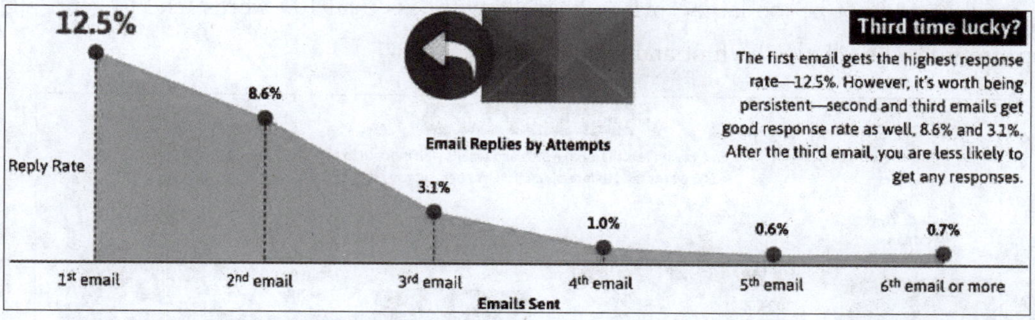

Figure 2 - 3 The Respective Response Rate When Multiple Letters are Sent

2.2 Highlight the subject line with appropriate number of words

It is commonly suggested that the subject line should be short, but this study found that the subject line of an appropriate length received a higher response rate. Emails with subject lines over 10 words tend to have a significantly higher response rate (46%), compared to emails with shorter subject lines. However, such differences are most effective and common in the first attempt. After the second attempt, the number of words in the subject line does not really matter.

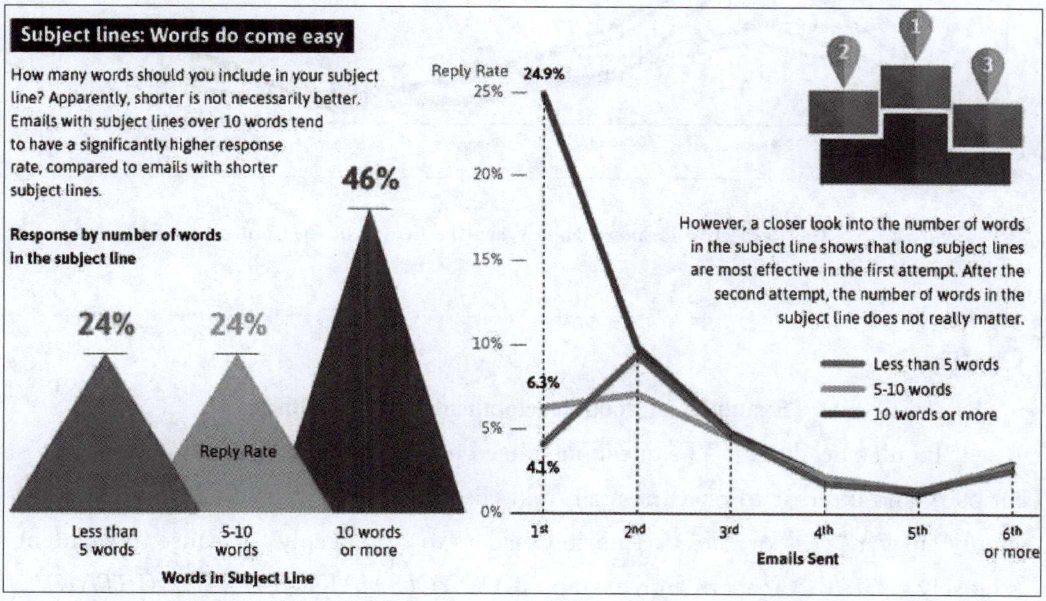

Figure 2 - 4 The Respective Response Rate When the Different Number of Words in the Subject Line

2.3 Keep concise content

In terms of content, the body of a development letter is mostly divided into three paragraphs, generally including a company's strength, products and values, services and characteristics, experience and other information. A company's advantages should be simply described, avoiding long description. In terms of language, the body of a development letter consists mainly of short sentences with appropriate colloquialism. In addition, the number of words in the body of the email should not be too large, meaning emails with less than 100 words tend to get a higher response rate, usually in the first and second email.

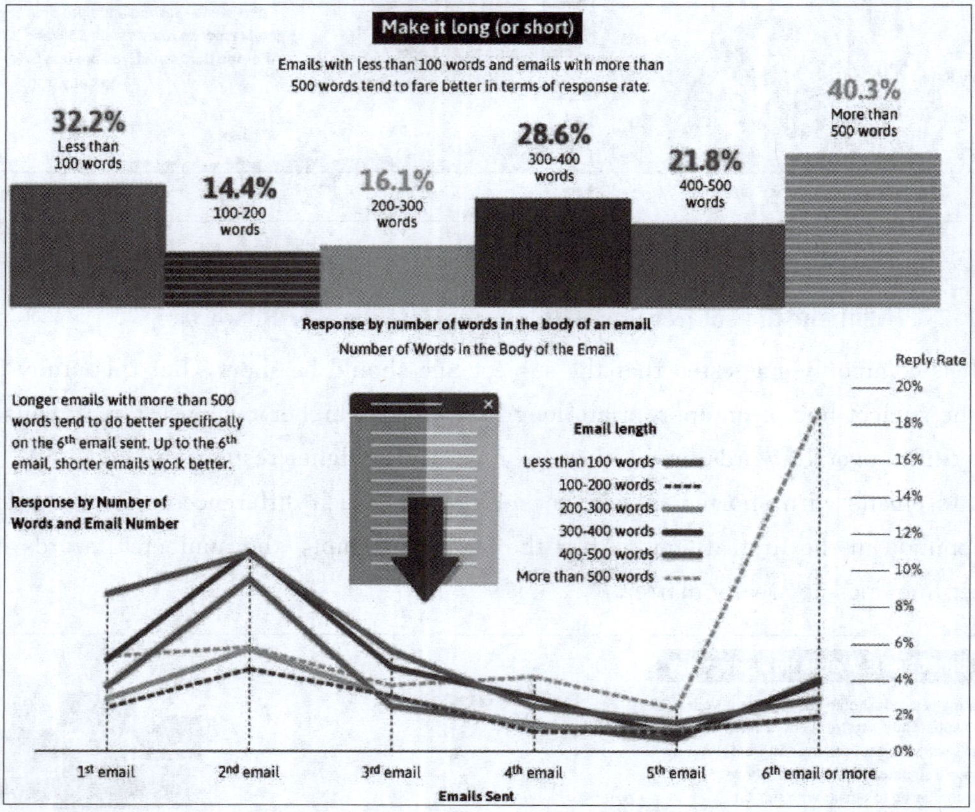

Figure 2 - 5 The Respective Response Rate When the Length of the Content are Different

Tips

Examples of good development letter headings

1. Inquiry headings: The questions raised by these headings can arouse people's curiosity and interest to read the main text that follows, and make it impossible to simply answer "yes" or "no", requiring readers to read deeply, because the content is closely related to readers. For example, *DO YOU MAKE THESE MISTAKES IN ENGLISH*? This title directly challenges readers, and the word "*these*" attracts readers to think and explore more.

2. Specific expression: The heading contains specific words to assure readers that what specific content will be involved in the text, and even contains precise quantifiers and specific values. For example, the heading *DOCTORS PROVE 2 OUT OF 3 WOMEN CAN HAVE MORE BEAUTIFUL SKIN* attract many women to read and have a try because it's women's nature to be beautiful and desire beautiful skin.

3. Typical Problems and Counter Measures of CBEC Pre-sales Customer Service

The work of CBEC pre-sales customer service is relatively difficult. The most important task is to guide consumers, increase conversion rate, and promote the smooth progress of closing a deal, so customer service personnel should pay attention to details and improve customer satisfaction. Pre-sales customer service personnel must be familiar with the products and equipped with specialized knowledge to carry out product promotion plans. Typical problems of CBEC pre-sales customer service mainly involve with inquiry, commodity details, payment method, freight and tariff, etc. The main job of pre-sales customer service will be illustrated from the five categories as follows.

3.1 Inquiry

On CBEC platforms, inquiries mainly refer to overseas customers sending information to sellers to consult the price or other factors of a certain product. Facing customers' inquiries, pre-sales customer service personnel should first assess the quality of the inquiries, to classify them as high-quality inquiries, junk inquiries or suspicious inquiries. When a high-quality inquiry is identified, it is necessary to respond to the inquiry according to the following six principles: analysis before reply, timely reply, communication features-based reply, increased number of words to reply, correct format and language.

In reply, it's necessary to thank customers for their inquiry, express the hope of establishing business with them, inform them of the terms and conditions of the order and then quote prices. The following is an example of a customer's inquiry for a large order:

Q: Hello, I want to order ×××pieces for this item, how about the price?
A:
Dear buyer,
Thanks for your inquiry. We cherish this chance to do business with you very much. The order of a single sample product costs ×××USD with shipping fees included. If you order ××× pieces in one order, we can offer you the bulk price of ××× USD/piece with free shipping. I look forward to your reply. Regards!
(Your name)

3.2 Product detail

The dialogue between pre-sales customer service personnel and customers mostly centers around the product itself. A clear product description can help customers quickly get the information they need, so personnel with sufficient product knowledge is the basis of communication and negotiation with customers. The more details a customer service specialist knows, the more trust will be gained from the customers.

For example, in CBEC, the wrong clothing size may cause a lot of returns and bad reviews, because there is no uniformed size for clothing, so the customer needs to convert sizes between international, China, European and American standards. Therefore, pre-sales customer service personnel should provide customers with specific size recommendations, and even Size Chart if necessary.

Q: Hi, seller, I usually wear an American size 8 dress. What size should I buy?
A: Hello, dear customer, our suggestion is that size M suits you well. If you have any questions, please contact us. Thanks!

3.3 Payment

Order conversion rate is very important for a store, and the payment system is one of the keys to improve conversion rate. Cross-border collection and payment is an important factor to be considered in the operation. A good method can reduce a large amount of expenditure. Generally speaking, for customers who do not have a PayPal account, customer service personnel can make a reply with the following example for a reference and recommend customers to use PayPal as much as possible.

Q: Do you accept check or bank transfer? I do not have a PayPal account.
A: We shall be glad to answer your inquiry as to the price of the goods.

For the sake of simplifying the process, I suggest that you pay through PayPal. As you know, it always takes at least 2-3 months to clear international check so that the dealing and shipping time will cost too much time.

PayPal is a faster, easier and safer payment method. It is widely used in international online business. Even if you do not want to register a PayPal account, you can still use your credit card to go through checkout process without any extra steps.

I hope my answer was helpful to you.

3.4 Shipping fee

When customers place a one-off purchase order with multiple items, they may ask for combined shipping, so the customer service personnel should modify and send the invoice, because customers will only be charged one shipping fee for multiple purchases. After the shipping document is sent successfully, the staff should timely inform the customer that the freight has been combined and the customer can pay directly through the electronic invoice.

Q: Hello, seller, can the shipping fee be paid together as I've bought several items from you? Please send me just in one package, thanks!
A: Hello, dear customer, thanks for your business!

We have combined the shipping already and only charge you the shipping fee once. You can check the invoice I've just sent to you and please make the payment through the invoice directly. Please feel free to contact us if you have any other questions. Thanks!

3.5 Tax

During shopping, tariff is the most concerned issue for customers. In the following example, the customer service personnel gave patient and detailed answers to the tax issues, and clearly informed customers that there will be no additional fees for small amounts of goods under normal circumstances. In case of special circumstances, consulting the local customs department will be suggested.

Q: Hi, I want to buy this and ship it to New York in the United States. What are the import duties or customs charges?

A: Thank you for your inquiry. I understand that you are worrying about any possible extra expense for this item. According to past experience, it did not involve any extra expense at buyer side for similar small or low-cost items. Please do not worry about it too much.

However, in some individual cases, buyer might need to take some import taxes or customs charges in import countries. As to specific rates, please consult your local custom office.

Appreciate your understanding.

Exercises

1. Multiple Choices

(1) Nowadays the mainstream search engines commonly used in China and abroad include ( ).

A. Baidu B. Google

C. Bing D. Above all

(2) When using search engine to search for tape buyers, we can search the words like ( ).

A. adhesive tape B. pressure-sensitive tape

C. PVC adhesive tape D. Above all

(3) Which of the following is not the disadvantage of using traditional yellow pages to develop customers? ( )

A. Slow update B. Inconvenient search

C. Higher charges D. Single communication mode

(4) It is not suggested to ( ) when writing an effective development letter.

A. insert hyperlink or pictures B. use white mail background

C. use oral expression D. use three-paragraph structure

(5) Which of the following job content belongs to pre-sales customer service? ( )

A. Notify customers have received payment

B. Handle customer disputes

C. Respond to customers' consultation and conduct shopping conduct

D. Deal with refund

2. True or False

(1) Pre-sales customer service personnel are mainly engaged in guiding services, such as recommending products, replying to customer inquiries, etc. ( )

(2) CBEC customer service is the international version of Taobao customer service. ( )

(3) According to the quality of inquiries, common inquiries can be divided into high quality inquiries, junk inquiries and suspicious inquiries. ( )

(4) It is recommended that the title of a development letter be as short as possible. ( )

(5) CBEC customer service personnel need to master the application of searching engines. ( )

Skills&Drills

Please return a letter according to the following instructions.

Hangzhou Miracle E-Commerce Co., Ltd. established an online store on the AliExpress platform in 2019. It is mainly engaged in daily household products. The product categories include bedding, kitchen and bathroom appliances, indoor accessories and other common daily necessities. Mr. John consulted Eyre on the matters of a new bedsheet, so how Eyre, the pre-sale customer service personnel, make a recommendation?

- List the product features briefly;
- Describe product price, logistics, payment, etc.

Reference answer

Role Play in Moral Education

In the context of "Internet + Foreign Trade", CBEC customer service has increasingly become an important part of the CBEC system, which is subdivided into pre-sales, in-sales and after-sales service. Among them, pre-sales customer service mainly involves developing potential customers, receiving customers, recommending products, replying to consultation, guiding customers to place orders and so on. Due to the job nature and working environment, pre-sales customer service personnel not only need basic professional ethics such as love and dedication, law-abiding integrity, but also need specific qualities and abilities such as resilience and discernment. On one hand, pre-sales customer service personnel need to constantly develop customers, often in the face of sending development letters without reply, or facing all kinds of customers to answer product details, payment methods, freight, tariffs and other problems, which requires pre-sales customer service personnel to be resilient and enthusiastic; on the other hand, pre-sales customer service personnel will receive lots of inquiries from customers. Some of them are customers with real purchase needs, and some of them are those who want to elicit your account or other information. Therefore, pre-sales customer service personnel should be able to identify and distinguish which are high-quality inquiries, junk inquiries or suspicious inquiries.

Resilience, often presented in the face of difficulties and setbacks, measures the degree of adherence to ideals and goals, reflecting the mental state of resistance to pressure and frustration. Chinese Nobel Prize winner Tu Youyou failed 190 times to extract artemisinin, which is a common phenomenon in the scientific community. The same goes for pre-sales customer service personnel who may send numerous development letters and answer complicated questions before successfully establishing a successful customer relationship.

1. Stress Resistance Test

Psychological Test—Let's see how well you can handle pressure	
Questions	You may not have ridden a bicycle for a long time, but think about what kind of bicycle you prefer or you are using: A. Light bicycles B. Electric bicycles C. Variable speed mountain bicycles
Analysis	Option A: 50% pressure tolerance. The biggest characteristic of light bicycles is that it is lighter to ride on any road and much easier for people to ride. People who choose this option generally can't stand the pressure they are under. Because of this, you can save yourself a lot of effort by choosing a light bicycle. But it doesn't mean you can't handle stress. Sometimes stress can be your motivation and make you work hard to achieve what you want. Such people are not in the minority. Option B: 20% pressure tolerance. It is classified as a bicycle because it has two pedals. As long as there is enough electricity, a cyclist can drive on the road without effort. If you choose this option, you are very sensitive to stress. In real life, you should never allow yourself to be overwhelmed. You are easy to give up when you're out of your comfort zone. However, sometimes stress can help you get a lot done. Give it a try and let the pressure become your motivation. Option C: 80% pressure tolerance. Many people like its characteristics of being able to change gears anytime and anywhere. Cyclists can choose different patterns to be relaxed on different roads. Like this feature, you have a good tolerance for stress. You will be very sensible about what level of stress is good for you. And when the pressure is too much, your excellent ability to self-regulation shows. You can adjust your attitude or do something to instantly relieve a lot of external stress. Sometimes stress can be a way for you to express yourself.

Discernment refers to distinction and analysis. Independent identification means thinking and judging independently about the nature and significance of things or events. Independent capacity of discernment is a symbol of one's mature thought and independent abstract thinking ability, which is also the basic quality requirement for one to smoothly integrate into social life. In the face of all kinds of inquiries, it is critical for pre-sales customer service personnel to improve the capacity of discernment.

2. Role Play

Student A plays the role of pre-sales customer service specialist, while student B and C play the role of the staff of a rival firm disguising as customers to make inquiries to student A and ask for samples. The Pre-sales customer service specialist do not know the real identity of the two "customers". In the actual performance process, the two "customers" improvise, putting forward the need for a number of samples and insisting that they do not want to pay the sample fee and the freight. Think over the following questions: How would student A react to student B and C's "improvisation"? How to help student A to distinguish between real and fake inquiries?

Analysis:

(1) Send samples or not: If customers just say they are interested in your products, want to place a large order, and ask for samples, but not specify a product, this kind of customers are invalid basically. It is recommended not to send samples. If customers have the specific requirements of specifications, quantity, they may be effective customers, but you still have to search his company name and website for further confirmation. Most of those who provide the free email 163, Gmail, Hotmail, Foxmail, Outlook and Yahoo are invalid customers. The email addresses are paid enterprise email addresses with the suffix of company domain name at the end of @, then the customers can be regard as valid. You must send samples to them.

(2) Sample charge problem: You need to distinguish customers' strength. If the customer is a big one with websites and brands, samples can be sent for free.

(3) Delivery freight problem: Generally speaking, if the sample is free, the freight is borne by the customer. If the customer is a big customer, and the freight is not expensive, you can consider asking your boss for free freight.

项目三

跨境电商售中客服

知识目标

1. 理解跨境电商售中客户服务工作的总体步骤与技巧；
2. 掌握跨境电商售中客户服务的纠纷解决办法；
3. 掌握包裹在物流递送阶段的客户问题解决与客户维护。

能力目标

1. 能够回答售中产品咨询和服务咨询的相关问题；
2. 能够解答售中客服产品咨询和服务咨询。

素质目标

具备较强的团队意识和服务意识，有较高的辨别力与共情力。

知识点索引

项目三　跨境电商售中客服

- 项目背景
- 任务分解
- 任务完成
- 知识要点
  - 一、订单处理
    - （一）等待客户付款
    - （二）客户已经付款
  - 二、卖家发货
    - （一）线下发货
    - （二）线上发货
  - 三、物流跟踪
  - 四、关联产品定向推介
  - 五、特殊订单处理与沟通
    - （一）发货前的特殊订单处理与沟通
    - （二）发货后的特殊订单处理与沟通
  - 六、跨境电子商务售中客户服务案例
    - （一）收到订单
    - （二）物流跟踪
    - （三）关联产品推介
    - （四）特殊订单处理

项目背景

小艾在公司已经工作两个月，处理了一些 B2B 平台售中服务业务，有了些许售中服务经验。部门经理告诉小艾、B2C平台售中客服的工作与B2B售中客服有很多不同，同时售中客服的工作在推动客户购买和解决售中出现的问题和纠纷上起着十分重要的作用，影响客户的满意度和公司的形象。所以小艾对接下来的B2C平台售中服务工作既期待又有些忐忑。

任务分解

今天是小艾第一天处理B2C平台的客户，虽然有了前期处理B2B平台的一些经验，但是对于初次接触B2C平台客户提出的各种问题，小艾还是感到无法从容应对。前期的简单咨询之后，一位客户已经下单，但是在售中出现了一系列问题，让小艾感到有些棘手。来自客户各种各样的询盘和咨询让小艾有些力不从心了。很多客户在询盘之后便消失不见，让不停回复信息的小艾甚感希望落空和疲惫。此外，有几个订单的交接不是很顺利。在不断地回复询盘和咨询之外，一些客户下单却迟迟未付款。另外一些客户针对物流运输也提出了各种相关问题，有一些订单被客户提起了纠纷；有的订单被海关扣了，原因还不是很清楚。

对此，部门经理对小艾进行了培训，并且提出了以下问题：

1. 跨境电子商务售中客户服务常见的问题主要涉及哪些方面？

2. 常见的售中客户提问可能会针对哪些方面？

任务完成

1. 跨境电子商务售中客户服务与沟通涉及的主要业务范围包括订单处理、卖家发货、物流跟踪、关联产品定向推介、特殊订单处理与沟通。

2. 针对售中服务客户的不同状态，通常出现的特殊情况主要有如下几种：

（1）客户未及时付款；

（2）客户付款而卖家逾期未发货导致“成交不卖”；

（3）卖家发货后的物流纷争和关税问题。

知识要点

售中是指从客户下单后到客户签收货物这个阶段。这一阶段的客户服务与沟通也是体现卖家服务质量的重要环节。售中客户服务与沟通涉及的业务范围包括订单处理、卖家发货、物流跟踪、关联产品定向推介、特殊订单处理与沟通。售中客户服务既是满足客户购买商品欲望的服务行为，又是不断满足客户心理需要的服务行为。在售中阶段，卖家的服务质量是决定客户是否最终会购买的重要因素。因此，提高服务质量对售中客户服务来说至关重要，卖家应该实行售中客户服务规范化，对具体的内容和要求分别制定规则。

一、订单处理

售中订单的控制与处理是跨境电子商务客户服务和沟通的关键环节，直接关系到交易能否达成，是跨境电子商务的核心业务流程。订单处理过程包括的细节和关键点较多。因此，优化订单处理过程，缩短订单处理周期，提高订单满足率和供货的准确率，可以进一步提高客户服务人员的服务水准，并提升客户满意度。良好的订单处理能力在店铺运营中可以节省大量的人力、物力、时间和金钱。

从客户进店拍下产品开始，会出现很多个订单节点，也就是常说的订单状态。对于跨境电商售中客服，订单状态分为等待客户付款和客户已付款两个环节，每一个环节都需要客户服务人员去做相应的工作。

（一）等待客户付款

对于客户已经拍下但还未付款的订单，卖家不可以直接关闭订单。客户未付款情况的处理方式主要有以下几种。

1. 提醒客户及时付款

通常情况下，如果客户下单后未及时付款，卖家可以通过提醒客户是否有产品价格、尺寸等问题，使用委婉的办法来提醒客户付款，并承诺付款后尽快发货。本项目后续提供了提醒客户及时付款的示例邮件。

2. 打消客户对产品质量或服务的疑虑

拍下产品半天未付款的客户可能正在犹豫不决，卖家可以抓住机会强化客户对产品和服务的信心。

3. 提供礼物或折扣以促成客户付款

有的客户下单 1～2 天后仍未付款，且未回复之前的付款提醒邮件，出现这种情况的原因可能是客户觉得价格偏高，正在考虑更加优惠的卖家。这时，客户服务人员可以在说明利润较低之后，提出为客户提供礼物或者折扣，促成交易。

（二）客户已经付款

客户付款并通过跨境电子商务平台风控管理部门的资金审核后，卖家可以通知客户已收到货款，并承诺尽快发货。以速卖通平台为例，客户付款成功之后卖家在卖家端查看订单详情。根据规定，除特殊类目外的所有类目发货期最长设定限制为 7 天，即卖家必须在客户付款后 7 天内发货。如果卖家逾期未发货而导致“成交不卖”，影响客户购物体验，也可能会影响卖家等级考核。

二、卖家发货

继续以速卖通平台为例，进入发货界面后，有两种发货方式供卖家选择，一种是线下发货，另一种是线上发货。如果卖家选择线下发货，在面对客户提起的物流纠纷时，有扣除卖家店铺服务分的风险；如果卖家选择线上发货，客户提起物流纠纷将不会扣除卖家店铺服务分。

（一）线下发货

卖家可以选择货运代理公司发货，然后在发货界面单击“填写发货通知”按钮，在

“货物跟踪号”文本框中填写快递单号。

（二）线上发货

图 3－1 为线上发货操作流程，包括七个主要步骤。

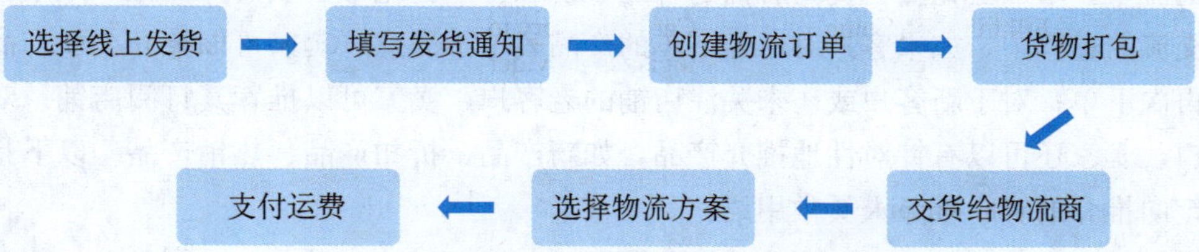

图 3－1　线上发货流程图

三、物流跟踪

发货结束并不意味着卖家的工作就完结了。良好的购物体验有助于提升店铺的考核指标。卖家关注物流情况，及时将物流进展告诉客户，能提升客户的购物体验。卖家应在产品进入客户所在地的时候告知客户货物的投递进展。如果遇到货物拥堵情况，卖家应对客户表示歉意；如果产品需要报关，可以预先告知客户。卖家需要经常跟踪包裹并把进展情况及时地告诉客户。通过对细节的把控和周到的服务，客户可以感受到卖家在发货速度、物流运送时间、货物情况、工作人员的服务意识等。

在物流跟踪过程中，卖家需要与客户沟通两方面内容：一是货物运输的进展情况；二是货物在运输途中可能遇到的情况。如果货物顺利出运，卖家可以根据物流显示的信息，在货物出运、货物抵达海关、货物到达客户当地邮局、货物妥投等时间节点及时告知客户，让客户在第一时间掌握货物运输情况，这有利于拉近与客户的关系并获得好评。

货物发出后，可能会遇到各种各样的问题，例如：物流信息未能及时更新，货物没能按照预期时间到达客户所在地，由于特殊原因造成物流延误等。这些问题均会引起客户的不满，卖家需要及时掌握物流信息，积极与客户沟通，尽量安抚客户的不满情绪，避免引起与客户的纠纷。虽然客户可通过物流详情页面了解时事物流信息，但是客户服务人员仍然应该在以下三个关键节点和客户及时沟通联系：货物抵达海关、货物到达邮局、货物投妥。

小贴士

包裹物流跟踪常见的状态

包裹查无信息“Not found”（当包裹记录还未上网，官网未更新）

包裹正在运输中“Transit”（当包裹还在运输中）

包裹到达待取“Pick Up”（当包裹显示已经到达目的地国家）

包裹投递成功“Delivered”（当包裹显示投妥，而收件人声称未收到时）

包裹运输过久“Expired”（时效延误/目的地国家不能查到投妥/官网不更新状态）

包裹可能异常“Alert”（大部分为退件/海关单号/损坏/丢失等问题）

四、关联产品定向推介

在售中阶段，为了让客户看到和接触到更多的产品，做好关联营销可以有效利用来之不易的流量，增加曝光量，提高店铺的客户单价和订单转化率，从而降低推广成本。在与客户交流的过程中，如果客户对已经下单的产品表示不满意，卖家可以推介关联产品，引导其再次下单；对于新客户或还未关注店铺的老客户，卖家可以推荐其订阅店铺；对于潜在客户，卖家还可以有针对性地推介产品，如新产品、折扣产品、热销产品。以下是关联产品定向推介的客户服务人员常用语：

(1) I am sorry that you are not satisfied with the product. I would like to recommend some other items of similar styles. Please click the link ×××（此为链接）for more specific information.

（很抱歉，您对该产品不满意。我想为您推荐相似款式的其他产品。请您单击以下链接×××了解更多产品详情。）

(2) Thank you for ordering our skirt. We are selling a nice and popular belt which matches the dress ordered. For more information, please click the link ×××（此为链接）.

（感谢您下单购买我们店的裙装。我们店有一条漂亮而且销量不错的腰带与您订购的该裙装很般配。若要了解腰带详情，请您单击以下链接×××。）

(3) Thanks a lot for your message. If you buy it along with the product in the link ×××（此为链接），you will be offered discount of 50%.

（多谢您的留言。如果您在购买它的同时也购买×××链接中的产品的话，可以享受五折优惠。）

(4) Sorry for interrupting you. But we would like to recommend our new product ×××, which is also a best-seller in real stores. If you are interested, refer to the link ×××（此为链接）.

（很抱歉打扰您。我们想向您推荐新品×××，这也是一款实体店中的热销产品。如果您有兴趣，可以在以下链接×××中查询。）

(5) Christmas/Thanksgiving is around the corner. The following link ×××（此为链接）shows warm package of considerate gifts. You will enjoy wholesale price of × dollars if interested.

（圣诞节/感恩节就要到了。链接×××中展示的是我们温暖又贴心的礼物套餐。如果您感兴趣的话，可以享受×美元的批发价。）

五、特殊订单处理与沟通

售中客户服务除了对订单进行正常的跟踪之外，还会在订单处理的过程中遇到一些特殊情况。那些由于发货、物流、海关等原因导致的不能正常出货或退货的订单，称之为特殊订单。

特殊订单可能出现在发货前，原因包括订单支付、海关税收、发货困难等；出现在发货后，可能是由节假日或者不可抗力因素导致的物流延误、发错货、漏发货、客户不清等。遇到这种订单时，卖家不能消极等待甚至逃避，而是应该积极、主动地和客户沟通，为客户着想，及时缓解客户的不满情绪，避免不必要的纠纷。

特殊订单处理方式主要包括：

（一）发货前的特殊订单处理与沟通

合并支付与价格优惠；包邮问题；海关税收相关事宜；发货困难。

（二）发货后的特殊订单处理与沟通

节假日等引起的可预测物流延误；不可抗力因素导致的物流延误；发错货或漏发货的问题；清关事宜的沟通。

六、跨境电子商务售中客户服务案例

以下为客户售中服务回复常见咨询的问题与模板，仅供参考。

（一）收到订单

- 提醒买家尽快付款

Dear costumer,

We appreciated your purchase from us. However, we noticed that you haven't made the payment yet. This is a friendly reminder to you to complete the payment transaction as soon as possible. Instant payments are very important; the earlier you pay, the sooner you will get the item.

If you have any problems making the payment, please let us know. We can help you to resolve the payment problems or cancel the order.

Thanks again! Looking forward to hearing from you soon.

Best Regards,

(Your name)

尊敬的顾客：

我们十分感谢您从我们这里购买商品。但是，我们注意到您尚未付款。谨此友情提醒您尽快完成支付交易。及时付款非常重要；您越早付款，将越早收到商品。

如果您在付款时遇到任何问题，或者希望取消订单，请告知我们。我们可以帮助您解决付款问题或取消订单。

再次感谢！期待很快可以收到你的来信。

最诚挚的祝福，

（卖家姓名）

- 取消订单回复

Dear customer,

Orders can only be canceled before the package is handle to shipping company. For canceled orders and refunds, AliExpress usually takes 1-2 weeks to make the refund the buyer.

Best Regards,

(Your name)

尊敬的顾客：

只有在包裹尚未交给运输公司之前才能取消订单。对于取消的订单和退款，速卖通退款时间通常需要 1～2 周。

最诚挚的祝福，

（卖家姓名）

（二）物流跟踪

● 已发货并告知买家

Dear customer,

Thank you for your purchase.

We have shipped out your order (order ID: ×××) on Feb. 15th by EMS. The tracking number is ×××. It will take 5-10 workdays to reach your destination, please check the tracking information for updated information. Thank you for your patience!

If you have any further questions, please feel free to contact me.

Best Regards,

(Your name)

尊敬的顾客：

感谢您的购买。

我们已于2月15日通过EMS发出您的订单（订单ID：×××）。订单号码是×××。到达目的地需要5～10个工作日，请查看跟踪信息以获取更新信息。感谢您的耐心等待！

如果您还有任何问题，请随时与我联系。

最诚挚的祝福，

（卖家姓名）

● 物流信息未及时更新

Dear customer,

We are sorry that now it's the busiest time of the shopping season and the logistics companies are running at maximum capacity. Your delivery information has not update yet, but don't worry about it. We will let you know as the update is available. Thank you for your patience.

Best Regards,

(Your name)

尊敬的顾客：

很抱歉，现在是购物旺季最繁忙的时候，物流公司正在全力以赴。您的收货信息尚未更新，但请不要担心。一旦更新物流信息，我们会第一时间通知您。感谢您的耐心等待。

最诚挚的祝福，

（卖家姓名）

（三）关联产品推介

● 客户不满意所选产品，推介关联产品

Dear customer,

I am sorry that you are not satisfied with the goods you inquired. According to your information, I would like to recommend some other items of similar styles and hope you will like them. These are our best-selling goods right now. Please check the link below: http://www.XXX.com.

If you have any questions about this product, please contact us.

Best wishes,

(Your name)

尊敬的顾客：

很抱歉您对您询问的商品不满意。根据您的信息，我想推荐一些其他类似款式的单品，希望您会喜欢。这些是我们目前最畅销的商品。请查看以下链接：http://www.XXX.com。

如果您对此产品有任何疑问，请联系我们。

最诚挚的祝福，

（卖家姓名）

- 着重向新客户推介新产品和促销活动信息

Dear customer,

Thanks for your order and hope it will meet your satisfaction. In order to keep you update with our latest promotion and products, please subscribe to our store. If you have any problems, please refer to: http://XXXX. com.

Looking forward to your future order.

Yours faithfully,

(Your name)

尊敬的顾客:

感谢您的订购，希望它会满足您的需求。为了让您了解我们最新的促销和产品，请订阅我们的商店。如有问题请查询网址: http://XXXX. com。

期待您未来的订单。

您忠实的，

(卖家姓名)

(四) 特殊订单处理

- 丢件问题出现时的告知

Dear costumer,

Sorry to tell you that we cannot get the tracking information. We are afraid the package might be lost. If you still want to buy the product, please place another order and I'll offer you a 5% discount. If not, please apply for refund. Thank you for your understanding.

Best Regards,

(Your name)

尊敬的顾客:

很抱歉告诉您，我们无法获取物流跟踪信息。我们恐怕包裹可能已经丢失。如果您仍想购买该产品，请再次下单，我们将为您提供 5% 的折扣。如果您不想重新购买，请申请退款。感谢您的理解。

最诚挚的祝福，

(卖家名字)

- 超重订单 (无法使用小包邮寄)

Dear costumer,

We are sorry to tell you that free shipping for this item is not available.

Free shipping by China Post Air Mail is only for package weighing less than 2 kgs. However, the weight of the item you choose is 2. 5 kgs which is higher. Therefore, would you please choose another express company, like EMS or UPS which may cost higher shipping fees, but is much faster. Or you can place the order separately and make sure the weight of each order is less than 2 kgs so as to take advantage of free shipping.

Yours faithfully,

(Your name)

尊敬的顾客:

我们很遗憾地告诉您，此商品不提供免费送货服务。

中国邮政航空邮件免费送货仅适用于重量小于 2 公斤的包裹。但是，您选择的物品重量为 2. 5 公斤，超过了重量限制。因此，请您选择其他快递公司，例如 EMS 或 UPS，它们运费可能更高，但运货速度更快。或者，您可以单独下单，并确保每个订单的重量小于 2 公斤，以享受免费送货服务。

您忠实的，

(卖家名字)

小贴士

客户沟通技巧

1. 向客户提供专业服务：（1）从专业的角度解决问题；（2）提供可信赖的数据与证据；（3）采取多样化的回复方式。

2. 控制客户对事件的认知与情绪：（1）淡化事件的严重性，保障问题顺利解决，先给买家吃定心丸；（2）向买家展示永远感恩的态度；（3）最后一次的邮件回复一定来自卖家。

3. 卖家积极提供有选择的解决方案：（1）方案应由卖家主动提供，而不是买家提出；（2）尽量提供多个方案（至少 2 个）供买家备选。

4. 坚持主动承担责任，第三方承担错误：（1）寻找合适的解释理由；（2）真诚地承担责任。

5. 注重回复邮件的技巧：（1）基本功扎实，避免拼写与语法错误；（2）邮件中不要有成段的大写；（3）尽量使用结构简单、用词平实的短句；（4）巧用分段与空行，让客户尽快找到想看到的重点。

习题测验

（一）选择题

1. 以下属于跨境电商客服售中服务范畴的是（　　）。

A. 回答客户咨询并进行导购

B. 通知客户运输中的物流与关税问题

C. 回应客户询价和商品细节等问题

D. 进行退换货处理

2. 以下关于跨境电商售中客服的说法，错误的是（　　）。

A. 邮件回复要及时且有礼貌

B. 建立同理心，让客人感到安心

C. 处理问题的时候，要善于给客人提供选择

D. 当产品到达目的国家，任务便完成

3. 在处理客户售中问题时，以下哪项不正确？（　　）

A. 如遇节日天气等人为不可控情况，应及时通知客户

B. 发货后及时告知发货情况

C. 发现错发或漏发等情况，不予以告知，等待客户自行询问

D. 货物到达海关、邮局和货物投妥等节点及时告知

4. 以下情况，跨境电商售中客服需要注意的有（　　）。

A. 产品运输方式

B. 海关申报清关

C. 产品是否符合其他国家的安全标准

D. 以上都是

5. 在订单处理过程中，如果客人迟迟未付款，以下哪种做法是错误的？（　　）

A. 打消客人关于产品的疑虑

B. 提供礼物或折扣以促成客户付款

C. 不断催促客人付款

D. 主动询问并了解客人的疑惑和担忧

（二）判断题

1. 跨境电商的售中服务阶段是指客户下单后到货物出运的时间段。售中沟通与服务是体现卖家服务质量的重要环节。（　　）

2. 客户下订单，但是仓库无货属于跨境电商售中沟通与服务的内容。（　　）

3. 包裹超出预计收货时间属于跨境电商售中沟通与服务的内容。（　　）

4. 发货前的特殊订单情况包括：海关税收问题、因物流风险而无法向客户所在国家发货、特定节假日导致无法向客户所在国家发货。（　　）

5. 优秀的跨境电商客服人员可以适时地向客户推荐更多的产品，增加产品的曝光量，提高店铺的客单价和订单转化率，降低推广成本，我们称这种营销方式为关联营销。（　　）

能力实训

阅读以下速卖通平台上真实的售中客户服务案例，分析并评价此案例中客户服务的优点。

1. 客户投诉

客户在一家女装店购买了一条裤子，还未收货之前产品就发现已经降价，遂在速卖通平台上进行投诉，具体内容如下。

订单号：××××××
订单金额：120 USD
订单创建时间：Dec. 12. 28. 2021
收货地址：×××××××

2. 卖家处理

卖家打开“我的速卖通”卖家端，单击“纠纷列表”，查看“纠纷详情”，具体内容如下。

订单号：××××××
纠纷原因：产品降价

订单创建时间：Dec. 12. 28. 2021
2022-01-03 22:30:51 Rosalie：That's unfair. Could I cancel the former order and place another one at the discount price ?
2022-01-04 20:11:47 Wen：Just as you said，there has been a price change. However，we have not changed the price randomly. Customers can get 10% off at AliExpress from Jan. 1-3 to celebrate the New Year's Day. You placed your order on December 28，right before the discount became available. We apologize for not letting you know immediately.
2022-01-05 19:56:24 Wen：We feel so sorry for your inconvenience. We will verify the price change as quickly as possible. Thank you for your patience.
2022-01-05 20:51:21 Wen：Thanks for your consideration，since the product has been shipped，I am afraid it is not advisable for a cancel. But in compensate，we will refund you the 20 dollar's markdown as soon as possible. How do you like it?
2022-01-06 11:51:09 Rosalie：OK，I understand that. So a 20 dollar refund is agreed.

3. 解决投诉

当卖家和客户就瑕疵产品的解决方案达成一致，投诉就解决了。卖家可以在“我的速卖通”中单击“纠纷列表”，打开“纠纷详情”进行查看，详情如下。

订单号：××××××
纠纷原因：产品降价
纠纷状态：纠纷结果 仅退款 USD20.00，由卖家出资

请分析该则投诉解决案例中客户服务与沟通的原则与优点，如沟通技巧、态度等。

参考答案

思政微训营

[坚忍力训练]

在跨境电商客服的售中服务与咨询过程中，经常会面临多样的困难与挫折，来自不同国家、地区和文化背景的客户对于产品、服务的概念各不相同，在交流与沟通中容易造成摩擦。此外，各种情景下的订单处理，特殊问题处理，包括对于物流的追踪，都是巨大的考验，无一不磨炼着跨境电商客服工作人员的意志。中华优秀传统文化历来强调人的意志力、坚忍力、自制力培养塑造。而坚忍力的培养，既是客服人员的工作现实所需，也是个人内在成长的要求。心理学家将坚忍力定义为在面对逆境或重大压力来源（例如家庭和人际关系问题、严重的健康问题或工作场所和财务压力）时能够很好地适应的能力。跨境电商客服工作人员坚忍力的把握应该从忍耐力、忍压力、忍挫力三个维度加以把握。

图 3－2、图 3－3 是加利福尼亚 DoveTail 学习中心针对坚忍力与抗压能力进行的心理研究调查，分别展现了不同程度下的坚忍力在应对工作压力时呈现出的模式曲线。对比两张图上的曲线，我们可以发现，低坚忍力与高坚忍力应对压力的模式差异主要在于对待压力和外界刺激的态度。低坚忍力情况下，存在的是一种对于压力和刺激的反射性保护机制。但是在高坚忍力情况下，面对压力采取的是一种事前的预测，开放性的好奇心，由此，能够进行较为冷静的评估，从而更加冷静和理智地处理问题。

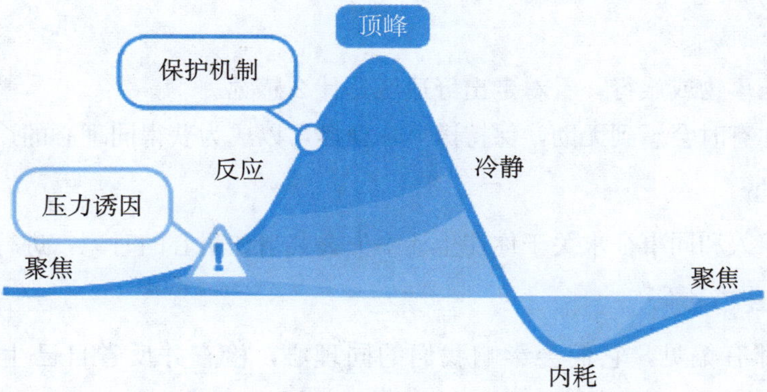

图 3－2　低坚忍力下的抗压模式曲线

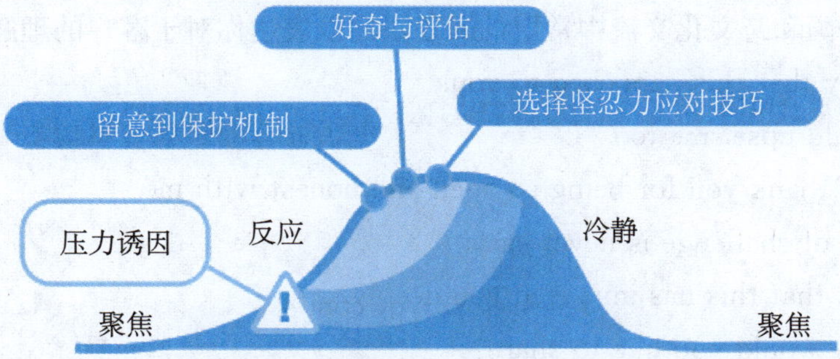

图 3－3　高坚忍力下的抗压模式曲线

根据哈佛商学院的报告，以下是培养坚忍力的小技巧：

（1）当灾难来临时，在做出反应之前从 1 数到 10，想一想自己能够从此次经历中得到什么。

（2）建立联系，与亲近的人建立健康的关系。

（3）避免将危机视为无法克服的问题，通过重新评估，重构和调整我们对压力事件的反应。

（4）接受改变是生活的一部分——专注于我们能改变的，而不是不能改变的。

[**共情力训练**]

具有强烈同理心的跨境电商客服人员能够迅速抓住机会，在面对变化时减少焦虑，创造更积极的工作环境，并以更好的耐心和理解提供优质的解决方案。项目一已经向大家介绍了同理心的定义，并通过问卷测试了每个人的同理心水平。在本项目中，我们将学习有效提升同理心的技巧：

以下是几个有助于提升共情力的小技巧：

1. 培养好奇心

（1）花时间和你不太了解的人在一起，问问他们自己，他们怎么样，他们的生活是什么样的。

（2）在社交媒体上关注来自不同背景（宗教、种族、政治）的人们，并聆听他们的意见。

（3）参观新的地方，结识当地人，同时沉浸在他们的生活方式中。

2. 走出舒适区

（1）学习新事物或旅行，看看走出舒适区是什么感觉。

（2）接受你有时会感到无助，保持谦卑，谦虚可以成为获得同理心的途径。

3. 接收反馈

向朋友、家人和同事征求关于你在生活中失去共情和耐心的时刻，进行反思。

4. 审视你自己的偏见

（1）我们都有偏见，它们会影响我们的同理心，检查并反省自己生活和工作中的偏见。

（2）寻找机会与来自其他背景的人交往，在不同之处进行包容和理解。

以下是在跨国和跨文化交流中常用的回复，用以表达你对于客户的理解和共情：

- I am sorry that this happened to you.
- That would upset me too.
- I want to thank you for being so open and honest with me.
- This sort of challenge is never easy.
- It is clear that this has impacted you deeply.
- What else would you like to share?
- It sounds like you had a very stressful time.
- Yes，what has happened makes no sense at all.
- I am on your side.
- It's no surprise you are upset.
- You are making complete sense.

提升共情力小组活动：创建共情图（充分发挥想象力来构建他人情况的全景图像）。

①从报纸或杂志上剪下一个场景中的人物。

②将图片贴在一张较大的纸上。

③小组活动，询问有关此人及其生活的问题并想象可能的答案：

- 这个人是谁？给他一个名字，假设一个家庭背景、工作背景、财务背景。
- 动用想象力，思考他们当下可能处在怎样的情景中，他们需要做出什么决定。
- 是什么影响了他们的决定？
- 他们会说什么？
- 其他人（朋友、同事、伙伴、家人）会让他们做什么？

④在图片周围的空白处写下答案，小组成员之间进行交流和沟通。

Project 3

CBEC In-sales Customer Service

Knowledge Objectives

1. To master the general procedure and techniques of in-sales service work of CBEC;

2. To understand the dispute resolution methods for CBEC in-sales service;

3. To master the skills of customer problem solving and customer relationship maintenance in the logistics delivery stage of CBEC in-sales service.

Competency Objectives

1. Understand the related questions of in-sales product consultation and be able to respond to the service consultation and give targeted answers;

2. Be able to answer in-sales customer service consultation regarding product and service.

Quality Objectives

Be able to have a strong sense of cooperation, high discernment and empathy in teamwork.

Key Points Index

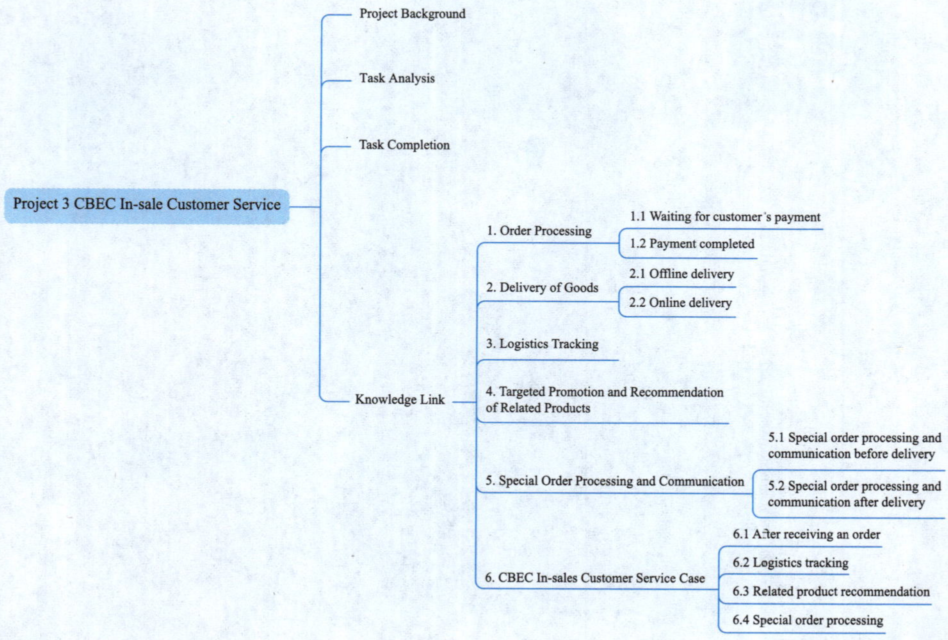

Project Background

Eyre has been working in the company for two months, and also has some in-sales service experience while dealing with B2B in-sales service business. The department manager told Eyre that the work of in-sales customer service on the B2C platform is very different from that of B2B in-sales customer service. At the same time, in-sales service of CBEC plays a very important role in promoting customer purchases and solving problems and disputes during the sales. In-sales customer service also greatly affects customer satisfaction and the company's image. Therefore, while looking forward to the following B2C in-sales service work, Eyre also feels a little bit nervous.

Task Analysis

Today is Eyre's first day dealing with customer problems on the B2C platform. Despite her abundant experience on B2B platforms, she finds herself slightly overwhelmed with the various problems put forward by customers on the B2C platform. After a simple consultation in the early stage, a customer has placed an order, yet a series of problems appeared later, involving all kinds of inquiries and consultations. On one hand, many customers disappeared after enquiry, making Eyre, who kept replying information, felt hopeless and exhausted. On the other hand, the handover of several orders also proved to be tricky. Apart from constant inquiries, some customers placed orders yet delayed payment. In addition, some customers have also raised various related issues regarding logistics and delivery. While some customers raised disputes, some orders have been detained by the customs with reasons not clear.

As a result, the department manager trained Eyre and asked her the following questions:

1. What are the common problems of CBEC in-sales customer service?
2. What are some of the most encountered in-sales questions you may face?

Task Completion

1. The business scope of CBEC in-sales customer service and communication includes order processing, logistics tracking, recommendation of related products, special order processing and communication.

2. According to the different status of in-sales customer service, special situations that usually occur mainly include the following:

(1) Customers do not pay in time;

(2) Customers pay and sellers fail to deliver the goods within the time limit, resulting in "Failure of deal after payment";

(3) Logistics disputes and tariff issues after goods are delivered.

Knowledge Link

In-sales customer service refers to the stage after the customer places an order to the time when customer receive goods. This stage of customer service and communication is also an important part of sellers' service. The business scope of in-sales customer service and communication includes order processing, logistics tracking, recommendation of related products, special order processing and communication. In-sales customer service is not only a service behavior that satisfies customers' desire to purchase goods, but also a service part that continuously satisfies customers' psychological needs. During this stage, the service quality is an important factor in deciding whether the customer will buy the products. Therefore, improving service quality is essential for in-sales customer service. Sellers should implement measures to standardize the in-sales customer service and formulate rules regarding specific content and requirements. The following are the four aspects of in-sales customer service.

1. Order Processing

The control and processing of in-sales service is a key part in CBEC customer service and communication, directly related to whether the transaction could be completed. The order processing includes numerous details and key points. Therefore, optimizing the order processing process, shortening the order processing cycle, increasing the order fulfillment rate and the accuracy rate of supply can further elevate the service of customer service personnel and customer satisfaction. Excellent order processing capabilities can save a lot of manpower, material resources, time and cost for business operation.

From the moment the customer enters the store and buys the product, there exist many stages, defined as different order status. The order status is divided into tuo steps: waiting customer payment, after payment and before shipment. Each step requires customer service personnel to complete different corresponding task.

1.1 Waiting for customer's payment

For orders that have been placed by the customer but have not been paid, the seller cannot close the order directly. The following are the many approaches to deal with customer non-payment.

1.1.1 Remind customers to pay in time

Under normal circumstances, if the customer does not pay in time after placing the order, the seller can remind the customer to pay by asking customer whether there are problems with the product price, size, etc., and using polite wording to remind the customer to pay while promising to ship the goods as soon as possible after payment. In the later part of this chapter, different sample email reminding customers to pay in time are provided.

1.1.2 Dispel customers' doubts about product quality or service

Customers who have not paid for a product after half a day may be hesitant. Sellers can seize the opportunity to strengthen their confidence in products and services.

1.1.3 Provide gifts or discounts to facilitate customer payment

Some customers do not pay for 1-2 days after placing an order, and do not respond to the previous payment reminder email. The reason for this situation may vary. The customer may be unsatisfied with the price and is considering more preferential sellers. At this time, the customer service personal can offer gifts or discounts to customers to facilitate the transaction.

1.2 Payment completed

After the customer completes the payment and passes the fund inspection of the risk control management department of the CBEC platform, the seller can notify the customer that the payment has been received and promise to deliver the goods as soon as possible. After the customer's payment is successfully completed, the seller shall check the order details on the AliExpress seller terminal. According to regulations, the maximum delivery period for all categories except special categories is set for 7 days, in other words, the seller must deliver the goods within 7 days after the customer finishes the payment. If the seller fails to deliver the goods within the due date, it will affect the customer's shopping experience and may also affect the seller's rating assessment.

2. Delivery of Goods

Let's take AliExpress as an example. After entering the shipping interface, the sellers can choose from two shipping methods. One is offline shipping, and the other is online shipping. If the seller chooses to ship offline, there is a risk of influencing the seller's store service assessment points while facing a logistics dispute raised by the customer; if the seller chooses to ship online, the customer's logistics dispute will not influence the store's service assessment points.

2.1 Offline delivery

the seller can choose a freight forwarding company to deliver the goods, and then click the "Fill in Delivery Notification" button on the delivery interface, and fill in the courier number in the "Cargo Tracking Number" text box.

2.2 Online delivery

The following figure shows the online delivery operation process, including seven main steps.

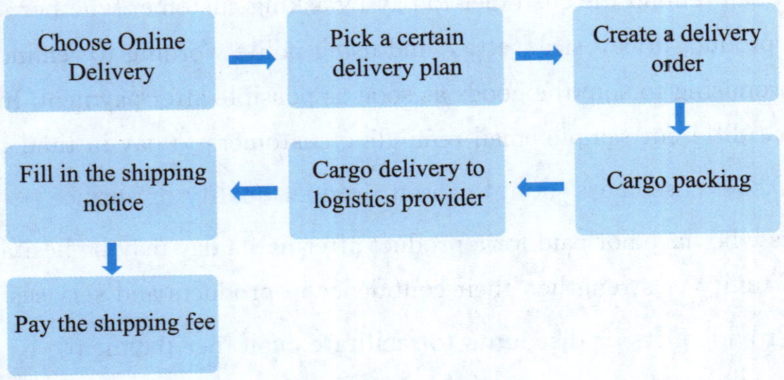

Figure 3 - 1 Online Delivery Operation Process

3. Logistics Tracking

The completion of the shipment does not mean that the seller's work is over. A good shopping experience helps to improve the evaluation indicators of the store. Sellers who pay attention to the logistics situation and inform customers of the logistics progress in a timely manner can enhance the customer's shopping experience. The seller shall inform the customer of the delivery progress of the goods when the product enters the customer's location. If a cargo congestion is encountered, the seller should apologize to the customer. If the product needs to be declared, you can inform the customer in advance. Sellers need to keep track of packages and inform customers of the progress in a timely manner. Through detailed control and thoughtful service, customers would have a clear understanding of the seller's delivery speed and the personnel's service performance.

In the process of logistics tracking, sellers need to communicate with customers about two aspects: one is the progress of the delivery; the other being the unexpected situation that the shipment may encounter. If the shipment is successfully completed, the seller can inform the customer in time according to the information of the logistics system. In this way, the customer can have a timely information of the shipment situation in the first time, which is conducive to strengthen the relationship with customers.

After the goods are delivered, various problems may be encountered, for example, the logistics information is not updated in time, the goods cannot reach the customer's location as expected as well as logistics delays due to special reasons. These problems will lead to customer dissatisfaction. Sellers need to be provided with logistics information in a timely manner, actively communicate with customers, try to appease customers' dissatisfaction and avoid disputes with customers.

Although customers can learn about logistics information on the logistics details webpage, customer service personnel should still communicate with customers in a timely manner at the following key time nodes: when goods arrive at the customs, when goods arrive at the post office and when goods are received by the customer.

Tips

Frequent Logistics Statue

The general status of parcel logistics tracking is as follows:

"Not found": when the package's information has not been updated on the official website.

"Transit": when the package is still in delivery.

"Pick Up": when the package shows that it has arrived in the destination country.

"Delivered": when the package shows that it has been delivered.

"Expired": when delays occurred/when the official website does not update the delivery information.

"Alert": when packages are returned/damaged or lost.

4. Targeted Promotion and Recommendation of Related Products

During the in-sales stage, in order to allow customers to get in touch with more products, a wonderful work of affiliated marketing can make full use of hard-won store flow, increase exposure, increase the store's customer unit price and order conversion rate, thereby reducing promotion costs. In the process of communicating with customers, if the customer is dissatisfied with the product ordered, the seller can recommend related products and guide them to place an order again; for new customers or old customers who have not followed the store, the seller can recommend them to subscribe to the store; for potential customers, sellers can also recommend targeted products such as new products, discounted products and hot-selling products.

The following are some samples maybe frequently used by customer service personnel for targeted promotion and recommendation of related products:

■ I am sorry that you are not satisfied with the product. I would like to recommend some other items of similar styles. Please click the link ××× for more specific information.

■ Thank you for ordering our skirt. We are selling a nice and popular belt which matches the dress ordered. For more information, please click the link ×××.

■ Thanks a lot for your message. If you buy it along with the product in the link ×××, you will be offered a discount of 50%.

■ Sorry for interrupting you. But we would like to recommend our new product ×××, which is also a best-seller in offline stores. If you are interested, refer to the link ×××.

■ Christmas/Thanksgiving is around the corner. The following link ××× shows warm package of considerate gifts. You will enjoy wholesale price of × dollars if interested.

5. Special Order Processing and Communication

In addition to the normal tracking of orders, in-sales customer service would also encounter some special situations in order processing. Orders that cannot be shipped or returned due to problems regarding shipping, logistics, customs, etc. are called special orders.

Special orders may appear before delivery. The reasons include order payment, customs taxes, delivery difficulties, etc., after delivery, logistics delays caused by holidays or inevitable factors, wrong delivery, missed delivery, unclear customers, etc. When encountering these orders, the seller can't passively wait or even evade, but should actively communicate with the customer and relieve the customer's dissatisfaction in time, in order to avoid unnecessary disputes.

The methods of special order processing mainly include the following types:

5.1 Special order processing and communication before delivery

combined payment and price discounts; offer free shipping; customs tax related matters; delivery difficulties.

5.2 Special order processing and communication after delivery

predictable logistics delays caused by holidays, etc.; logistics delays caused by inevitable factors; issues of wrong or missing shipments; communication on customs clearance matters.

6. CBEC In-sales Customer Service Case

The following are some of the common templates for CBEC customer in-sales service responses, for reference only.

6.1 After receiving an order

- Remind buyers to pay as soon as possible

Dear customer,

We appreciated your purchase from us. However, we noticed that you haven't made the payment yet. This is a friendly reminder to you to complete the payment transaction as soon as possible. Instant payments are very important; the earlier you pay, the sooner you will get the item.

If you have any problems making the payment, please let us know. We can help you to resolve the payment problems or cancel the order.

Thanks again! Looking forward to hearing from you soon.

Best Regards,

(Your name)

- Responses to canceled order

Dear customer,

Orders can only be canceled before the package is handle to shipping company. For canceled orders and refunds AliExpress usually takes 1-2 weeks to make the refund get to the buyer.

Best Regards,

(Your name)

6.2 Logistics tracking

● Notification to buyers after shipment

Dear customer,

Thank you for your purchase.

We have shipped out your order (order ID: ×××) on Feb. 15th by EMS. The tracking number is ×××. It will take 5-10 workdays to reach your destination, please check the tracking information for updated information. Thank you for your patience!

If you have any further questions, please feel free to contact me.

Best Regards,

(Your name)

● Responses when logistics information is not updated in time

Dear customer,

We are sorry that now it's the busiest time of the shopping season and the logistics companies are running at maximum capacity. Your delivery information has not been updated yet, but don't worry about it. We will let you know as the update is available. Thank you for your patience.

Best Regards,

(Your name)

6.3 Related product recommendation

● Recommend of related products when customers are not satisfied with the products

Dear customer,

I am sorry that you are not satisfied with the goods you inquired about'. According to your information, I would like to recommend some other items of similar styles and hope you will like them. These are our best-selling goods right now. Please check the link below: http://www.×××.com.

If you have any questions about this product, please contact us.

Best wishes,

(Your name)

● Introduction of new products and promotions to new customers

Dear customer,

Thanks for your order and hope it will meet your satisfaction. In order to keep you update with our latest promotion and products, please subscribe to our store. If you have any problems, please refer to: http://XXXX.com.

Looking forward to your future order.

Yours faithfully,

(Your name)

6.4 Special order processing

● Notification of lost items

Dear customer,

Sorry to tell you that we cannot get the tracking information. We are afraid the package might be lost. If you still want to buy the product, please place another order and I'll offer you a 5% discount. If not, please apply for refund. Thank you for your understanding.

Best Regards,

(Your name)

● Notification of overweight orders (when goods are overweight and cannct be mailed in small packages)

Dear customer,

We are sorry to tell you that free shipping for this item is not available.

Free shipping by China Post Air Mail is only for package weighing less than 2 kgs. However, the weight of the item you choose is 2.5 kgs which is higher. Therefore, would you please choose another express courier, like EMS or UPS which may cost higher shipping fees, but is much faster. Or you can place the order separately and make sure the weight of each order is less than 2 kgs so as to take advantage of free shipping.

Yours faithfully,

(Your name)

Tips

Customer communication skills

1. Provide professional services to customers:

(1) Solve the problem from a professional perspective;

(2) Provide reliable data and evidence;

(3) Adopt diversified response methods.

2. Alleviate customers' anxiety of the event:

(1) Downplay the seriousness of the incident and ensure that the problem will be resolved smoothly, and the top priority is to give the buyer reassurance;

(2) Display to buyers an attitude of eternal gratitude;

(3) The last email for reply must come from the seller.

3. Actively provide selective solutions:

(1) The plan should be provided by the seller, not by the buyer;

(2) Try to provide multiple solutions (at least 2) for buyers to choose from.

4. Persist in taking the initiative to take the responsibility:

(1) Make a suitable explanation;

(2) Take responsibility with sincerity.

5. Pay attention to the skills of email responses:

(1) The responses should be written with solid basic skills, avoid spelling and grammatical errors;

(2) Do not include paragraphs in capital letters in the email;

(3) Try to use short sentences with simple structure and plain words;

(4) Cleverly use segmentation and blank lines, so that customers can find the key points they want to see as soon as possible.

Exercises

1. Multiple Choices

(1) Which of the following is included in the in-sales service of CBEC service? ( )

A. Answer customer inquiries and guide shopping

B. Notify customers of logistics and customs issues in transportation

C. Respond to customer inquiries and product details

D. Return and exchange

(2) Which of the following statement about in-sales service in CBEC is wrong? ( )

A. Email responses should be prompt and courteous

B. Cultivate empathy and make guests feel at ease

C. When dealing with problems, try to provide customers with various alternative choices

D. When the product reaches the destination country, the task is completed

(3) Which of the following is incorrect when dealing with customer sales problems? ( )

A. In case of uncontrollable circumstances such as festive weather, customers should be notified in time

B. Inform the customer of the delivery status in time after delivery

C. On spotting wrong delivery or missing delivery problems, wait passively for customers' inquiry instead of notifying them first

D. Timely notification of the arrival of the goods at the customs, post office and delivery of goods and othertime nodes

(4) Which of the following scenario should in-sales service personnel of CBEC pay attention to? ( )

A. Product shipping method

B. Customs declaration and clearance

C. Whether the product meets the safety standards of other countries

D. All of the above

(5) During the order processing phase, if the customer fails to pay, which of the following is wrong? ( )

A. Reassure customers about the product

B. Offer gifts or discounts to encourage customers to pay

C. Constantly urge customers to pay

D. Take the initiative to learn about the doubts and concerns of customers

2. True or False

(1) The in-sales service stage of CBEC refers to the time period from when a customer

places an order to the time when goods are shipped. In-sales communication and service are an important part to reflect the quality of sellers' services. ( )

(2) The customer places an order, but the warehouse is out of stock, which is the content of communication and service in CBEC in-sales process. ( )

(3) The delivery of the package beyond the estimated delivery time is the content of communication and service in CBEC in-sales process. ( )

(4) Special order situations before shipment include: customs tax issues, inability to ship to the customer's country due to logistics risks, and inability to ship to the customer's country due to specific holidays. ( )

(5) Excellent in-sales service of CEBC personnel can recommend more products to customers in a timely manner, increase product exposure, increase the store's customer unit price and order conversion rate, and reduce promotion costs. We call this marketing method as Affiliated Marketing. ( )

Skills&Drills

Read the in-sales customer service case on the AliExpress platform below, analyze and evaluate the advantages of customer service in this case.

1. Customer complaints

A customer bought a pair of pants in a women's clothing store, and found that the price of the product had been reduced before receiving the goods, so he complained on the AliExpress platform. The details are as follows.

Order number: ××××××
Price: 120 USD
Time: Dec. 12. 28. 2021
Shipping address: ×××××××

2. Treatment

The seller opens "My AliExpress" seller interface, clicks "Dispute List" to view "Dispute Details", the details are as follows.

Order Number: ××××××
Dispute reason: product price reduction
Order time: Dec. 12. 28. 2021
2022-01-03 22:30:51 Rosalie: That's unfair. Could I cancel the former order and place another one at the discount price?

2022-01-04 20:11:47 Wen: Just as you said, there has been a price change. However, we have not changed the price randomly. Customers can get 10% off at AliExpress from Jan. 1-3 to celebrate the New Year's Day. You placed your order on December 28, right before the discount became available. We apologize for not letting you know immediately.
2022-01-05 19:56:24 Wen: We feel so sorry for your inconvenience. We will verify the price change as quickly as possible. Thank you for your patience.
2022-01-05 20:51:21 Wen: Thanks for your consideration, since the product has been shipped, I am afraid it is not advisable for a cancel. But in compensate, we will refund you the 20 dollar's markdown as soon as possible. How do you like it?
2022-01-06 11:51:09 Rosalie: OK, I understand that. So a 20 dollar refund is agreed.

3. Complaint Resolution

Complaints are resolved when the seller and customer agree on a solution for the product. Sellers can click "Dispute List" in "My AliExpress" and open "Dispute Details" to view, the details are as follows.

Order: ××××××
Dispute reason: product price reduction
Dispute Status: Dispute Outcome Refund only USD20.00, funded by the seller

Please analyze the principles and advantages of customer service and communication in this complaint resolution case (from the aspect of attitude, communication skills, etc.).

Reference answer

Training Camp in Moral Education

【Resilience Training】

During the in-sales service and consultation, personnel of CBEC are often confronted with various difficulties. Customers from different countries, regions and cultural backgrounds have different demand of products and services, entailing frictions and issues. In addition, order processing, tracking of logistics all proved to be tests challenging customer service personnel. Traditional Chinese culture has long emphasized the cultivation and shaping of people's resilience, perseverance and self-control. The cultivation of resilience is not only a professional requirement for customer service personnel, but also a requirement for personal growth. Psychologists define resilience as the process of adaptability in the face of adversity or daunting stress, such as family and relationship problems, serious health problems or workplace and financial stress. While resilience involves "bouncing back" from difficult experiences, it also promotes personal growth.

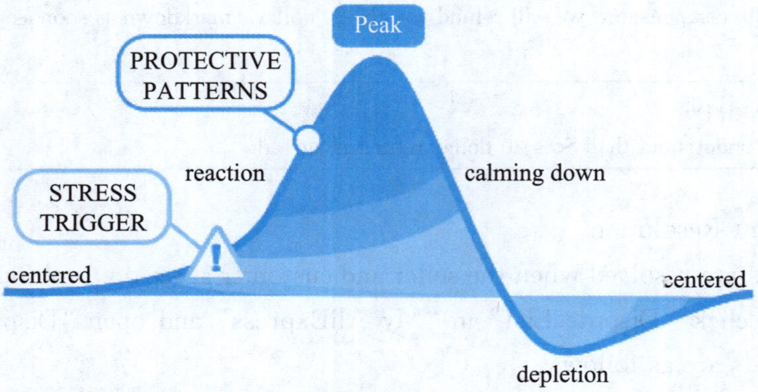

Figure 3 - 2　Stress tolerance mode curve at low endurance level

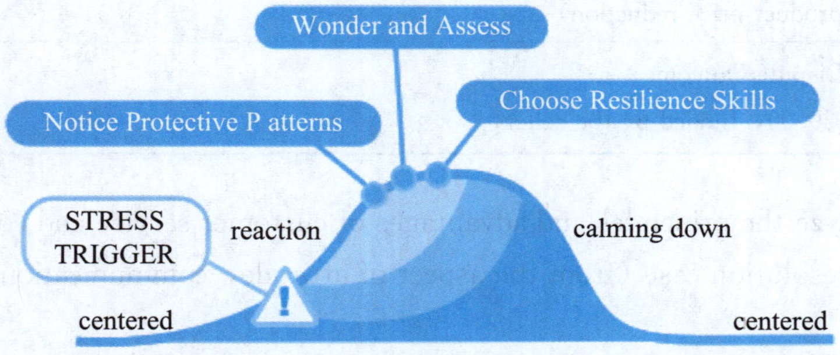

Figure 3 - 3　Stress tolerance mode curve at high endurance level

The above is a psychological research survey conducted by the DoveTail Learning Center in California on endurance and stress resistance, respectively showing the pattern curves of different levels of endurance in coping with work pressure: Comparing the two curves, we can conclude that the differences in coping with stress between low endurance and high endurance mainly lie in the attitude towards stress and external stimuli. In the case of low endurance, there is a reflex protection mechanism against stress and stimuli. However, in the case of high endurance, it adopts a mechanism of prior prediction and curiosity, necessitating a calmer assessment and more rational treatment of pressure.

According to the Harvard Business School Report, here are some tips for developing resilience:

(1) When disaster strikes, count from 1 to 10 before reacting, thinking of one positive lesson you can derive from this experience.

(2) Build connections, cultivate resilience by building healthy relationships with those close to us.

(3) Avoid viewing crises as insurmountable problems through reassessing, restructuring and adjusting our responses to stressful events.

(4) Accept that change is part of life—focus on what we can change instead of what we can't.

[**Empathy Training**]

Customer service personnel with strong empathy can quickly seize opportunities, experience less anxiety in the face of changes, create a more positive work environment and provide solutions with patience and understanding. The first chapter introduces the definition of empathy and tests everyone's empathy level via a questionnaire. In this chapter, we provide you with several effective tips to help boost your empathy:

1. Cultivate curiosity

(1) Spend time with people you don't know well and ask themselves how they are and what their life is like.

(2) Follow and listen to people from different backgrounds (religion, race, politics) on social media while listening to their opinion.

(3) Visit new places and meet the locals while immersing yourself in their way of life.

2. Get out of your comfort zone

(1) Learn new things, travel and see how to step out of your comfort zone.

(2) Accept how helpless you sometimes feel and stay humble. Humility can be a useful way to gain empathy.

3. Receive feedback

Ask friends, family, and colleagues for reflection on moments in life when you lost empathy and patience.

4. Examine your own biases

(1) We all have biases which affect our empathy. Reflect your own biases during life and work.

(2) Look for opportunities to interact with people from other backgrounds and develop an inclusive understanding of differences.

The following responses are commonly used in cross-border and cross-cultural communication to express your understanding and empathy for customers:

- I am sorry that this happened to you.
- That would upset me too.
- I want to thank you for being so open and honest with me.

- This sort of challenge is never easy.
- It is clear that this has impacted you deeply.
- What else would you like to share?
- It sounds like you had a very stressful time.
- Yes，what has happened makes no sense at all.
- I am on your side.
- It's no surprise you are upset.
- You are making complete sense.

Activity for boosting empathy：Create an empathy map（use your imagination to build a panoramic image of someone's situation）.

① Cut out a character in a certain scenario from a newspaper or magazine.

② Paste the picture on a larger piece of paper.

③Group activity，ask questions about the person and their life stories and imagine possible answers：

- Who is this guy? Give him a name，assume a family background，work experience，and financial background.
- Use your imagination to come up with what situations they might be in right now and what decisions do they need to make.
- What influenced their decision?
- What will they say?
- What would other people（friends，colleagues，partners，family）ask them to do?

④ Write the answer in the blank space，and communicate among the group members.

项目四

跨境电商售后客服

知识目标

1. 熟悉平台售后规则；
2. 掌握新老客户维护和管理的方法。

能力目标

1. 能够利用信函提醒客户留评；
2. 能够正确处理、积极化解订单纠纷；
3. 能够对新老客户进行日常维护和管理。

素质目标

培养商务沟通中的共情力与合作力。

知识点索引

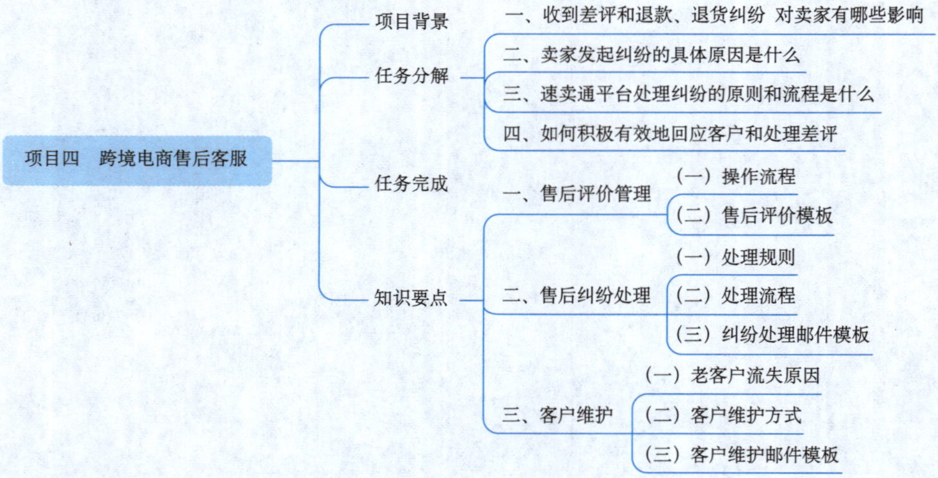

项目背景

从接触 B2C 售中客服以来，小艾的工作都比较顺利，对客服务中遇到的问题在同事的帮助下也都成功化解，自己也学到很多方法和技巧。但是，今天，小艾看到有一位名叫 Judus 的客户给出了一星差评，并提起退款退货。作为公司新人的小艾遇到这么棘手的问题，真有点手足无措。你能帮助小艾处理这个问题吗？

任务分解

在这个案例中，我们要考虑哪些问题?

一、收到差评和退款、退货纠纷对卖家有哪些影响

收到退款、退货，对卖家的影响有好有坏。有利的方面是：首先，可以提高卖家的选品能力，为产品优化提供意见。一些质量不好的产品，退货率肯定会偏高，那卖家就可以趁机淘汰此产品，或者改进产品。其次，可以提升卖家的综合能力，包括提高产品供应链管理质量、仓库管理水平、配送服务水平等，提高卖家的市场竞争力。当然，不好的影响也挺多的，比如退货会影响卖家的绩效指标中的订单缺陷率（ODR，亚马逊平台）或纠纷提起率（速卖通平台）。如果卖家的退货处理措施令买家不满意，可能会使买家留差评或者发起索赔，增加封号的风险。另外，增加退货成本，对产品造成损耗，增加二次销售的压力，以及卖家其他方面的损失。当然，最严重的后果就是损害品牌形象，降低店铺的信誉度，造成买家流失，影响店铺的销量与业绩。所以，退款退货纠纷要尽量减少，遇到差评最好能在问题妥善解决后争取让客户修改评价。

二、卖家发起纠纷的具体原因是什么

客服小艾通过查询速卖通后台的“纠纷详情”，查到买家 Judus 购买的产品是雾化器，他的反馈如下：

“I have tried 3 of them at my battery and all have problem at the thread connection and have damaged my battery! This atomizer is totally DEFECTIVE is no way to sell them. I want a full refund as soon as possible.”

客户测试了三件产品，发现都在接线处出现问题，而且损坏了自己的电池，因此要求全额退款。此纠纷属于货不对版。

三、速卖通平台处理纠纷的原则和流程是什么

根据《阿里巴巴平台交易争议规则》（2018 年），质量问题是指卖方交付的产品的材料、工艺和/或质量不符合采购合同的规定，或存在损坏、功能故障、零件缺失或其他可能妨碍其正常使用的问题。上述案件中的争议有关质量问题。

如果买方声称所交付产品的质量问题和描述不一致可以用肉眼识别，买方应首先提供照片、视频或阿里巴巴平台认可的其他证据来证明。然后，卖方应提供证据和合理的解释，证明产品不存在质量问题或描述不一致，或此类问题的原因不可归咎于卖方。如果卖方未能在规定的期限内提交有效证据，平台将认定产品存在质量问题或描述不一致。

如果卖方交付的产品存在质量问题、描述不一致或侵权问题，阿里巴巴平台应支持将产品退回并退款给买方。

四、如何积极有效地回应客户和处理差评

首先，认真倾听，显示出共情力，让客户体会到你的关心和诚意。其次，注意冷静分析订单争议的来龙去脉。注意电子证据，如聊天记录和物流记录，通过电子证据跟客户真诚沟通，获得客户理解。理解客户的心情，引导客户的负面情绪。最后，真诚恰当地解决纠纷，并提出合理的修改评价的要求。

任务完成

小艾及时进行了如下处理：

首先，小艾积极地通过邮件与客户沟通：

Dear Judus,

Thank you for your letter. We feel really sorry for the troubles and frustration our products brought to you. You can be assured to have a full refund if these products are really problematic. So, in order for us to see the problems clearly, could you please take a picture of all the 3 damaged atomizers in one picture, and show us how you tried them by a video. We really appreciate your help and feedback. We will contact you soon.

Have a good day!

Best regards,

Eyre

随后，小艾把此款产品的问题录入系统，向公司有关部门反馈。Judus 发来了图片和操作视频。经过技术人员分析，认为有可能为操作问题。所以，小艾跟 Judus 进一步沟通：

Dear Judus,

Sorry to keep you waiting. Our technicians have watched your video and suggested you to try them again according to the procedures in the product instruction. We also made a video for you to follow. We believe you can get them work well. If you would still like to get them back, you surely can get a full refund. Sorry for the inconvenience. We hope sincerely to continue our business relation. We would highly appreciate it if you could modify the negative evaluation.

Yours sincerely,

Eyre

同时，小艾对顾客的评价及时回复，提醒顾客仔细阅读产品说明书，按正确的操作步骤启动产品。

Judus 按照为他录制的视频重新适用了产品，结果产品工作正常。他对客服服务非常

满意，不仅撤销了退款纠纷，而且更改了评价。

知识要点

售后客服从买家签收货物后开始，具体工作内容如图 4－1 所示：

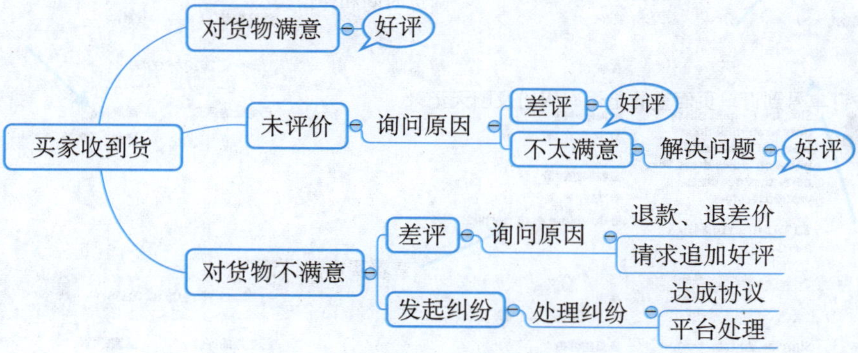

图 4－1　跨境电商售后客服任务图

一、售后评价管理

跨境电商售后客服工作很重要的一个环节就是客户评价管理。客户评价对网店未来的经营至关重要。据调查，90%的客户会在购物之前查看商品的售后评价，以决定选择哪个卖家下单。人们愿意多花 30%以上的价格来购买服务等级为优的卖家销售的商品。

在跨境电子商务领域的各大平台上，售后评价一般分为好评、中评、差评和未评价。无论是哪种评价，客服人员都要认真对待，及时沟通。对于客户的好评要给予及时的感谢；对于未及时给出评价的客户要进行催评；如果收到中差评，客服人员一定要及时联系客户，弄清原因，并想办法弥补，争取获得客户的谅解，让客户修改为好评。

（一）操作流程

以速卖通平台为例，针对中差评，交易评价管理包括如下操作：

- 速卖通交易→等待您的评价→已生效的评价

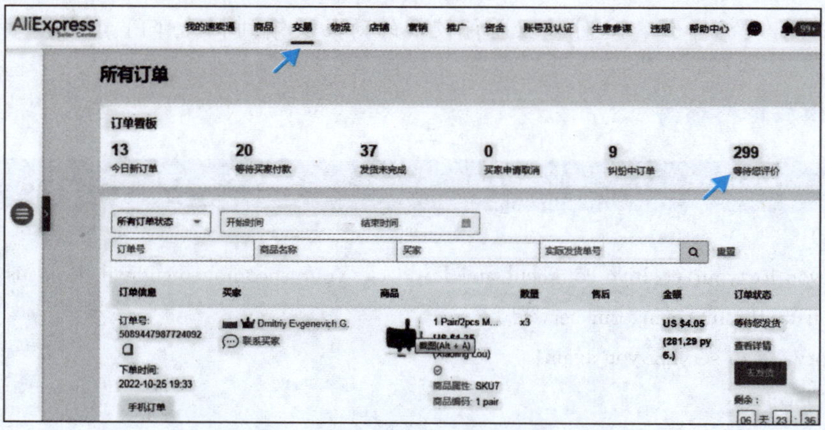

图 4－2　查看已生效的评价

● 筛选一周内的中/差评→搜索→查看买家评价的具体问题以及订单里的沟通记录→点击回复评价

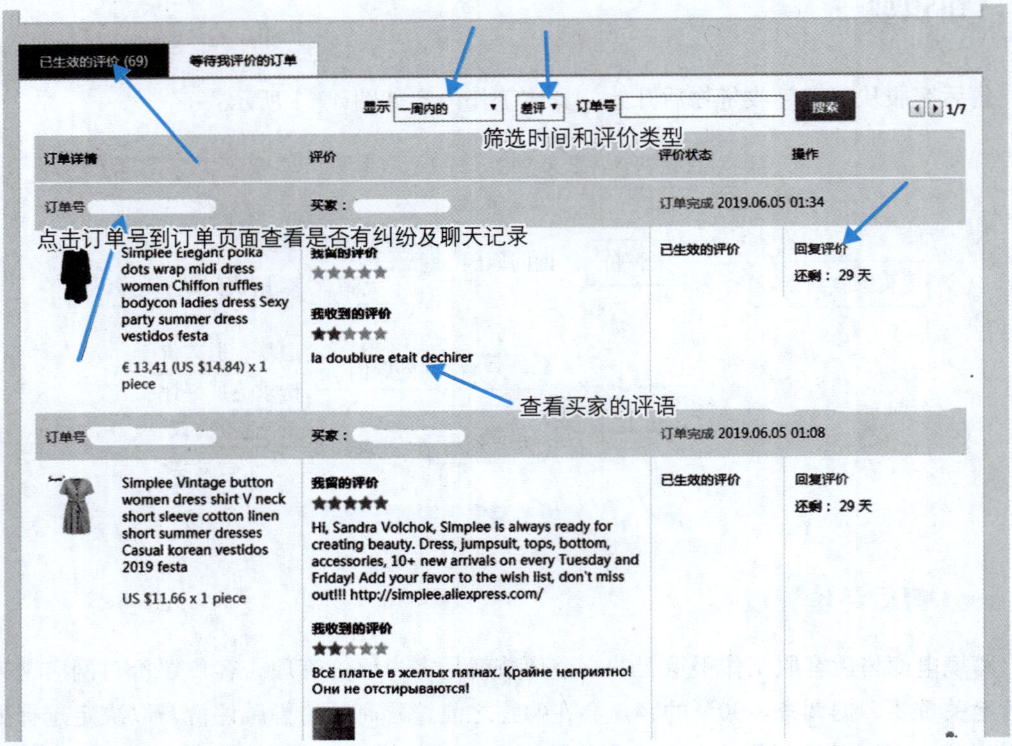

图 4-3　回复评价

小贴士

回复差评

回复差评的主要目的是消除其他买家的顾虑并且证明商家的产品和服务做得好。因此，应该注意以下几点：

- 理解买家差评的真正原因并且有针对性地回复。
- 及时处理。
- 以周/月为单位，定时整理差评较多的商品反馈到相关部门。

（二）售后评价模板

模板 1：好评回复

Dear (buyer),

Thank you for your positive comment and feedback. Your encouragement will keep us moving forward and constantly improving our service.

Look forward to serving you again!

Yours Sincerely,

(seller)

［参考译文］

亲爱的（买家名）：

感谢您的积极评价和反馈。您的鼓励将使我们继续前进并不断改进我们的服务。

期待再次为您服务！

你的诚挚的，

（卖家名）

模板 2：催评

Dear (buyer),

We've made a transaction already in some other day and you purchased items from us. We've greatly appreciated your favor and hope you are satisfied with us. The detailed information of our last transaction as follows:

Item Name: ____________________

Item Number: ____________________

Total Deal Price: ____________________

If you are satisfied with your purchase as well as the services provided, please do spare tine to leave us positive feedback for us.

Your positive feedback is critical for us, and we highly appreciate it. If you have any problem or concerns about your purchase, please don't hesitate to tell us and we will try our best to help.

Thank you again. And we look forward to serving you again soon.

Yours Sincerely,

(seller)

［参考译文］

亲爱的（买家名）：

我们之前已经进行了交易，您从我们这里购买了商品。我们非常感谢您的青睐，希望您对我们感到满意。我们上次交易的详细信息如下：

商品名称：____________________

商品编号：____________________

总交易价格：____________________

如果您对我们的产品以及我们的服务感到满意，请留下积极反馈。

您的积极反馈对我们至关重要，我们万分感谢。

如果您有任何问题，请不要犹豫，告诉我们，我们会尽力帮助。

再次感谢您的帮助。希望很快有再次服务您的机会。

你的诚挚的，

（卖家名）

模板 3：修改评价

Dear (buyer),

We are sorry to see that you left negative feedback relating to your recent purchase experience from our store. But I'm pleased we have solved the problem together. I hope you are satisfied with our solution.

Now that we have solved the problem, would you please spare some time to change your feedback into positive feedback? You know 5-star is really important to us.

Thanks again and we sincerely look forward to establishing long business relationship with you .

Best wishes,

(seller)

［参考译文］

尊敬的（买家名）：

我们很遗憾地看到您从我们的商店留下了与您最近的购买体验相关的负面反馈。但是我很高兴我们一起解决了这个问题。我希望您对我们的解决方案满意。

既然我们已经解决了问题，您能抽出一些时间把您的反馈变成积极的反馈吗？（修改反馈的链接）您知道五星好评对我们来说真的很重要。

再次感谢，我们真诚期待与您建立长期的业务关系。

最美好的祝愿，

（卖家名）

二、售后纠纷处理

（一）处理规则

买方可以在卖方装运（或应该装运）货物后 5 日内提出争议。

下列规则应适用于每一类争端：

1. 未收到货物的争议

（1）如果买方在卖方规定的交货期限到期后就未收到的货物提出争议，卖方应在 72 小时内做出答复。

（2）如果卖方没有在上述期限内做出回应，货款将自动全额退还给买方。经买卖双方协商无法解决争议的，可提交平台解决争议。

（3）尽管有上述规定，如果货物交付延迟（即不是上面定义的准时交货），买方可以获得全额退款（并保留产品）。

2. 无理由退货争议（相关交易保护期内）

（1）一旦买方申请该争议程序，系统应自动提示卖方在 24 小时内上传退货订单号。如果卖家没有回应或时间流逝，买家将被直接退款。

（2）一旦卖方上传退货订单号，买方应下载退货信息，然后：

■ 如果在 20 天内卖方确认收到产品的退货，货款将退还给买方；

■ 如果在 20 日之后，卖方仍未确认收到退货，且卖方未提出争议，货款将退还给买方；

■ 如果在 20 天内，卖方没有收到产品的退货，或者收到的商品有问题（如已经损坏、没有完全退货、已经使用和/或不处于可转售状态），卖方也可以申请平台解决纠纷。

3. 其他纠纷

一旦买方提出其他类型的纠纷，卖方必须在 72 小时内做出回应。如果当事人无法解决争议，平台将根据买卖双方提供的证据来决定。

为提高买家对平台、对卖家的体验和信心，平台鼓励卖家积极与买家协商；如果协商没有达成解决方案，平台有权积极参与提案解决。但在此种情况下，平台的参与不应损害买卖双方在谈判中的平等地位。

(二) 处理流程

1. 接受纠纷流程

交易→纠纷中订单→按纠纷响应剩余时间（由少到多）→点击“纠纷详情”→查看聊天记录并查看订单情况，确定是否要退款给买家→联系买家。

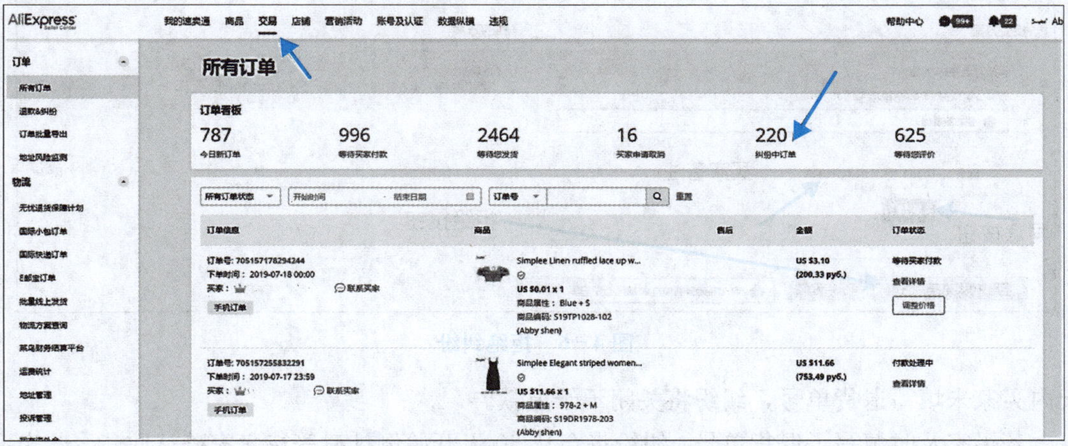

图 4-4 查询纠纷中的订单

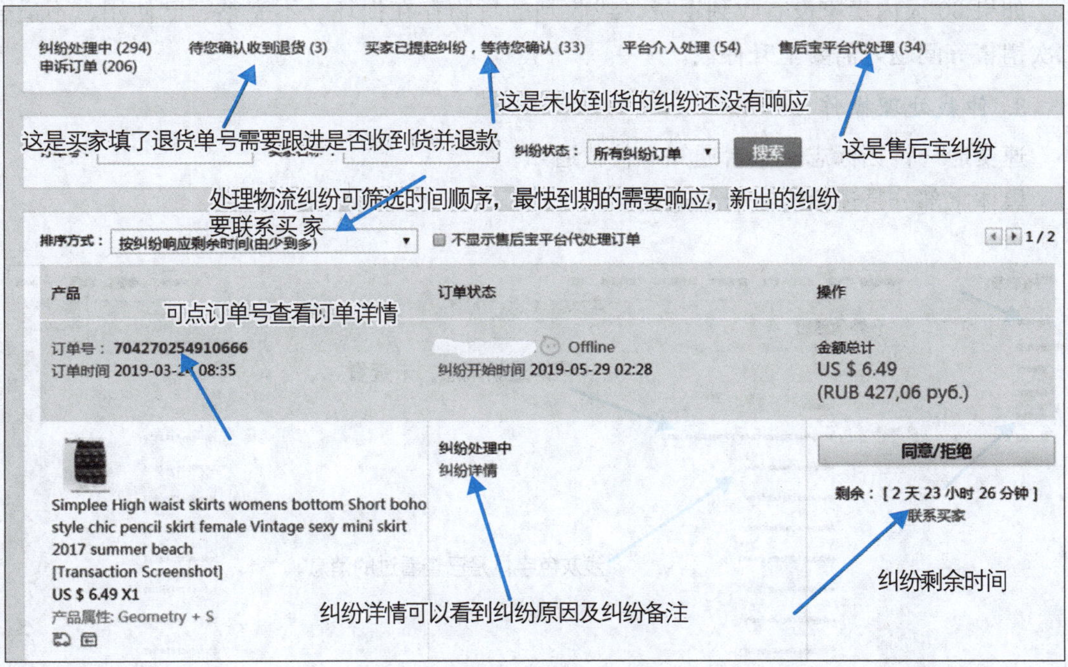

图 4-5 查询纠纷详情

2. 拒绝纠纷流程

点击“拒绝并新增仅退款方案”（拒绝需要提供证据）→ 退款金额写 0→请详细描述您的问题（必填）就写具体情况。

一般纠纷状态是退货退款的，平台会先给予 10 天的时间让买家填写退货单号，若 10

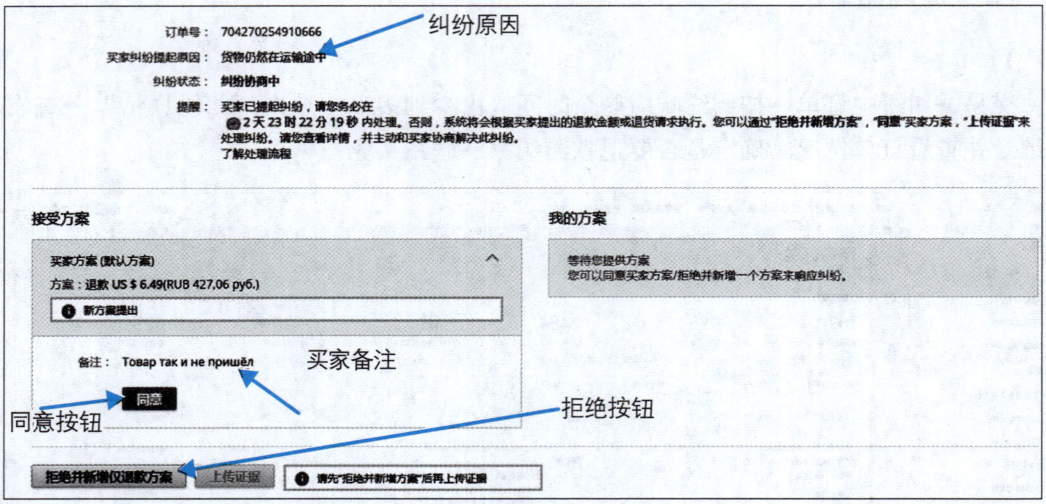

图 4-6 拒绝纠纷

天内买家未填写退货单号，纠纷将关闭不予退款。

若买家及时填写了退货单号，纠纷将会从 30 天开始倒计时等待卖家确认收货。若卖家未在 30 天内确认收货，到期后平台将会直接结束纠纷并退款给买家。

如果 30 天内卖家没有收到退货，或收到的货物存在损坏、不完整、已使用、不适合二次销售等问题，需要上升仲裁。

3. 仲裁处理操作

速卖通→铃铛标志→平台通知→仲裁通知。

黑体字部分是还没有查看的通知。

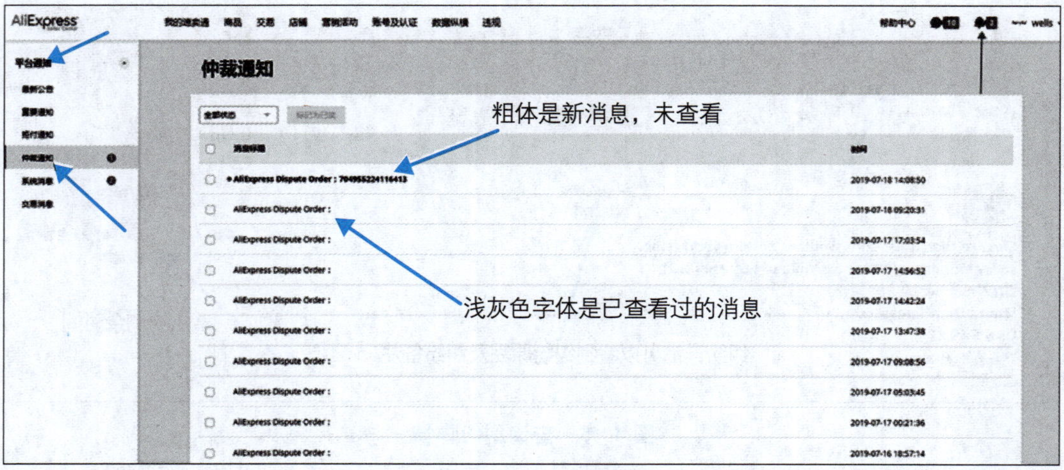

图 4-7 查看仲裁通知

判为不成立的一般不用处理；

如果成立，则需查看订单状态，确认是否应该退款并备注原因，然后查看响应时间还有多久并做出响应。

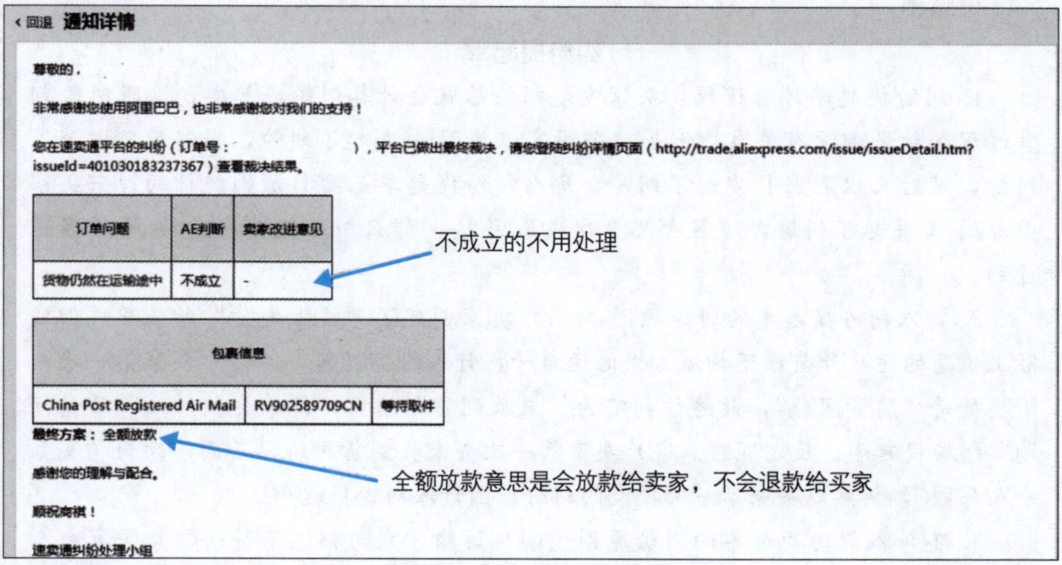

‹ 回退　**通知详情**

尊敬的，

非常感谢您使用阿里巴巴，也非常感谢您对我们的支持！

您在速卖通平台的纠纷（订单号：　　　　　　　　），平台已做出最终裁决，请您登陆纠纷详情页面（http://trade.aliexpress.com/issue/issueDetail.htm?issueId=401030183237367）查看裁决结果。

订单问题	AE判断	卖家改进意见
货物仍然在运输途中	不成立	-

包裹信息		
China Post Registered Air Mail	RV902589709CN	等待取件

最终方案：全额放款

感谢您的理解与配合。

顺祝商祺！

速卖通纠纷处理小组

图 4-8　判为不成立的纠纷

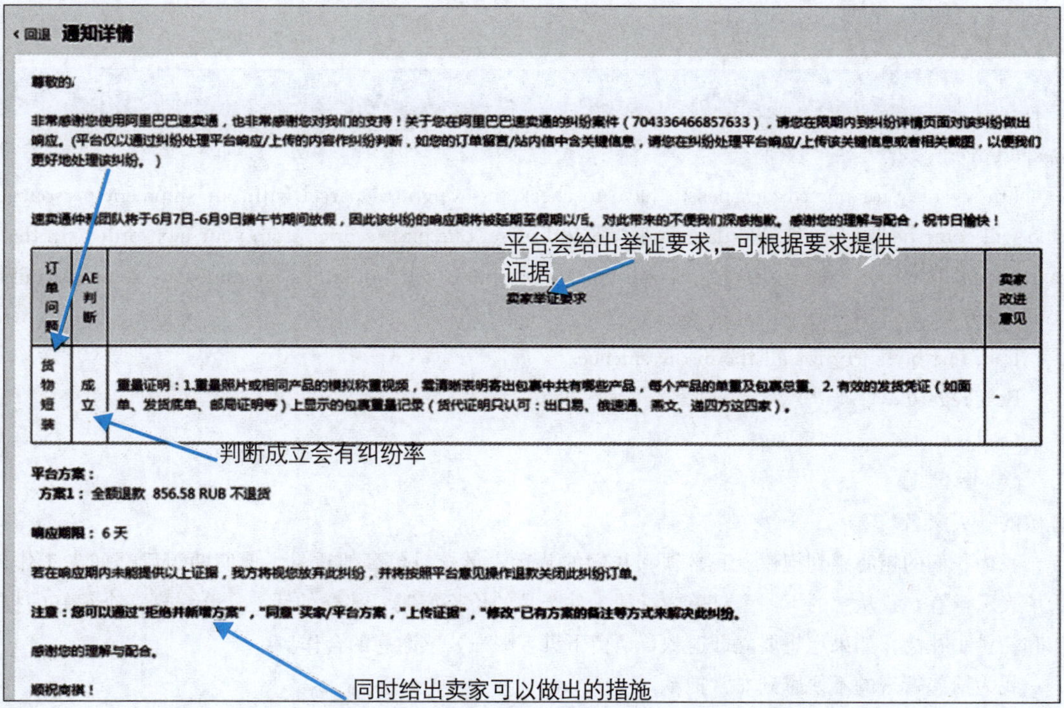

‹ 回退　**通知详情**

尊敬的/

非常感谢您使用阿里巴巴速卖通，也非常感谢您对我们的支持！关于您在阿里巴巴速卖通的纠纷案件（704336466857633），请您在限期内到纠纷详情页面对该纠纷做出响应。(平台仅以通过纠纷处理平台响应/上传的内容作纠纷判断，如您的订单留言/站内信中含关键信息，请您在纠纷处理平台响应/上传该关键信息或者相关截图，以便我们更好地处理该纠纷。)

速卖通仲裁团队将于6月7日-6月9日端午节期间放假，因此该纠纷的响应期将被延期至假期以后。对此带来的不便我们深感抱歉。感谢您的理解与配合，祝节日愉快！

订单问题	AE判断	卖家举证要求	卖家改进意见
货物短装	成立	重量证明：1.重量照片或相同产品的模拟称重视频，需清晰表明寄出包裹中共有哪些产品，每个产品的单重及包裹总重。2. 有效的发货凭证（如面单、发货底单、邮局证明等）上显示的包裹重量记录（货代证明只认可：出口易、俄速通、燕文、递四方这四家）。	-

平台方案：

方案1：全额退款 856.58 RUB 不退货

响应期限：6 天

若在响应期内未能提供以上证据，我方将视您放弃此纠纷，并将按照平台意见操作退款关闭此纠纷订单。

注意：您可以通过"拒绝并新增方案"，"同意"买家/平台方案，"上传证据"，"修改"已有方案的备注等方式来解决此纠纷。

感谢您的理解与配合。

顺祝商祺！

图 4-9　判为成立的纠纷

小贴士

纠纷提起率

1. 纠纷提起率计算逻辑：买家发起纠纷后就会计算纠纷提起率，这跟纠纷判责过程和结果都没有关系。例如：若买家以原因 A 发起了纠纷，发起后又取消了纠纷，然后又以原因 B 发起了纠纷，那么纠纷提起率是按 B 原因统计的；若买家以原因 A 发起了纠纷，过程中又更改成原因 B，那么纠纷提起率是按 A 原因统计的。

2. 计入纠纷提起率的纠纷原因：(1) 卖家创建了“线上发货”物流单，但实际上填写的运单号是线下物流方式的运单号，计入纠纷提起率。(2) 买家第一次纠纷类型是“质量问题”，最终被判定为“未收到货”结案，订单会被计入“质量问题”纠纷提起率；反之同理。(3) 买家第一次提未收到货纠纷，后面修改为“买家个人原因”，仍然以买家第一次提交的纠纷原因计入纠纷提起率。

3. 不计入纠纷提起率的纠纷原因：(1) 运输方式与描述不符；(2) 买家个人原因（我不喜欢、我不想要、我买错了）或“无理由退换货”，则不计入纠纷提起率。

（三）纠纷处理邮件模板

模板 1：货物短装

Dear (buyer),

I'm so sorry for our carelessness. I have to check the weight of parcel with our shipment personnel who will come back to work two days later. Could I offset one piece's price from your next order? In that case, a good discount and a simple gift will be sent to you. If you would like an immediate refund, could you please let me have your PayPal account?

I am terribly sorry for all the inconvenience.

Best regards,

(seller)

[参考译文]

尊敬的（买家名）：

我为我们的粗心感到抱歉。我必须和我们的装运人员核对包裹的重量，他们两天后会回来工作。为了表示歉意，我从您的下一个订单中抵消 1 件产品的价格好吗？那样的话，您会拿到一个很好的折扣和一份小礼物。如果您想要立即退款，请留下贝宝账户，感谢您的合作。

我为给您带来的不便感到非常抱歉。

最诚挚的问候，

（卖家名）

模板 2：产品质量纠纷

Dear (buyer),

We are sorry for the quality problem and would pay more attention to the product quality.

We accept your requirement and please kindly return the good to the following address: ...

By the way, we've got a plan B. That is, we send you a new one with 50% discount and you close the dispute. Hope you consider it. Thank you!

Best regards,

(seller)

[参考译文]

尊敬的（买家名）：

我们对质量问题感到抱歉，并将更加关注产品质量。

我们接受您的要求，请将货物退回以下地址：……

顺便说一下，我们提供另一个选择。那就是我们给您发一个新货，有 50%的折扣，但请您关闭纠纷。希望您考虑一下。谢谢！

最诚挚的问候，

（卖家名）

三、客户维护

新客户重要还是老客户重要？这基本是一个没有答案的问题：新客户给企业带来朝气，老客户给企业带来保障，只能新老兼顾。但是我们最终的目的不过是把所有的新客户都变成老客户，而良好的跨境售后服务则是把新客户变成老客户的有效关键。请看一组数据：

- 发展新客户的成本是挽留老客户的 3～10 倍；
- 客户的忠诚度下降 5%，你的利润会降低 25%；
- 向新客户推销产品的成功率是 15%，老客户是 50%；
- 每年的老客户保持率增加 5%，利润会增加 25%；
- 60%的新客户都来自老客户的推荐；
- 20%的老客户会给你带来 85%的利润。

可见，新客户开发比较困难，卖家应重视老客户。要知道如何维护老客户，我们就要先知道老客户流失的一些原因。

（一）老客户流失原因

1. 缺乏服务意识

提到服务意识，可能很多人会想到服务态度，事实上服务意识还包括解决问题的时效、工作效率低下等。服务意识淡薄是直接导致客户流失的重要因素。就像纠纷，很多人不知道如何处理就干脆拖着，这是客户最讨厌的事情。

2. 产品缺乏创新度

随着市场成熟及产品价格透明度的提高，产品带来的利益空间越来越小。若企业不能及时进行产品创新，客户为了获得利益，势必会选择有创新性的企业合作，毕竟利益才是维系双方关系的纽带。

3. 客户遇到新"诱惑"

如今行业竞争日益激烈，而客户毕竟是有限的，这时"多金"的客户自然而然会成为大家争夺的对象。竞争对手有时候比你自己更了解你的产品，一旦让他们抓到软肋，就会不择手段地进行扩大，迅速占领市场有利地位，获得更多客户。

（二）客户维护方式

针对以上问题，我们总结了一些维护客户的方法：

（1）及时有效地回复客人，优化投诉处理的流程以提升投诉处理速度，缩短退款时间。不仅如此，跨境电商还可以将在线聊天工具与电话相结合，作为解决用户售后服务渠道，减少用户被动式等待，从而高效率处理用户投诉事件。

（2）定期更换网页内容。将新产品信息发布上网，或者将产品的图片替换一下，这些都会让买家及时了解公司的最新信息，吸引新客户的同时让老客户也不至于因为没有新鲜感而流失。

（3）定期给老客户或者潜在的客户发送公司的最新产品信息，坚持就会有回报，开发一个新客户所花费的费用可能相当于维持几个老客户所花费的费用，因此在开发新客户的时候一定不能忽视老客户的维持，可以在节日的时候给客人发送卡片祝福，客人都会觉得很亲切，合作得会很愉快。

（4）抽时间关注竞争对手有哪些做得比我们更好的地方，一个好的竞争对手就像一面镜子，可以让我们清楚地看到自身的不足并加以改进。

遇到客户流失的时候，不管是主观因素还是客观因素，都建议企业先从自身入手，分析产生问题的根源，找到深层次原因。如果有时间，可以对已经离去的客户做一个简单的问卷调查，看看他们对产品和服务最不满意的地方是什么。

（三）客户维护邮件模板

模板 1：问候老客户

Dear (buyer),

Long time no see! How are you doing?

You ordered a pair of shoes from us. How do you like them? Please feel free to tell us if you've got any problem with them.

We've got some new stuff recently. Attached is the updated catalogue for your reference . If you have any new inquiry, please let us know.

Best wishes,

(seller)

[参考译文]

尊敬的（买家名）：

好久不见！您好吗？

您向我们订购了一双鞋。您觉得他们怎么样？如果您在使用中遇到任何问题，请随时告诉我们。

我们最近有一些新产品。附上最新目录供您参考。如果您有任何新的需求，请告诉我们。

最美好的祝愿，

（卖家名）

模板 2：推荐订阅店铺

Dear (buyer),

Welcome to subscribe to our store. By a few clicks you can enjoy our VIP service such as the latest updates from new arrivals to best-selling products on a weekly basis etc. Any problem on subscribing, please refer to...

(seller)

[参考译文]

尊敬的（买家名）：

欢迎订阅我们店铺。只需点击几下，您就可以享受我们的贵宾服务，及时了解到每周所上新品及畅销产品的最新信息等。订阅有任何问题，请参考……

（卖家名）

模板 3：营销活动推荐

Dear (buyer),

Thank you for shopping in my shop.

To express our gratitude to our customers, a series of promotional activities will be held from June 1st to 7th , including $15 off orders of $99 or more, 12% off for all the products and various coupons for your choices. There are only 7 days to go!

Come on and join us now!

(seller)

[参考译文]

尊敬的（买家名）：

谢谢您的惠顾。

为了表达我们对客户的谢意，我们将在 6 月 1 日至 7 日期间举办一系列促销活动，包括 99 美元或以上订单的 15 美元折扣、全场八八折以及供您选择的各种优惠券。只剩 7 天了！

快来加入我们吧！

（卖家名）

习题测验

（一）选择题

1. 下列哪一项不是跨境电子商务售后客户服务的主要工作？（ ）

A. 客户管理　　B. 纠纷处理

C. 售后评价管理　　D. 邮寄货物

2. 跨境电子商务领域的各大平台上，售后评价一般分为（ ）。

A. 好评、差评　　B. 好评、中评、差评

C. 五星好评、差评　　D. 好评、中评、差评、未评价

3. 如果当事人无法通过协商解决纠纷，则纠纷将交由（ ）来解决。

A. 平台　　B. 买方

C. 卖方　　D. 法庭

4. （ ）指卖方交付的产品的材料、工艺和/或质量不符合采购合同的规定，或存在损坏、功能故障、零件缺失或其他可能妨碍其正常使用的问题。

A. 与描述不符　　B. 质量问题

C. 侵权　　D. 海关扣留

5. 若买家提交的纠纷是（　　），则不计入卖家的纠纷提起率。

A. personal reasons　　B. quality problems

C. color not as described　　D. size not as described

（二）判断题

1. 如果买方声称所交付产品具有质量问题或与描述不符，若问题肉眼可见，卖方应首先提供照片、视频或其他 Alibaba. com 认可的证据来证明。（　　）

2. 对于客户的好评不需要回复。（　　）

3. 若买家以原因 A 发起了纠纷，发起后又取消了纠纷，然后又以原因 B 发起了纠纷，那么纠纷提起率是按 B 原因统计的。（　　）

4. 买家第一次提未收到货，后面修改为“买家个人原因”，将不计入纠纷提起率。（　　）

5. 一般纠纷状态是退货退款的，平台会先给予 10 天的时间让买家填写退货单号，若 10 天内买家未填写退货单号，纠纷将关闭不予退款。（　　）

能力实训

假设你在速卖通平台经营一家主营女士休闲鞋的网店，英国客户 Judy 一周前曾经在你的店铺买过一双鞋子。

1. Judy 来信反映收到的鞋子与产品描述不符，对订单表示不满，并在平台上开启纠纷，要求退款。请回复她的邮件，并尽量说服她关闭纠纷。

2. 感恩节即将到来，请你向 Judy 表示节日祝贺。你的店铺开启了一系列促销活动，如满 100 美元减 10 美元的活动，请在信中推荐给她。

参考答案

思政微情景

小艾成功地处理了客户的纠纷，心情轻松而快乐。在休息区，小艾遇到了部门主管王总。王总阅历深厚，在客户服务方面很有经验。小艾入职以来，得到王总很多指点，所以见到王总，小艾迫不及待地把经过说了一遍。王总不无赞赏地说：“新入职就能这么圆满地解决客户的问题，很不简单。”接着，他又说：“在整个处理过程中，你知道成败的关键在哪里吗？”这个问题让小艾陷入了沉思……

请以此情景为基础，与你的学习伙伴构思对话内容，共同完成角色扮演的任务。

参考答案：

小艾说："是不是客户发火时，我控制住没有生气也没有气馁，而是给予他最大的理解和选择？"

"是的，你在这项业务中显示出极强的共情力。这是作为客服专员最难能可贵的素质。"王总接着说，"当客户因为产品问题而发牢骚时，如果你急着为产品、为公司辩护，会让客户更加生气，结果必然会适得其反。而你处处体现出对客户的理解和歉意，反而使客户感受到被倾听、被尊重，因此有利于平复客户的情绪，为后续处理创造一个合作的氛围。"

"其次，你能够及时解决纠纷，得益于与其他部门特别是技术支持部门的及时沟通和反馈，显示出较强的合作力。在得知有可能是误操作而导致问题出现时，你不仅提示了正确的操作步骤而且还为客户录制了视频，演示操作程序。最后，还留给客户退款的选择权。在这样宽松温暖的氛围中，客户比较容易配合你的工作，提供相关资料或再进行尝试，直至问题最终解决。"

"哦。"小艾努力地点点头，"共情与合作，这就是这份工作的真谛啊！"

Project 4
CBEC After-sales Customer Service

Knowledge Objectives

1. Be familiar with after-sales policy of common platforms;
2. Master the approaches of managing and retaining the new and existing customers.

Competency Objectives

1. Able to use letters to manage feedback;
2. Able to properly handle and actively resolve disputes with orders;
3. Able to retain and manage new and existing customers.

Quality Objectives

Develop empathy and cooperation in business communication.

Key Points Index

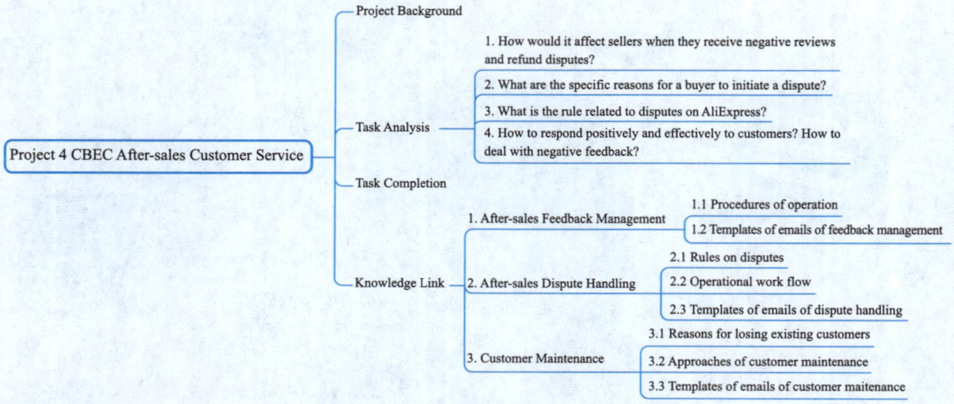

Project Background

Since Eyre began to work on in-sales customer service, she has improved quite a lot and the problems at work have been perfectly settled with the help of some experienced colleagues. Today Eyre found that a customer named Judus left a one-star bad review and opened a dispute for a full refund. As a newcomer, Eyre was a bit overwhelmed by such a tough situation. Could you please offer some advice for her to cope with the problem?

Task Analysis

How to make the response? The questions to consider are shown in the following mind map.

1. How would it affect sellers when they receive negative reviews and refund disputes?

Receiving a refund and return request, the online store will get loss as well as benefit. Firstly, the seller will benefit from the optimization of product selection. Since the defective products are more likely to be returned, the seller could take the chance to shake out the products or improve them. Secondly, it can improve the comprehensive ability of the seller, such as management of product supply chain, warehouse management, and distribution services, etc. , and it will enhance the market competitiveness of sellers. However, it may also bring some negative effects. For example, returns may affect negatively the indicators of the seller's performance by raising the order defect rate (ODR) on Amazon or dispute rate on AliExpress. What's worse, if the seller's handling measures are unsatisfactory to the buyer, it may cause the buyer to post a negative review or initiate a dispute, which will expose the seller to the risk of blocking the account. In addition, it may also cause increase of returning costs, risk of product damaging, pressure for resales, and other losses to the seller. And the most serious consequence is undoubtedly the damage of the brand image and the store's credibility, which will result in the loss of buyers and affect the sales and performance of the store. Therefore, refund requests should be minimized, and it is best to encourage customers to revise their negative feedback after the problem is properly resolved.

2. What are the specific reasons for a buyer to initiate a dispute?

Eyre, as a customer service specialist, checked the dispute details shown on AliExpress, and learnt the product Judus purchased is an atomizer. His feedback is as follows.

"I have tried 3 of them at my battery and all have problem at the thread connection and have damaged my battery! This atomizer is totally DEFECTIVE is no way to sell them. I want a full refund as soon as possible."

The situation is the customer has tested three products and found that they all had problems with thread connection. What's worse, the trial damaged his own batteries. That's why he requested a full refund.

3. What is the rule related to disputes on AliExpress?

According to Alibaba.com Transaction Dispute Rules (2018), quality problems means the material, craftsmanship, and/or quality of the products delivered by the seller fails to meet the provisions of the purchase contract, or there is damage, functional failure, missing parts or other issues that may prevent their normal use. The dispute is related to quality problem.

Where the buyer claims that the quality problem and inconsistency in description of the products delivered are identifiable with naked eyes, the buyer shall first provide photos, videos, or other evidence approved by Alibaba. com to prove it. The Seller shall then provide evidence and reasonable explanations establishing that the products do not have quality problems or inconsistent descriptions or the reasons for such issues are not attributable to the seller. If the seller fails to submit the valid evidence within the specified time limit, Alibaba. com shall determine that the products have quality problems or inconsistent descriptions.

Where the products delivered by the seller have quality problems, inconsistent descriptions, or infringement issue, Alibaba. com shall support returning of products and refund to the buyer.

4. How to respond positively and effectively to customers? How to deal with negative feedback?

Firstly, listen carefully and show empathy, and let your customers feel your concern and sincerity. Secondly, scrutinize the context of the dispute to identify the cause and the party who should take the responsibility. Pay attention to electronic evidence, such as chat records and logistics records. With them, communicate sincerely with customers. Understand the customer's mood and channel their negative emotions. Finally, resolve disputes with faith and appropriateness, and propose reasonably revisions to the evaluation.

Task Completion

Eyre timely carried out the following treatment.

First, Eyre actively communicated with the client via email.

Dear Judus,

Thank you for your letter. We feel really sorry for the troubles and frustration our products brought to you. You can be assured to have a full refund if these products are really problematic. So, in order for us to see the problems clearly, could you please take a picture of all the 3 damaged atomizers in one picture, and show us how you tried them by a video. We really appreciate your help and feedback. We will contact you soon.

Have a good day!

Best regards,

Eyre

Next, Eyre entered the problem of this product into the system and gave feedback to the relevant departments of the company. Technical staff analyzed the photos and video Judus sent to Eyre, and then found that the problem of the products could be caused by improper operation. So, Eyre contacted Judus by email.

> Dear Judus,
>
> Sorry to keep you waiting. Our technicians have watched your video and suggested you to try them again according to the procedures in the product instruction. We also made a video for you to follow. We believe you can get them work well. If you would still like to get them back, you surely can get a full refund. Sorry for the inconvenience. We hope sincerely to continue our business relation. We would highly appreciate it if you could modify the negative evaluation.
>
> Yours sincerely,
>
> Eyre

Judus retried the product according to the instruction of the video recorded specially for him and he found the product worked well. He was very satisfied with the customer service so that he not only withdrew the refund dispute, but also modified his rating.

Knowledge Link

The detailed work of after-sales customer service is as follows.

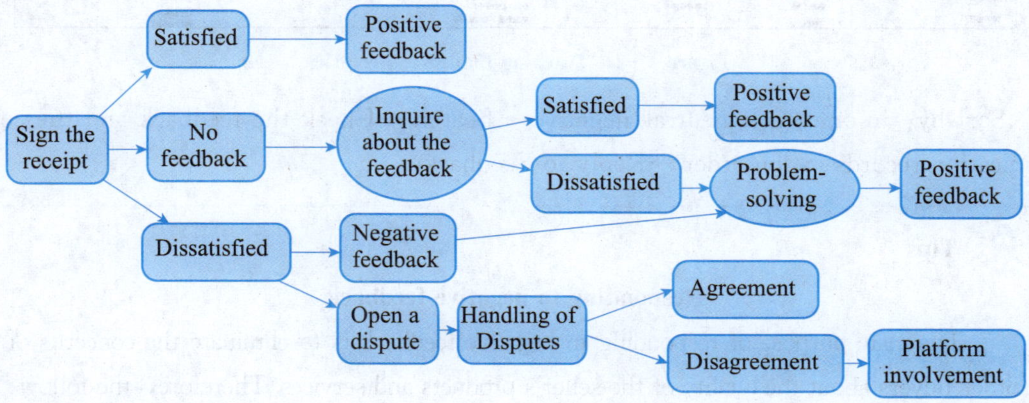

Figure 4 - 1 Tasks of After-sales Customer Service

1. After-sales Feedback Management

Customer feedback management is indispensable in CBEC after-sales customer service. Customer reviews are crucial to the future of an online store. According to a survey,

90% of customers will check customer reviews before deciding the seller they would like to place an order. People are willing to pay 30% more for the goods sold by the sellers with superior service ratings.

On major platforms in CBEC, after-sales feedback of customers is generally divided into positive, mutual, negative and unevaluated. No matter what kind of feedback it is, customer service personnel should take it seriously and answer customers in a timely manner. Specifically, the customer's positive feedback is supposed to have timely thanks; customers who do not give timely evaluation should be reminded; facing negative feedback, customer service personnel must clarify the reasons on time and find ways to make up for it, which may obtain the customer's understanding, and their agreement to modify their feedback.

1.1 Procedures of operation

Take the AliExpress as an example, for mutual and negative reviews, the feedback management includes the following operations:

Orders →To review→ Published Feedback

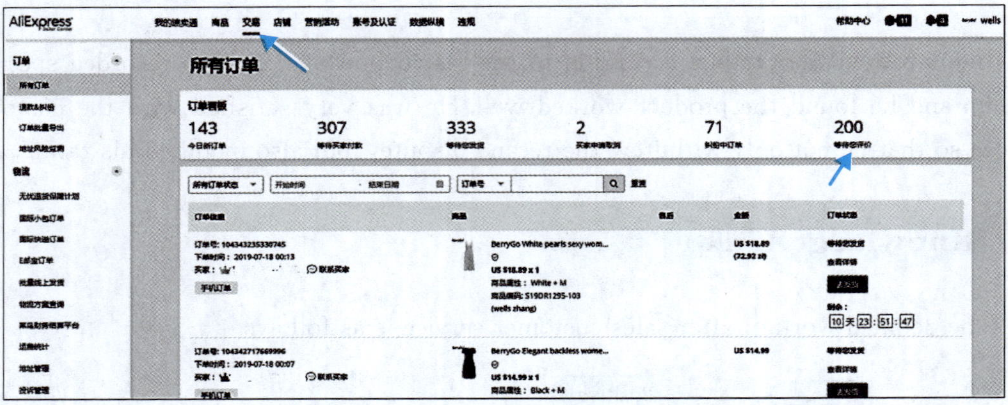

Figure 4-2 Tracking Published Feedback

Sort by: in one week/neutral/negative→ Search →Check the feedback and the communication records in the order →Reply to Feedback

Tips

Responding to negative feedback

The main purpose of responding to negative feedback is to eliminate the concerns of other buyers about the quality of the seller's products and services. Therefore, the following points should be noted.

- Identify the root cause of the buyer's negative feedback and respond to the point.
- Timely process.
- On a weekly or monthly basis, sort out the items with more negative feedback and report them to the relevant departments.

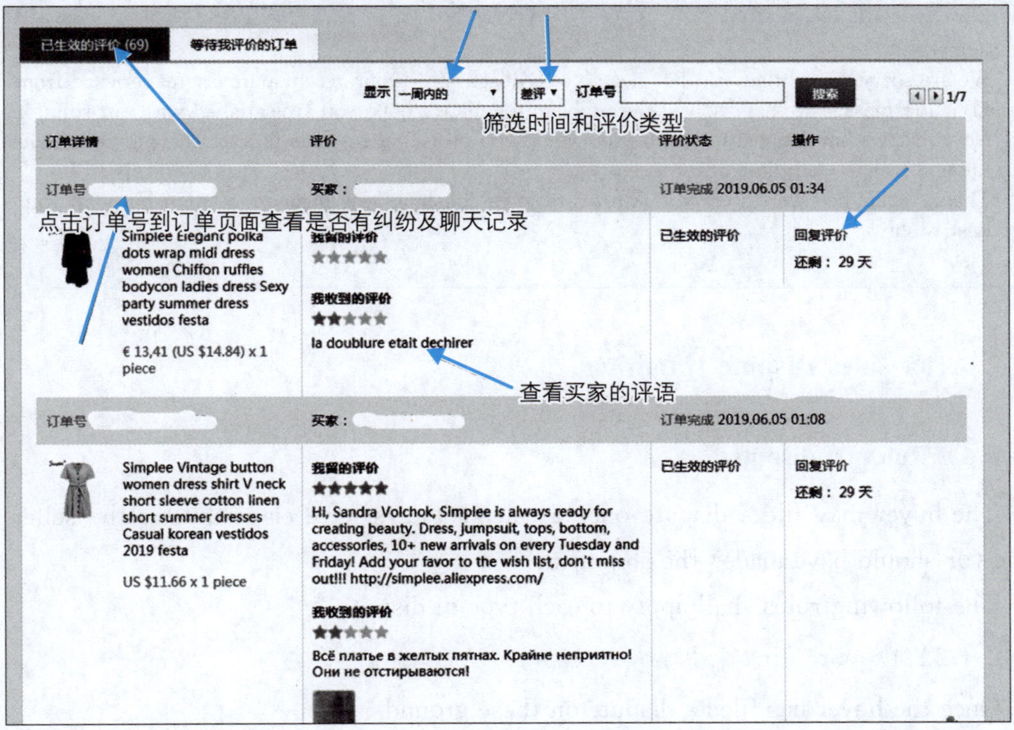

Figure 4－3 Replying to Feedback

1.2 Templates of emails of feedback management

Sample 1: Reply to positive feedback

Dear (buyer),

Thank you for your positive comment and feedback. Your encouragement will keep us moving forward and constantly improving our service.

Look forward to serving you again!

Yours Sincerely,

(seller)

Sample 2: Remind customers of giving feedback

Dear (buyer),

We've made a transaction already in some other day and you purchased items from us. We've greatly appreciated your favor and hope you are satisfied with us. The detailed information of our last transaction is as follows:

Item Name: ____________________

Item Number: __________________

Total Deal Price: ______________

If you are satisfied with your purchase as well as the services provided, please do spare time to leave us positive feedback.

Your positive feedback is critical for us, and we highly appreciate it. If you have any problem or concerns about your purchase, please don't hesitate to tell us and we will try our best to help.

Thank you again. And we look forward to serving you again soon.

Yours Sincerely,

(seller)

Sample 3：Modify feedback

Dear (buyer),

We are sorry to see that you left negative feedback after your recent purchase experience from our store. But I'm pleased we have solved the problem together. I hope you are satisfied with our solution.

Now that we have solved the problem, would you please spare some time to change your feedback? You know 5-star is really important to us.

Thanks again and we sincerely look forward to establishing long business relationship with you.

Best wishes,

(seller)

2. After-sales Dispute Handling

2.1 Rules on disputes

The buyer may file a dispute once 5 calendar days have elapsed after the seller has made (or should have made) the shipment.

The following rules shall apply to each type of dispute:

2.1.1 Dispute for goods not received

Once the buyer has filed a dispute on these grounds:

(1) The seller shall respond within 72 hours provided that the buyer may not submit a dispute for goods not received until the delivery term set by the seller has elapsed.

(2) If the seller does not respond within the term set forth above, the payment will be automatically refunded to the buyer in full. If the dispute cannot be resolved after negotiation between buyer and seller, it can be submitted to the platform to settle the dispute.

(3) Not with standing the above, if the delivery of the goods is late (i. e., is not an On-time Delivery as defined above), the buyer can get a full refund (and keep the product).

2.1.2 No-reason return dispute (within the relevant Transaction Protection Period)

(1) Once the buyer applies for this dispute procedure, the system shall automatically prompt the seller to upload the return order number within 24 hours. If the seller does not respond or the time elapses, the buyer will be directly refunded.

(2) Once the seller uploads the return order number, the buyer shall download the return information, then:

■ If within 20 calendar days the seller confirms receipt of the return of the products, the payment will be refunded to the buyer;

■ If after 20 calendar days the seller has not confirmed receipt of the return of the products and the seller has not filed a dispute, the payment will be refunded to the buyer;

■ If within 20 calendar days the seller has not received the return of the products or the goods received have issues (e. g. they have been damaged, not fully returned, they have been used and/or are not in resalable condition), the seller can also apply for a dispute to be settled by the platform.

2.1.3 Other disputes

Once the buyer files for other types of disputes, the seller must respond within 72 hours. If the parties cannot resolve the dispute, the platform will decide according to the evidence provided by the buyer and the seller.

In order to improve the buyer's experience and confidence in the platform and in the sellers, the platform encourages sellers to actively negotiate with buyers; if the negotiation does not result in a settlement being reached, the platform has the right to actively participate in the proposal solution. However, in such cases, the involvement of the platform shall not prejudice the equal standing in the negotiation of the buyer and the seller.

2.2 Operational work flow

2.2.1 Acceptance of proposals from the buyer

Operations: Orders →In dispute.

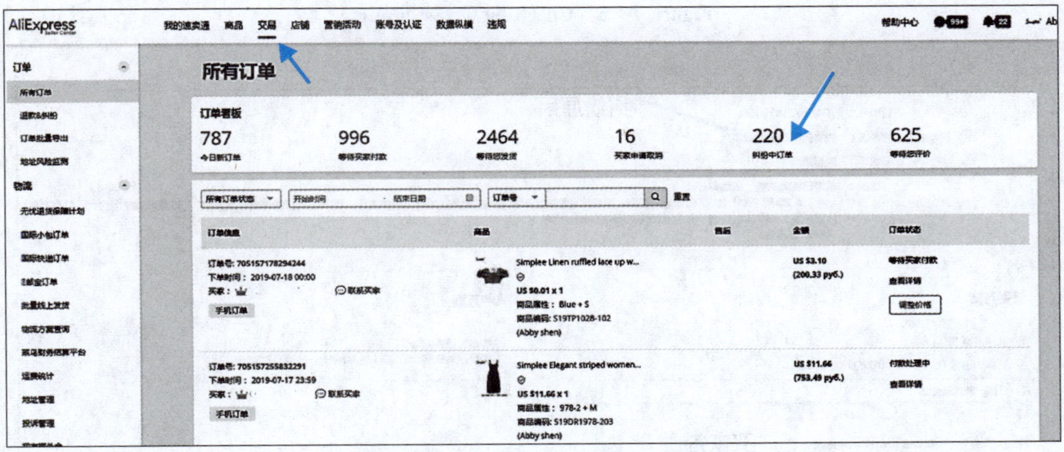

Figure 4 - 4 Tracking In Dispute

Click "View Details" → check chat record and order status to determine if you are supposed to refund the buyer→contact buyer.

2.2.2 Rejection of proposals from the buyer

Click "add only refund proposal" (rejection requires evidence) →Refund amount: 0 →Describe your problem: describe the specific situations.

If a dispute is refund & return, the platform will give 10 calendar days for the buyer to fill in the return order number. If the buyer does not fill in the return order number within the stipulated period, the dispute will be closed without refund.

If the buyer fills in the return order number in time, the dispute will start counting down from 30 calendar days to await the seller's confirmation of receipt. If after 30 calendar

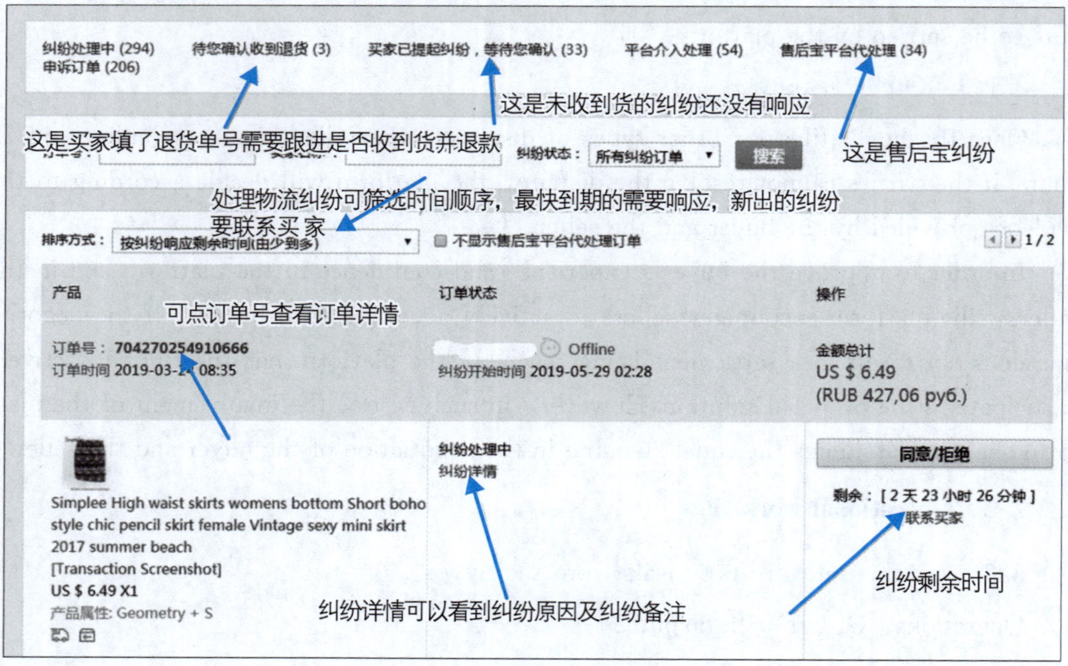

Figure 4-5　Checking Order Status

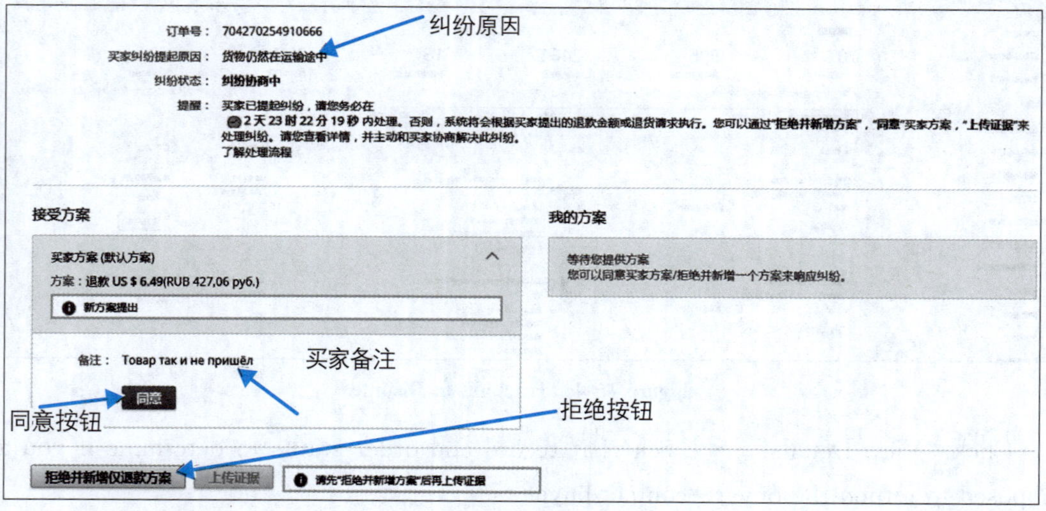

Figure 4-6　Rejection

days the seller has not confirmed receipt of the return of the products and the seller has not filed a dispute, the payment will be refunded to the buyer.

If within 30 calendar days the seller has not received the return of the products or the goods received have issues (e. g. they have been damaged, not fully returned, they have been used and/or are not in resalable condition), the seller can also apply for a dispute to be settled by the platform.

2.2.3 Operations of arbitration

Operations: AliExpress. com→Bell logo→platform notice→arbitration notice. The item in bold is the notice that has not been viewed yet.

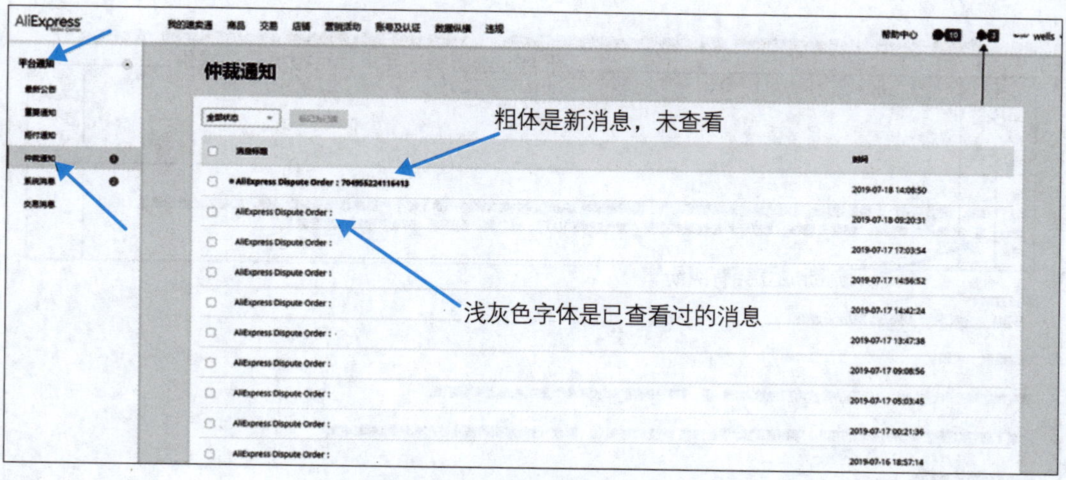

Figure 4 - 7 Arbitration Notice Checking

Those disputes whose judgments are not upheld generally do not need processing.

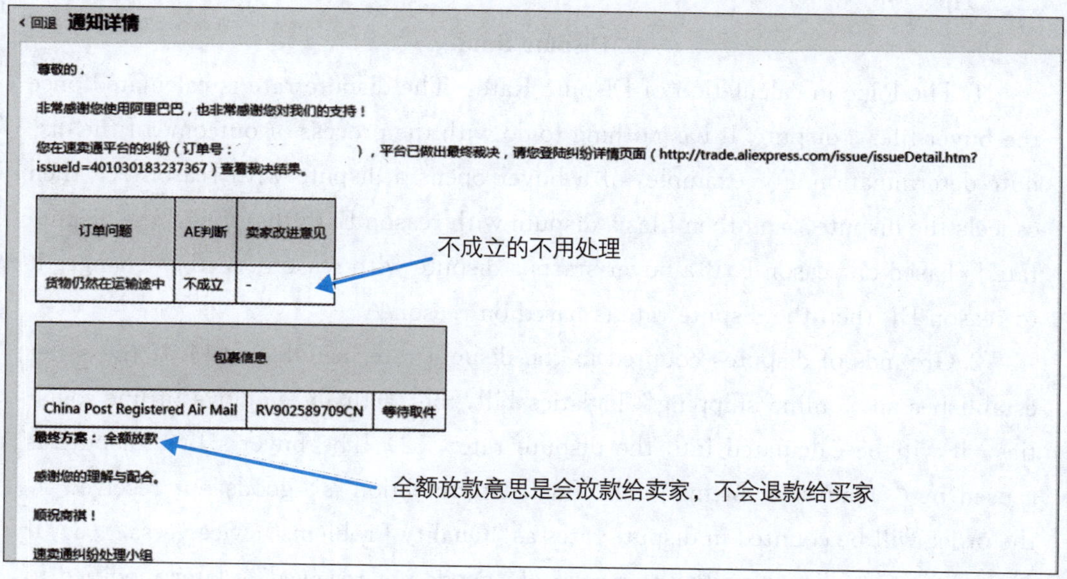

Figure 4 - 8 Unestablished Dispute

If the dispute is established, check the order status to confirm if you should refund and note the reason and check how long the response time is left and make response.

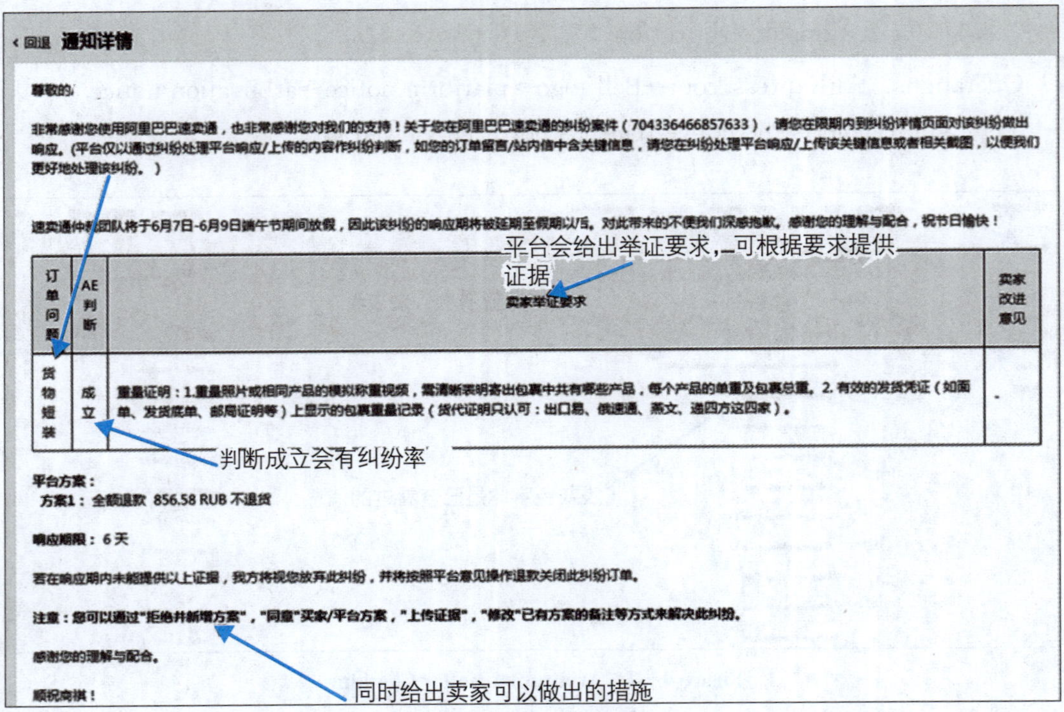
‹ 回退 **通知详情**

尊敬的

非常感谢您使用阿里巴巴速卖通，也非常感谢您对我们的支持！关于您在阿里巴巴速卖通的纠纷案件（704336466857633），请您在限期内到纠纷详情页面对该纠纷做出响应。(平台仅以通过纠纷处理平台响应/上传的内容作纠纷判断，如您的订单留言/站内信中含关键信息，请您在纠纷处理平台响应/上传该关键信息或者相关截图，以便我们更好地处理该纠纷。)

速卖通仲裁团队将于6月7日-6月9日端午节期间放假，因此该纠纷的响应期将被延期至假期以后。对此带来的不便我们深感抱歉。感谢您的理解与配合，祝节日愉快！

订单问题	AE判断	卖家举证要求	卖家改进意见
货物短装	成立	重量证明：1.重量照片或相同产品的模拟称重视频，需清晰表明寄出包裹中共有哪些产品，每个产品的单重及包裹总重。2. 有效的发货凭证（如面单、发货底单、邮局证明等）上显示的包裹重量记录（货代证明只认可：出口易、俄速通、燕文、递四方这四家）。	-

平台方案：

方案1：全额退款 856.58 RUB 不退货

响应期限：6天

若在响应期内未能提供以上证据，我方将视您放弃此纠纷，并将按照平台意见操作退款关闭此纠纷订单。

注意：您可以通过"拒绝并新增方案"，"同意"买家/平台方案，"上传证据"，"修改"已有方案的备注等方式来解决此纠纷。

感谢您的理解与配合。

顺祝商祺！

Figure 4 - 9 Established Dispute

Tips

Dispute Rate

1. The logic in calculation of Dispute Rate: The dispute rate is calculated once the buyer files a dispute. It has nothing to do with the process or outcome of the dispute determination. For example, if a buyer opens a dispute with reason A, then cancels the dispute, and then files a dispute with reason B. In that case, the dispute rate is based on reason B. If a buyer starts a dispute with reason A, then changes it to reason B, then the dispute rate is based on reason A.

2. Grounds of disputes counted in the dispute rate include: (1) If the seller establishes an "online shipping" logistics bill, but actually employs offline logistics, it will be calculated into the dispute rate. (2) The buyer's first dispute is caused by "Quality Problems", the final determination is "goods not received", the order will be counted in dispute rates as "Quality Problems"; vice versa. (3) If a buyer opens a dispute with the reason of "goods not received", later modified to "personal reasons", the first reason will be treated as the cause of disputes counted into the dispute rate.

3. Grounds of disputes that do not be counted into the dispute rate include: (1) Shipping modes not as described. (2) The buyer start a dispute with personal reasons (I don't like it, I don't want it, I bought the wrong one), or for "Easy Return".

2.3 Templates of emails of dispute handling

Sample 1: Short loading

Dear (buyer),

I'm so sorry for our carelessness. I have to check the weight of parcel with our shipment personnel who will come back to work two days later. Could I offset 1 piece's price from your next order? In that case, a good discount and a simple gift will be sent to you. If you would like an immediate refund, could you please let me have your PayPal account?

I am terribly sorry for all the inconvenience.

Best regards,

(seller)

Sample 2: Product quality disputes

Dear (buyer),

We are sorry for the quality problem and would pay more attention to the product quality.

We accept your requirement and please kindly return the good to the following address: ...

By the way, we've got a plan B. That is we send you a new one with 50% discount and you close the dispute. Hope you consider it. Thank you!

Best regards,

(seller)

3. Customer Maintenance

Who are more important, new customers or existing customers? There has been no answer to the question. New customers bring dynamism to the enterprise, while existing customers bring security. That's why we had better keep balance between them. However, our ultimate goal is just to turn all new customers into regular customers, and quality CBEC after-sales customer service means a lot to it. Let's look at a set of data:

- The cost of developing new customers is 3 to 10 times that of retaining regular ones;
- A 5% drop in customer loyalty will reduce your profits by 25%;
- The chance of selling products to new customers is 15% and it is 50% to existing customers;
- A 5% increase in retaining regular customers each year will result in a 25% increase in profits;
- 60% of new customers are by referral of existing customers;
- 20% of your regular customers bring 85% of profits.

Since new customers are so difficult to develop, existing customers definitely deserve attention. Before understanding how to maintain existing customers, we need to know some reasons for losing existing customers.

3.1 Reasons for losing existing customers

3.1.1 Lack of attentive service

When it comes to attentive service, many people may think of service attitude, but in fact, attentive service also includes the timeliness of problem solving. Low efficiency is an important factor that directly leads to customer loss. In coping with disputes, many cases remain untouched till the response timeout just because customer service personnel don't know how to do, which is last thing the customers would like to see.

3.1.2 Lack of product innovation

As the markets become increasingly mature and product prices more transparent, there is less margin of benefit left to customers. If companies fail to timely innovate products, customers are bound to choose more innovative manufacturers in order to enlarge benefits. After all, the interest is the bond that maintains the relationship between the two sides.

3.1.3 Customers encounter new "temptations"

Nowadays, the market is increasingly competitive in an industry, and customers are limited, so it is natural that the profitable customers will become the object of competition. Competitors sometimes know your products better than yourself. Once catching the shortcoming of your products, they will do whatever it takes to expand it and quickly occupy a favorable position in the market and get more customers.

In response to the above problems, we have summarized some ways to maintain customers.

3.2 Approaches of customer maintenance

3.2.1 Respond to customers in a timely and effective manner

Optimize the complaint handling process to shorten the refund time. What's more, CBEC companies can also combine online messengers with phone calls as channels to solve users' problems and avoid users passive waiting.

3.2.2 Update the web pages regularly

Post new product information, or replace the product images. These will keep buyers up to date with the latest information about the company, attracting new customers while preventing existing ones from leaving due to lack of novelty.

3.2.3 Regularly send the latest product information to existing customers

It will be rewarded. Since the cost of developing a new customer may be several times more than that of maintaining existing customers, the maintenance of existing customers must not be ignored. Just sending a greeting card to the customers in holidays will establish more friendly and joyful relationship with them.

3.2.4 Pay attention to where our competitors are superior

A good competitor is like a mirror that allows us to clearly identify your shortcomings and thus you can improve on them.

When encountering customer loss, regardless of subjective or objective factors, it is recommended that companies analyze the root cause of the problem from themselves. If possible, the companies can do a simple questionnaire to the customers who have already left to make clear what they are most dissatisfied with the products and services.

3.3 Templates of emails of customer maintenance

Sample 1: Greetings to our regular customers

Dear (buyer),

Long time no see! How are you doing?

You ordered a pair of shoes from us. How do you like them? Please feel free to tell us if you've got any problem with them.

We've got some new stuff recently. Attached is the updated catalogue for your reference. If you have any new inquiry, please let us know.

Best wishes,

(seller)

Sample 2: Recommending Subscription of the Shop

Dear (buyer),

Welcome to subscribe to our store. By a few clicks you can enjoy our VIP service such as the latest updates from new arrivals to best-selling products on a weekly basis etc. Any problem on subscribing, please refer to ...

(seller)

Sample 3: Marketing campaign recommendation

Dear (buyer),

Thank you for shopping in my shop.

To express our gratitude to our customers, a series of promotional activities will be held from June 1st to 7th , including $15 off orders of $99 or more, 12% off for all the products and various coupons for your choices. There are only 7 days to go!

Come on and join us now!

(seller)

Exercises

1. Multiple Choices

(1) Which is NOT the main task of CBEC after-sales customer service ? (　　)

A. customer management　　B. dispute handling

C. after-sales feedback management　　D. mailing goods

(2) On the major platforms of CBEC, after-sales feedback is generally divided into (　　).

A. positive & negative　　B. positive, negative, neutral

C. five-star & negative　　D. positive, negative, neutral, unevaluated

(3) If the dispute cannot be resolved after negotiation between buyer and seller, it can be submitted to (　　) to settle the dispute.

A. the platform　　B. the buyer

C. the seller　　D. the court

(4) (　　) means the material, craftsmanship, and/or quality of the products delivered by the seller fails to meet the provisions of the purchase contract, or there is damage, functional failure, missing parts or other issues that may prevent their normal use.

A. inconsistent description　　B. quality problems

C. infringement　　D. customs detention

(5) If the buyer submits a dispute is (　　), it will not be counted in the seller's dispute rate.

A. personal reasons　　B. quality problems

C. color not as described　　D. size not as described

2. True or False

(1) Where the buyer claims that the quality problem and inconsistency in description of the products delivered are identifiable with naked eyes, the Seller shall first provide photos, videos, or other evidence approved by Alibaba. com to prove it. (　　)

(2) The customer's positive comments do not need reply. (　　)

(3) If a buyer initiates a dispute with reason A, and then cancels the dispute, and then initiates a dispute with reason B, then the dispute rate is counted by reason B. (　　)

(4) The buyer opened a dispute with the reason "goods not received", later modified the reason into "for personal reasons ", then, it will not be counted in the Dispute Rate. (　　)

(5) General dispute status is Return of Products and Refund, the platform will first give 10 days for the buyer to fill in the return order number, if the buyer does not fill in the return order number within 10 days, the dispute will be closed without refund. (　　)

Skills&Drills

Suppose you run an online store specializing in women's casual shoes on AliExpress. Judy, a British customer, bought a pair of shoes from your store a week ago.

(1) Judy wrote to reflect that the shoes received did not match the product description, especially the color, which displeased her very much. She opened a dispute to demand a refund. Please reply to her by email and try to convince her to close the dispute.

(2) Thanksgiving Day is coming, please send her your greetings and recommend her the campaigns, like "$10 Off the Order of $100+".

Reference answer

Micro Scenario in Moral Education

Eyre is relaxed and happy after successfully handling the customer's dispute. In the break area， she meets Director of her department， Mr. Wang. Mr. Wang is an experienced customer service specialist. Since Eyre joined the company， she has received a lot of guidance from him. So， when she encounters him， Eyre couldn't wait to tell him what had happened. Mr. Wang said with appreciation， "It's not easy to solve the customer's problem so successfully when you are a newcomer." Then he asked， "In the case， do you know what's the key to success?" This question put Eyre in deep thought ...

Please work out the dialogue and complete the role play with your partners according to the situation.

Reference answer：

Eyre said： "Is it that when the customer blamed in an offensive way， I controlled myself from being angry or discouraged， and I gave him the greatest understanding?"

"Yes! You have shown great empathy in this business. That is the most uncommon and valuable quality of a customer service specialist." Mr. Wang continues， "If you had hastily defended our company， the customer would have been more crossed and the result more counter productive. Instead， you show understanding and apology for the customer in the whole process. These responses told the customer he was listened to and respected. And it is definitely helpful to calm the customer down and create a cooperative atmosphere for follow-up procedure."

"Secondly， you showed capacity of cooperation with others. You resolved the dispute in a timely manner， thanks to effective communication and feedback with other departments， especially the technical support department. When you learned from them that there was a possibility that the problem was caused by a misuse， you not only prompted the correct procedure but also recorded a video specifically for the customer to demonstrate the procedure. In such a relaxed and friendly atmosphere， the customer was more likely to cooperate with you and provide relevant information and try again until the problem was finally resolved."

"Oh，" Eyre nods， "Empathy and cooperation are the true meaning of this job!"

项目五

跨境电商客服技巧进阶

知识目标

1. 能够有效识别诚意客户并对客户进行分类；
2. 能够熟悉客户跟进流程并具备初步的管理策略。

能力目标

1. 掌握跨境电商客户的识别及分类方法；
2. 掌握跨境电商维护及管理客户的基本策略。

素质目标

具备较强的团队合作能力及思辨能力。

知识点索引

- 项目五 跨境电商客服技巧进阶
  - 项目背景
  - 任务分解
  - 任务完成
    - 一、培养挖掘客户价值的敏锐性
    - 二、保持跟进客户的耐心和耐力
    - 三、对客户进行科学归类
      - （一）社会属性
      - （二）行为属性
      - （三）价值属性
  - 知识要点
    - 一、客户关系管理基础
      - （一）新老客户购买流程对比
      - （二）老客户价值分析及维护策略
      - （三）客户信息收集
    - 二、客户分类及应对策略
      - （一）RFM分类模型
      - （二）其他分类方法及应对策略
    - 三、客户维护及沟通技巧
      - （一）客户维护技巧
      - （二）客户沟通技巧

项目背景

小艾刚入行跨境电商不久，她十分努力，日常“996”。从发布产品、收数据、做推广到拿货发货一刻不得闲。但数月下来，她发现订单不仅没有增多，收益也与自己想象中的相去甚远；反观小林，虽然他做跨境电商年数也不长，但却轻松自在得多。不仅赚到了钱，还时常能跟家人聚会、跟小伙伴健身运动，叫小艾好生羡慕。同是做跨境电商，为什么差别如此之大？

任务分解

原来，小林早早地就把打造本土化和个性化的客服体验作为自己的主要策略。他觉得，在如今产品同质化现象越来越普遍的跨境领域，有竞争力的价格、详尽的产品描述、全方位的音视频推广这些传统要素并非卖家的核心竞争力，能真正促成跨境消费转型升级的重要支柱之一实为优质的服务。于是，他细化经营产品，在日常客户维护上投入了更多的精力，积极研究客户背后的价值。经过一段时间的努力，小林店铺的客户复购率有了显著提升，新客户转成了老客户，而老客户也成了重要客户，店铺的运营也顺利走上了正轨。于是，小艾虚心向小林请教了以下三个关键问题：

1. 如何挖掘并识别有价值的客户？
2. 如何持续地跟进客户？
3. 如何更高效地管理客户？

任务完成

一、培养挖掘客户价值的敏锐性

老客户和重要客户往往是由零售客户转化而来，但并非所有的零售客户都是潜在的大额客户。因此，客服人员需要具有发现潜在价值客户的敏锐性。这个技能虽无法在短期内形成，但有些常用的技巧可供参考，比如，潜在的价值客户会比普通的客户更重视卖家的商品丰富度、商品线的备货供应情况，以及当购买数量提升时，是否能够得到相应的折扣。换言之，价值客户更关注利润空间、稳定的商品供应以及某个类目下丰富的商品种类。供货稳定、有较大的批发折扣以及灵活的运输方案，是博得价值客户的基本条件。因此，若客服人员能通过与客户的积极沟通，有意识地分析客户的历史交易数据和购买流程，就能形成较为可靠的观察与总结，从而培养发现潜在价值客户的敏锐性。

二、保持跟进客户的耐心和耐力

新手卖家之所以很少有人能谈成大额订单，原因之一就是他们在客服工作上欠缺对重点客户的持续跟进。大额客户在跨境电商平台上的询盘往往是同时向多个中国卖家批量发出的，在收到多个卖家的第一轮报价后，客户往往会对所有的报价以及运输服务进行横向比较。因此，在报价后，客服人员应定期主动联系买家，明确他们的需求和现状，并据此及时调整产品价格、运输方式、交货时间以及清关方式等条款，以更好地满足客户需求，积极促成订单。

三、对客户进行科学归类

相比其他电商，跨境电商的客户关系管理更具挑战性。因此，运用科学的分析方法来合理区分客户群体，并根据不同客户群的特点来提供差异化的商品和服务对提高店铺的营销效率大有裨益。一般情况下，通过分析归纳客户在购物时所产生的各项数据，我们可以从以下三个维度对客户进行归类：

（一）社会属性

由于来自不同国家的消费者天然就有着不同的文化背景和消费需求，因此，我们首先就能根据地址对客户进行国别分类，直观体现出店铺主要客户群体的国家分布情况，并以此调整产品营销的方式或优化产品本身。比如一款在美国客户群中好评如潮、销量较高的运动鞋却在巴西买家群里遇冷，遇到这种情况，我们可以有针对性地优化商品，或是针对巴西买家在葡语页面设计更适合该类客户群体的营销话术。

（二）行为属性

根据客户不同的消费行为，刻画出在不同消费行为属性下的典型客户画像，并依此采取不同的营销策略和沟通话术。比如，在分析客户数据后我们可能会发现，有的客户喜欢购买打折商品、习惯咨询优惠券和免运费等信息；而有的客户偏向选择高价的同类商品，尤其在意售后条款；还有的客户比较挑剔，沟通不当就有给中评甚至差评的可能。因此，总结不同客户群的消费行为实际上是了解客户的真正需求、提供更有针对性服务的基础。

（三）价值属性

在跨境电商的各交易平台中，卖家的等级制度十分严谨；与此同时，从购买行为、成交金额和评价情况等维度进行评估，各平台对买家等级也有规范。因此，根据买家积分和相应等级的差异，我们也能快速对不同客户进行分类和标签化管理。

小贴士

价值属性等级

根据企业需求和岗位权限的不同，价值属性的评估方法之一是以历史订单或搜索/购买历史为依据，可大致划分为以下四个等级：

一级：已下过订单的老客户、已参与预购的准客户；

二级：有明确下单意向、购买意愿强的客户；

三级：对产品有相对具体的规格或价格需求的客户；

四级：无明确意向、咨询历史的客户。

知识要点

一、客户关系管理基础

客户关系管理（Customer Relationship Management，CRM）指的是深入分析客户信息，挖掘客户潜在需求，提高客户满意度，增加客户黏性，是有利于提高运营效益的一种手段。在跨境电商领域，客户关系管理以产品为媒介，在挖掘客户潜在需求的同时有利于塑造店铺及品牌形象，赋予店铺活力，有助于提高店铺效益。换句话说，客户关系管理以客户为中心，辅以营销、管理、数据及软件等工具来搜集、整理、分析客户数据，主动且有选择地建立客户关系，有意识地将营销思维融入客户维护中，提升客户复购率。

（一）新老客户购买流程对比

从图5-1中我们可以发现，新老客户从搜索到成交的流程存在较大差异。一般而言，新客户通过关键词搜索、类目浏览或广告倒流进入店铺，在浏览店铺时会在不同程度上对产品款式、产品细节、评价情况、价格折扣以及店铺信誉等信息来进行主观辨别，只要稍有不满意就有可能退出店铺，这就是跳失率。如果有新客户对感兴趣的产品进行咨询、比价甚至完成下单，也有较大可能在成交后因物流、售后服务不及时或不到位而产生纠纷。

相比之下，老客户或回头客的购买流程就简单高效得多。只要有过良好的购物体验，老客户更关注店铺的新产品与促销活动，当看到感兴趣的产品时，他们倾向于简单咨询或直接购买；如果发生缺货或物流等问题，老客户也相对容易沟通，给出的产品评价也更为宽容感性，纠纷率少。不难发现，对客户进行积极管理且有针对性的维护是提高店铺营收的重要手段。

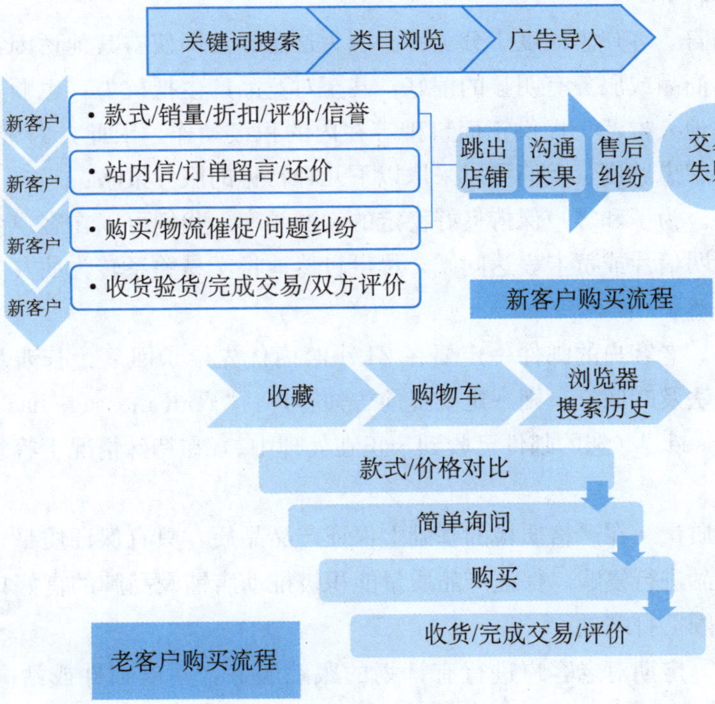

图5-1 新老客户购物流程

（二）老客户价值分析及维护策略

1. 提升复购率

从图5-1中我们可以明确，老客户的购买流程短。有数据表明，开发一个新客户的成本是维护一个老客户的7～8倍。因此，一次交易的完成并不意味着结束，挖掘客户及客户圈的潜在价值，对提升店铺的复购率以及店铺利润率有着十分积极的意义。

2. 优化开发产品

在拥有良好购物体验的前提下，老客户与店铺之间建立了信任基础。因此，有针对性地加强与客户线上和线下的双线沟通，可以更直接地获取老客户对产品的意见和建议，进而优化或开发满足客户真正需求的产品，以便在竞争激烈的跨境领域中抢占先机。

3. 用口碑建品牌

随着跨境购物的普及，好的产品有利于渗透国外终端用户的生活圈，从而赢得好的口碑。在成熟的社交媒体网络中，对客户社交圈的积极维护能有效地增加客户黏性，一旦与客户建立了长期稳定的关系，客户也乐于分享优秀的产品，在助力店铺口碑的同时收获品牌建设的基础。

通过对老客户的价值分析我们可以明确，在跨境领域积极维护老客户，不仅能进一步强化客户对店铺的忠诚度，更能大大降低销售成本。客户忠诚度通常包括再购买意愿、基本行为（购买时间、购置次数、购置数量等）和衍生行为（公开推荐、口碑、介绍客户、给小费等）三个方面。

4. 提升客户忠诚度

对品牌产品而言，客户忠诚度十分关键。因为这意味着即使有其他诱因，客户仍能保持对商家所提供的商品或服务有明显的偏好，甚至对竞品产生抵抗力，也顺其自然地完成包括重复购买、向他人推荐、提供正面口碑等在内的积极动作。因此，为维护好老客户，建立更具黏性的品牌忠诚度，我们可以采取以下几种常见的服务策略：

（1）定期问候。为了和客户保持良好稳定的沟通频率，我们可以在客户生日或是一些重大节日发邮件、明信片或贺卡表达问候，尽量自然地将交易关系转为朋友关系，这对后期跟进工作大有裨益。

（2）优先回复。老客户的邮件一定要在 24 小时内优先给予回复，若涉及需要多方配合的复杂问题而无法及时回复，则一定要提前告知客户："Your message has been received and is being processed."（您的邮件已收到，正在处理中。）在特殊情况下答复时间也不要超过三天。

（3）确保产品质量。在严格质检的基础上保证产品品质，只有保证质量，客户，尤其是老客户才会对产品进行复购。保证产品质量能积极推动店铺及品牌的良好口碑，为进一步建立良性"生态圈"打基础。

（4）定期回访。定期对老客户进行有计划的跟踪服务，并以邮件或站内信的方式回访，及时获得客户对产品质量和服务的反馈，同时收集改进意见。要让客户留有"店铺的产品和服务都是以客户为中心来不断提升和优化的"这一关键印象。

（三）客户信息收集

客户关系管理包括信息收集、客户分类、客户维护和客户营销四步（见图 5－2），在这一流程中，信息收集无疑是管理客户的第一步。为做好信息收集工作，首先要明确收集客户信息的路径。一般而言，收集信息的路径如下：

订单批量导出后，我们用 Excel 表格就能对客户信息进行梳理，按需筛选包括用户

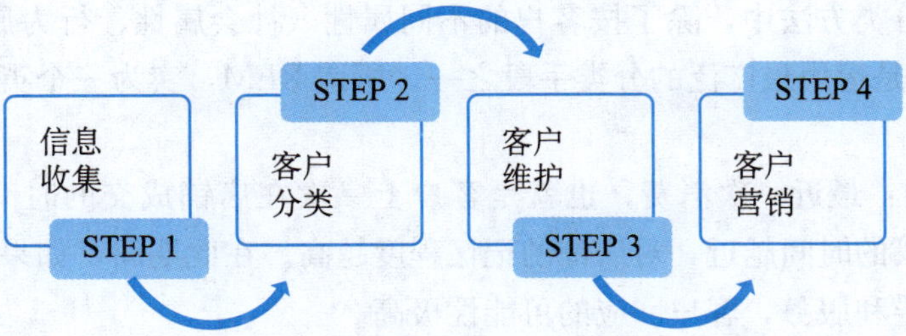

图 5-2　客户关系管理流程

图 5-3　信息收集路径流程

ID、邮箱、订单金额、产品信息、收货地址、国家、联系方式等内容，为进一步标签化管理打基础（见表 5-1）。

表 5-1　客户信息标签化管理表

用户名	邮箱	订单信息	地址	国家	联系方式	评价	活跃度

有了基础信息后我们就能有意识地抓取潜在目标客户，进行二次营销。比如重点查看买卖双方评价状况、购买频率和购买习惯，来判断该客户是否有批发意愿，倾向高价还是低价产品等。当然，二次营销也讲究时机。一般情况下，我们可以在下列几个时间节点通过邮件或站内留言等方式与重点客户进行沟通：

（1）优质产品上新，推广宣传新品时；

（2）特价促销活动，如“双 11”“黑五”等打折季；

（3）重要节日，如感恩节、圣诞节等消费需求急剧增长时；

（4）对有固定采购需求的买家，在下一次采购节点前。

此外，在收集客户信息时，我们不仅要及时整理显性信息，还要对客户数据所暗含的隐性信息做尽可能多的挖掘和归纳。

二、客户分类及应对策略

（一）RFM 分类模型

客户分类是为了方便卖家对买家的管理，差异化地对待客户，更有针对性地向客户提供服务。在众多分类方法中，除了按客户的不同属性（社会属性、行为属性、价值属性）来分，RFM 模型是运用最广泛的分类手段之一。所谓 RFM，实为三个英文关键词的首字母组合：

R（Recency）：最近一次消费，也就是客户上一次在店铺成交的时间和成交的产品。理论上，客户购买的时间越近，对店铺的记忆程度越高。在此期间，如果我们能通过客服来提供相应的引导和服务，客户回应的可能性极高。

F（Frequency）：消费频率，即在单位时间内的消费次数。消费次数越多，说明客户的满意度越高，如果卖家始终保持优质的服务和产品，买家就非常容易产生黏性，对店铺的忠诚度也会提升。

M（Monetary）：消费金额，即单位期间内的消费总额与平均消费额之比。当店铺成长到一定阶段，客群基数大于客服可以悉数维护的程度时，我们要学会合理利用资源，把重心放到重点客户群。由于店铺 80%的利润往往来自 20%的客户，因此花 80%的精力去维护那 20%能得到的回报率也就更高。

RFM 是一种简单易用的分类模型，它通过量化客户近期的购买行为、购买频率和消费金额 3 个指标就能直观地表达客户的价值状态。比如，我们可以将 RFM 设定为 3～5 个阶段：R 值参考开店时间、产品本身的特性及运输周期；F 值参考店铺的客户评价和购买频次；M 值参考产品单价（见表 5-2）。

表 5-2　RMF 客户价值评估框架

5	R≤90 天	F≥5 次	1000USD≤M
4	90 天<≤190 天	F=4 次	500USD≤M≤1000USD
3	180 天<R≤360 天	F=3 次	200USD≤M≤500USD
2	360 天<R≤720 天	F=2 次	100USD≤M≤200USD
1	720 天以上	F=1 次	M<100USD

根据确定的 RFM 模型框架，我们就能针对每个客户的具体情况来打分（见表 5-3）。

表 5-3　RMF 客户价值评估表

客户名称	R 值	R 值得分	F 值	F 值得分	M 值	M 值得分	RFM 得分
Jack	80	5	1	1	22	1	7
Lucy	320	3	2	2	734	4	9
John	600	2	3	3	280	3	8
Peter	106	4	3	3	586	4	11
Cici	736	1	4	4	102	2	7

客户 Jack 最近一次消费的时间是 80 天，对应的 R 值得分是 5；消费次数是 1，对应

的 F 得分是 1；消费金额是 22，对应的 M 得分是 1，因此该客户的 RFM 总得分为 7 分。通过 RFM 模型我们不难发现，得分最高的成交金额不一定最高；而得分最低也并不意味着成交额最低。因此，客户价值不单是成交金额的体现，通过对 RFM 的设计和量化，我们就能为店铺筛选出优质客户、为精准营销做准备。

（二）其他分类方法及应对策略

根据买家的消费行为、性格特征和特定心理，我们也可以对客群进行其他维度的标签化管理，并使用相应策略来提升客户服务质量。

1. 按性格特征分类及应对策略（见图 5-4）

友善型	·特质：性格随和，较为真诚和宽容； ·策略：提供优质服务，进行长期维护。
独断型	·特质：不善于理解他人，不易接受他人意见； ·策略：不怠慢，尽可能满足需求，适当维护。
分析型	·特质：懂道理、讲道理，善用法律手段维权； ·策略：真诚对待，合理解释，长期维护。
自我型	·特质：以自我为中心，有报复心理； ·策略：控制情绪，以礼相待，不做特殊维护。

图 5-4　客户常见性格特征分类及应对策略图

2. 按购买行为分类及应对策略（见图 5-5）

交际型	购买型	礼貌型	讲价型
·特质：喜聊天，较感性，得到积极回应下单概率高； ·策略：热情应对，重点维护。	·特质：直接购买，会给好评但甚少回应； ·策略：适当沟通，不过度维护。	·特质：有距离感，但会因为热情的服务成为回头客； ·策略：热情应对，重点维护。	·特质：喜还价，对促销和优惠极为在意，下单效率低； ·策略：礼貌回应，守好底线，适当维护。

图 5-5　客户常见购买行为分类及应对策略图

3. 按常见问题分类及应对策略（见图 5-6）

卖家信用是否可靠？	价格低是否为劣质产品？	同类商品选择多，不知选哪个好？	交易安全吗？有什么保障？	退换货、物品损坏、免邮怎么处理？
策略：用交易记录和用户评价来说服。	策略：说明价格由来以及对质量的保障。	策略：仔细询问客户需求，给出合理推荐。	策略：详细介绍安全交易的方方面面以打消买家顾虑。	策略：以售后服务、消费者保障服务给予买家信心。

图 5-6　按客户常见问题分类及应对策略图

4. 按消费心理分类及应对策略（见图 5－7）

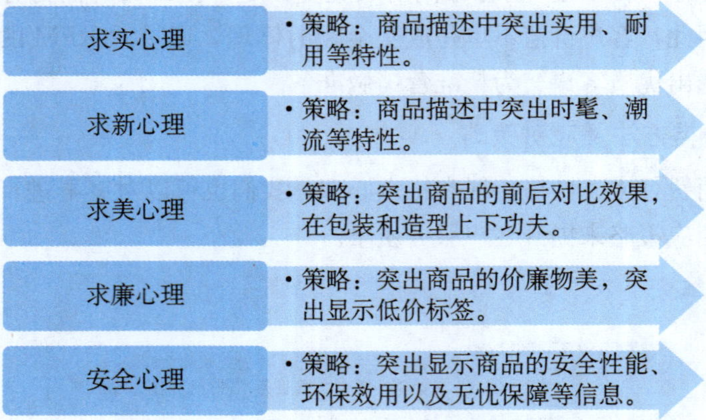

图 5－7　按客户消费心理分类及应对策略图

三、客户维护及沟通技巧

（一）客户维护技巧

满意度源于每一次的交易，满意度的持续累积不仅能增加客户对店铺的信赖，还能助力新老客户的转化。合理使用下列客户维护技巧，即可有效提升客户满意度。

1. 收货前

(1) 成交致谢。客户的成交是对卖家信任的开始，简单的感谢是对买家信任感的呵护。

(2) 赠送礼品。附赠礼品建议选择邮票、挂件、贺卡、剪纸等不占空间、重量较轻的物品。合适的小礼物能直接提升客户对店铺以及产品的好感。

(3) 发货通知。订单发货后，及时做好发货通知，时时关注包裹物流状态，如遇航线拥堵、延迟派送等异常情况应及时告知客户并延长收货日期。

2. 收货后

(1) 好评奖励。客户确认收货后对产品有了真实感受，叠加前期周到的服务印象，一般而言不会抗拒对购物体验做出好评。此时，卖家可通过发放优惠券、满立减、特别折扣等形式来积极促成满意评价，刺激客户再次下单。

(2) 分享有礼。一方面，分享有礼是对好评奖励的延伸；另一方面，分享有礼是加入客户社交圈的良好契机。

(3) 客户专享日。如果只是机械地进行商品打折宣传或上新通知，买家容易疲劳，反而会产生负面情绪。因此，我们可以设置几个时间节点为客户专享日，设计专门的活动回馈新老客户。比如，在交易完成后的“蜜月期”内，店铺特地送上“蜜月之礼”：“We are glad to find you were satisfied with our goods and give us five-star feedback, this means a lot to us and will keep us moving forward. Since now you are a VIP customer in our store, we have some special offers for you, please check out the following link to find out more.”

之后，我们还能借“满月之礼”“百日之礼”等节点来进行定向沟通：“My Dear VIP Friend，today is the 100th day since we met，a \$5 coupon has been prepared for you，enjoy shopping，my friend!”对买家而言，持续的定向联络会引起客户对店铺的再次关注，且时间越长意义越大。

（4）关联推荐。根据客户的已购商品来推荐相似产品。关联产品包括纵向推荐，比如客户买了假发，可推荐假发专用梳；以及横向推荐，比如客户买了直发假发，可推荐卷发假发等。

3. 维护频率

维护客户的目的之一是加强客户对店铺的记忆。因此，当我们进行维护时，不仅需要注意内容，也需要注重频率。切勿急功近利，应与客户保持长久的关系。可供参考的是，根据人的记忆周期规律，我们可以抓住 1、2、4、7、15 这几个时间节点进行维护。

例如：当客户拍下订单后，我们在第 1 天发出致谢和关联产品推荐，第 2 天告知货物状态及发放定向优惠券，第 4 天告知物流信息及好评有礼活动，第 7 天告知分享有礼活动、发送优惠券使用提醒，第 15 天更新物流状态及节假日问候。

（二）客户沟通技巧

1. 专业服务

（1）从专业的角度解决问题。客服首先就需要明确专业分工的思想，尽可能地在工作本身的专业性上下功夫，从专业的角度来帮助客户解决问题。首先，在解释问题发生的原因时，客服人员能清楚明了地向客户阐释问题产生的真实原因；其次，当涉及行业术语或概念时，客服人员要有“接地气”的能力，善用通俗易懂的语言向客户进行说明；最后，在协商解决方案时，客服人员能依照具体情况提出负责且有效的解决方案，而非敷衍了事或干脆拖延处理。

事实上，客户就所遇到的问题提出质疑或投诉，对卖家并非坏事。只要能顺利且彻底地解决问题，反而可以有效加深客户对店铺的信任感，进而形成客户黏性。换句话说，客服工作者应当把每次处理问题的过程当作展示自己专业能力的机会，用专业的方法与态度来妥善解决问题，让新客户变成老客户。

（2）提供可信赖的依据。由于距离远、流程多以及语言文化之间的差异，在跨境购物的过程中产生问题的概率远高于国内电商。因此，无论是面对客户的常规咨询还是处理棘手的投诉与问题，客服人员都应当尽可能地提供“看得见、摸得着”的依据。

对具体的产品而言，可信赖的依据可以是商品的细节图片、详尽的文字说明或是能讲解商品细节的短片等。在物流一侧，量化数据更为直观，比如包裹单号、追踪网址、物流动态等。需要注意的是，在客服人员向客户提供依据时，要尽可能提供完整的物流信息、买家所在国的物流追踪网站以及对专业数据的清晰解释。

（3）采用多样化的回复。在跨境平台中有许多优质产品，无论在组装、使用还是在后期维护的步骤上都较为复杂。大部分情况下，卖家会配上大量的说明性文本供客服人员参考。当客户就技术性问题进行咨询时，客服人员可以搜索技术参数、使用方法等进行大段描述与解释。然而，当面对复杂问题时，说得越多反而不一定能彻底解决问题。因此，通过制作“安装流程图”或拍摄简单的“使用演示录像”来直观地讲解可以更高效地解决问题。

2. 掌握主动

优秀的客服人员不仅能疏导客户情绪，还能自然地引导客户携手积极解决问题。掌握主动权的具体做法可参考以下几点：

（1）积极抚慰。在跨境电商中，买家通常不熟悉复杂的国际物流，甚至无法清晰理解产品的英文说明。因此，当出现问题时买家常常会呈现焦躁心态。针对这种情况，客服人员首先要积极安抚客户，从客户的视角出发，客观分析问题。待客户平静下来，第一时间向客户保证能顺利解决问题。

（2）表达感恩。“感恩”是西方文化中被普遍认可的美德，“感恩节”就是极为典型的代表。在实际工作中，如果客服人员能时时向买家呈现感恩的态度，这对顺利解决投诉、塑造良好的店铺形象有百利而无一害。

（3）最后一封邮件。电子邮件、站内信及订单留言是客服人员常用的沟通渠道。从商务礼仪的角度看，买卖双方在沟通过程中的最后一封邮件理应由卖家发出，这对赢得客户好感有一定的积极作用。此外，跨境电商平台的后台系统可以统计站内信或订单留言的平均回复时间，平均回复时间越短，时效越高，代表店铺的服务水平越高。因此，无论在何种情况下，由客服人员发出最后一封沟通邮件不仅是出于礼貌，也是服务技巧的体现。

3. 责任意识

（1）合理解释。当面对客户的不满情绪或投诉时，客服人员需要为买家找到一个合理的、能够接受的理由，且这个理由最好是由第三方或不可抗力引起的。事实上，找到这个合理的解释可以更容易地让客户接受卖家所提出的解决方案，有助于高效解决纠纷和争议。

（2）承担责任。合理解释并不代表不承担责任，客服人员的出发点是提高解决问题的效率，更好地服务客户。在实际情况中，把错误合理地推诿到第三方身上，并表明“即使错误不在我们，我们仍愿意为顾客解决问题”的态度，往往更能平息客户的怒气，也能更顺利地达成解决方案。长远来看，也只有把买家当作自己的朋友，以诚意相待，快捷、彻底地帮客户解决问题，才有可能在一次次的实践中积累买家信任。

习题测验

（一）选择题

1. 一般而言，我们可以从哪几个方面对跨境电商平台的客户进行归类？（　　）

A. 社会属性　　B. 行为属性

C. 价值属性　　D. 以上皆是

2. 客户关系管理的意义在于什么？（　　）

A. 深入分析客户信息，挖掘客户需求

B. 提升客户满意度，增加客户黏性

C. 有利于提高运营效益

D. 以上皆是

3. 我们要积极维护老客户的原因是（ ）。

A. 能够提升复购率、优化开发产品、确保产品质量

B. 能够提升复购率、提升产品口碑、优化开发产品

C. 优化开发产品、提升产品口碑、确保产品质量

D. 能够加快购买时间、提升产品口碑、确保产品质量

4. RFM 分类模型中的 RFM 分别指代的是（ ）。

A. Rates、Friendly、Money

B. Rates、Frequency、Money

C. Recency、Frequency、Monetary

D. Recency、Friendly、Money

5. 客户维护是客服人员日常工作的重要组成部分，我们可以依照相对合理的维护频率，适时与客户进行沟通。以下哪个选项的维护频率较为合理？（ ）

A. 1、2、4、7、9　　B. 1、2、4、7、15

C. 1、3、5、7、9　　D. 1、3、5、7、15

（二）判断题

1. 跨境电商客服的工作范畴仅包含与客户进行沟通。（ ）

2. 跨境电商客服人员不管在什么情况下都要主动承担错误。（ ）

3. 跨境电商客服人员在与客户进行沟通时应尽可能提供可靠的数据。（ ）

4. 跨境电商客服人员应专心服务新客户，老客户无须花大力气维护。（ ）

5. 客服人员与客户进行协商后顺利解决了问题，客户最后回复了“thank you”，客服人员无须对此类信息进行回复。（ ）

能力实训

（一）简答题

1. 简述适合客服人员进行二次营销的时间节点。

2. 简述跨境电商客服人员的客户沟通技巧。

（二）案例分析

正值圣诞消费旺季，盯着消费者钱包的不仅是大肆促销的商家，还有一批网络诈骗分子。大量亚马逊用户在 Facebook、Twitter 等社交平台上发帖称，自己曾遭遇虚假邮件诈骗，并有不少网友因此泄露了个人重要信息。

收到诈骗邮件的多为英国、美国、澳大利亚等地区的亚马逊用户，有些人被告知“订单无法发货”、无法访问亚马逊账户和其他订单，需要通过单击邮件中的链接确认信息方能恢复使用。据了解，收件人被要求输入的个人信息包括姓名、手机号、地址和银行卡号等。值得一提的是，受骗人在输入个人信息并单击保存后，会自动跳转到亚马逊官网，让

他们忽视了自己被骗的事实。

另一种常见的诈骗手法与之类似。诈骗人会向用户发送一封“订单确认”邮件，声称该用户的订单已确认，并附上订单详情以及预计的交货日期等信息。如用户未购买此商品，则可通过邮件中的链接取消订单。

除了以上两种常见的诈骗方式外，还有一种“领取礼品卡”的诈骗方式：有用户曾在Twitter上发帖并@亚马逊官方账号称，收到了一封邮件被告知获得了价值110欧元的礼品卡，可以通过点击邮件中提供的链接来激活。然而，亚马逊则回复该用户这并非官方发送的邮件。

随着跨境电商的不断普及，对消费者来说，不仅不能随意相信在购物时通过非官方渠道接收到的优惠，在购物时更应加强防范，不轻易泄露个人信息。

思考：如有买家遇到类似问题来店铺留言咨询，作为一名跨境电商客服人员，你该如何回复？

参考答案

思政微面试

想成为一名合格的跨境电商客服，要进一步提升自己的专业素养，除了要具备换位思考、高效处理、善于倾听、有韧性等多项基本素质之外，还应以创造新的客户价值体验为目标，积极掌握、实践辨析能力及合作能力两项关键技能。

（一）辨析能力

客服人员服务客户的根基在于“全面深入分析目标产品、目标客户”，即对企业自身环境、产品特点先知，对竞争对手产品信息先知，对行业发展态势先知，对目标客户（群）需求先知，才能做到“妙算”，取得战略上的成功。因此，为了实现“知彼知己”，我们必须潜心钻研业务，针对不同客户群体，着重培养信息的分析能力，精耕细作客服的高阶职业素养。事实上，清晰了解跨境电商的行业变化、知晓社会化媒体营销对跨境行业的影响力，不仅是一名优秀客服人员市场分析能力的直接体现，也是跨境企业赢得行业先机的先决条件。只有我们秉承改革创新、开拓进取的时代精神，才能深切践行“以眼力明辨真伪、以脑力深入思考、以实力服务客户”的职业价值观。

（二）合作能力

客服原本就是跨境电商运营流程中的重要环节，客服工作涉及仓库、产品及物流等方方面面的沟通和协调。因此，好的团队协作可以给到客户更快、更准确的回应；与跨职能团队之间保持良好的关系，也可以在需要时获得支持与帮助。

（三）微面试

1. 你问我答

假设你手握某跨境龙头企业的客服专员面试通知，为了能在面试中全面展现自己的专业素养，请你和同学搭档，从下列面试问题中挑 3～5 个相互问答，注意记录对方在面试中的表现。

序号	问题
1	Tell us about a time where a project did not go as planned. What can be done to avoid a similar problem in the future?
2	Have you ever needed to make an important decision quickly?
3	Tell us about a time you work successfully within a team.
4	Have you ever foreseen a problem before it happened? What did you do to prevent this from happening?
5	Imagine that you come to work to see that you have been sent 1,000 emails overnight. If you only have time to answer 200 of them, how would you decide which 200 emails to respond to?
6	A customer has come up to you with a problem while you are in the middle of talking to your manager about something very important. How would you react to this?
7	How do you keep yourself motivated when customers take their frustrations on you?
8	How do you measure success?
9	While in a meeting, your co-worker suggests a solution to a problem that you know will not work. Do you voice your concern to the team in the meeting?
10	What steps do you take when addressing a problem?
11	Describe a time when you noticed a problem at work and came up with a solution to fix it.
12	Tell us about a time when you set a lofty goal for yourself and achieved it. What steps did you take to make it happen?
13	If your manager made a mistake on an important document, how would you go about addressing it?
14	Is it better to increase prices to gain profit or lower prices to make customers happy?
15	Suppose you need to alert a customer because your product/service contains a major problem, how will you handle that task?

2. 评价与复盘

在小组通力合作完成微面试后，我们就要进入更为关键的包括自评以及互评在内的复盘环节。事实上，从回答上述面试问题到对表现做出评价的过程就是思辨的过程，而问题回答得越是具体细致有创意，我们就越能深挖其中的共性特征，以此来进行较为客观的评价。一般来说，我们可以从下面几个维度进行评价：

（1）逻辑清晰。有较强思辨能力的人不会让偏见或刻板印象左右他们的决策，在回答问题时他们善于从各个角度考虑不同情况，并能有逻辑地梳理整合自己的回答。因此，在听他们论述自己的观点时，听者很容易就能抓住重点，信息触达效率高。

（2）有理有据。善于思辨的面试者不受主观情绪左右，他们善于挖掘关键证据或是线索，根据已知事实进行适当的逻辑推演，不草率下结论。事实上，也正因为论据扎实，他们的观点普遍具有说服力。

（3）创新思维。有思辨能力的人也具备相当的创造力。如果在回答问题时给出“非黑即白”的答案，说明面试人不善于跳出框框思考。当然，创造力也不应跳脱基本的逻辑，因此，有批判性思维能力的人通常会提出一些具有一定创意但又不失逻辑的解决方案。

（4）答案完整。不少面试题原本就没有“正确”或“错误”的答案，出题者的目的在于测试面试人是否有能力给出一个逻辑清晰、结构完整、内容充实的论述，从而考查面试者的应变能力、语言表达能力和归纳演绎能力等。从某种意义上讲，在面试时我们能做到有理有据地自圆其说就是思辨能力良好的体现。

Project 5
Advanced Skills of Customer Service for CBEC

Knowledge Objectives

1. Master approaches to identify and classify CBEC customers;
2. Master basic strategies of customer maintenance and management.

Competency Objectives

1. Able to effectively identify and classify potential customers;
2. Able to be familiar with the customer follow-up process and have a preliminary management strategy.

Quality Objectives

Develop strong teamwork and critical thinking skills.

Key Points Index

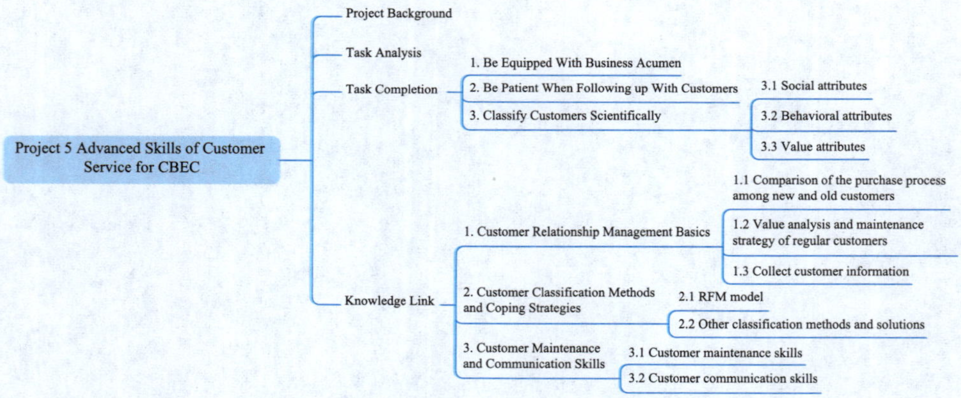

Project Background

Eyre worked very hard since she entered the CBEC business. She was busy in listing products, collecting data, setting up promotion and delivering goods, she simply had no time for herself. But months passed, she found that orders have not increased the way she expected, nor to mention the income he imagined he could receive. On the other hand, Xiao Lin, was much more relaxed. Not only did he make money, but he got the time to stay with his family and friends, which made Eyre really jealous. Why the difference?

Task Analysis

It turned out that Xiao Lin had taken the creation of a localized and personalized customer service experience as his main strategy from the very beginning. He believes that in the cross-border e-commerce field where product homogeneity is becoming more and more common nowadays, traditional elements such as competitive prices, detailed product descriptions, and comprehensive audio and video promotion are not the core competitiveness of sellers. As a result, he refined his business products, devoted more energy to daily customer maintenance, and actively studied the value behind his customers. After some hardwork, the store's customer repurchase rate has been significantly improved, new customers have become regular customers, and regular customers have become important customers, thus the operation of the store has been smoothly on track. Consequently, Eyre humbly asked Xiao Lin for advice:

- How to find and identify valuable customers?
- How to follow up customers?
- How to efficiently manage customers?

Task Completion

1. Be Equipped with Business Acumen

Regular customers and important customers are often converted from retail customers, but not all retail customers can turn to big customers. Therefore, customer service personnel need to have a business acumen to discover potential valuable customers. Although this skill cannot be formed in the short term, there are some commonly used techniques for reference, for example, valuable customers will pay more attention to product richness, pre-stocking, supply and whether they could get corresponding discounts when provided with an increased purchase quantity. In other words, valuable customers pay more attention to profit margins, stable supply of goods, and a wide selection of goods under a certain category, that is to say, stable supply, large wholesale discounts and flexible transportation schemes are the basics for winning valuable customers. As a result, if customer service personnel can actively communicate with customers and consciously analyze customers' historical transaction data and purchase processes, they can form more reliable observations and summaries, thereby fostering the acumen to discover potential valuable customers.

2. Be Patient when Following up with Customers

One of the important reasons why few novices can get big orders is that they lack continuous follow-up strategies to key customers in their customer service work. Inquiries from big customers on CBEC platforms are often sent in batches to multiple Chinese sellers at the same time. After receiving the first round of quotations from multiple sellers, they often make horizontal comparisons on all quotations and logistic services. Therefore, after the quotation, customer service personnel should actively contact the buyer on a regular basis to clarify their demands, and adjust the product price, logistic method, delivery time, and customs clearance methods in a timely manner.

3. Classify Customers Scientifically

Compared with other e-commerce, the customer relationship management of CBEC is more challenging. Therefore, using scientific analysis methods to reasonably distinguish customer groups and providing differentiated goods and services according to the characteristics of different customer groups is of great benefit to improving the marketing efficiency of stores. In general, by analyzing and summarizing various data generated by customers during shopping, we can classify customers from the following three perspectives:

3.1 Social attributes

Since consumers from different countries naturally have different cultural backgrounds and consumer needs, we can classify customers by country according to their addresses in the first place. By laying out country distribution of the main customer groups of the store, one can adjust marketing methods and optimizing products accordingly. For example, a sports shoe that has received rave reviews from the American customers and has a high sales volume may get cold shoulders from the Brazilian buyers. In this case, we can optimize the products in a targeted manner, or design a marketing strategy for Brazilian buyers in Portuguese pages that is suitable for this type of customer group.

3.2 Behavioral attributes

According to different consumption behaviors of customers, typical customer portraits can be depicted. Based on different customer portraits, one can adopt various marketing strategies and communication skills accordingly. For example, after analyzing customer data, we may find that some buyers like to buy discounted goods, they are used to consulting coupons and free shipping. While some customers prefer to choose high-priced products, they concerned about the after-sales terms. Some customers are fastidious, and they may give medium or even bad reviews if improper communication is confirmed. Therefore, summarizing the consumption behavior of different customer groups is actually the basis for understanding the true needs of customers and providing more targeted services.

3.3 Value attributes

In various trading platforms of CBEC, the seller's grading system is strict, meanwhile, each platform also regulates the buyer's level by evaluating their purchasing behavior, transaction amount and review status. Therefore, according to different buyer points and corresponding levels, we can quickly classify and label different customers.

Tips

Measurement of Customer Value

Catering to different enterprise needs and position authority, one of the evaluation methods of value attributes is based on historical orders or search/purchase history, which can be roughly divided into the following four levels:

Level 1: regular customers who have placed orders and potencial customers who have placed pre-orders;

Level 2: customers with strong purchase intention;

Level 3: customers who have clear specifications or price requirements for products;

Level 4: customers with no clear intention and consultation history.

Knowledge Link

1. Customer Relationship Management Basics

Customer Relationship Management (CRM for short) refers to in-depth analysis of customer information, mining potential customer needs, improving customer satisfaction and increasing customer stickiness. It is a means to improve operational efficiency. In the cross-border e-commerce field, customer relationship management uses products as a medium, which helps to shape the store and brand image while digging the potential needs of customers. In the meantime, it gives vitality to the store and helps to improve the store's profits. In other words, customer relationship management is customer-centric and to collect, organize and analyze customer data actively and selectively aiming to establish ideal customer relationships supplemented by tools of marketing, management, data and software. Consequently, marketing thinking is consciously integrated into customer maintenance to increase customer repurchase rate.

1.1 Comparison of the purchase process among new and old customers

The two charts above show us that there are big differences in the process from the search to the completion of a deal between new and regular customers. Generally speaking, new customers enter the store through keyword search, category browsing or advertising. When browsing the store, new customers will subjectively screen information such as product style, product details, evaluation status, price discounts and store reputation. Once they are dissatisfied with any details provided, they may exit the store. That is

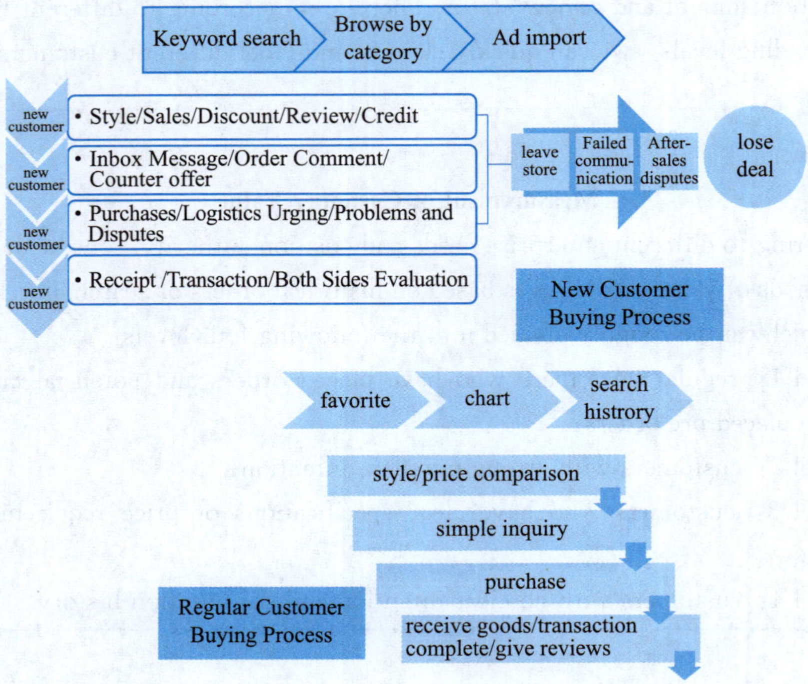

Figure 5 - 1 Purchase Process of Mew and Regular Customers

what we call as the bounce rate. If a new customer consults, compares prices or even completes an order for a product they are interested in, there is still a high possibility that disputes will arise after the transaction due to untimely or inadequate logistics and after-sales services.

In contrast, the buying process for regular or returned customers is much simpler and more efficient. As long as they have a good shopping experience, regular customers pay more attention to the new products and promotions of the store. When they see the products they are interested in, they tend to simply inquire or make the purchase directly; if stock or logistic problems appear, regular customers are relatively easy to communicate, they are more generous and emotional on giving the product reviews. As a result, the dispute rate of regular customers is low. It is not difficult to find that actively managing customers and maintaining them in a targeted manner is an important method to increase store revenue.

1.2 Value analysis and maintenance strategy of regular customers

1.2.1 Increase the repurchase rate

The above chart indicates that the purchase process of regular customers is relatively short. Data shows that the cost of developing a new customer is 7 to 8 times that of maintaining a regular customer. Therefore, the completion of a transaction is not the end of a deal, and mining the potential value of customers and customer circles has a positive significance for improving the repurchase rate of the store and the profit margin of it.

1. 2. 2 Optimize product

Based on good shopping experiences, trust has been built between regular customers and the store. Therefore, in order to seize the opportunity in this highly competitive field, strengthening online and offline communication with regular customers can help to directly obtain their opinions and suggestions on products, so as to optimize or develop products to meet the real needs.

1. 2. 3 Build a brand via word of mouth

With the popularity of cross-border shopping, good products are conducive to penetrating the life circle of foreign buyers, thereby winning a good reputation among customers. The active maintenance of customer social circles can effectively increase customer stickiness. Once a long-term and stable relationship is established, customers are more willing to share products with their family and friends, which can help to gain word of mouth from the customers and build store reputation from there.

Through the value analysis of customers, we can make it clear that actively maintaining customers can not only strengthen customer loyalty to the store, but also greatly reduce the cost of sales. Customer loyalty usually includes: repurchase intention, basic behavior (purchase timing, purchase frequency, purchase quantity, etc.) and derivative behavior (open recommendation, word-of-mouth, customer referral, tipping, etc.).

1. 2. 4 Increase customer loyalty

For brand products, customer loyalty is critical. Because it means that even with other incentives, customers can maintain a preference for the goods or services offered by the store, and even develop resistance to competing products. Moreover, they are willing to conduct positive actions such as re-purchasing, recommending products to others, providing positive word of mouth, etc. Therefore, in order to maintain customers and strengthen brand loyalty, we can adopt service strategies as follows:

1. 2. 4. 1 Regular greetings

In order to maintain a stable communication frequency with customers, we can send emails, postcards or greeting cards to express greetings on customer birthdays or some major festivals, and try to naturally turn transactional relationships into friendships, which is of great benefit to later follow-up work.

1. 2. 4. 2 Reply Priority

The emails of regular customers must be given priority to reply within 24 hours. If it involves complex problems that require much coordinated efforts and cannot be replied in time, be sure to inform the customer in advance: "Your message has been received and is being processed." In that case, make sure the response will be made in three days.

1. 2. 4. 3 Ensure product quality

Only if we ensure product quality under strict quality inspection, customers, especially regular customers will do the purchase repeatedly. Ensuring product quality can not only actively promote the reputation of stores and brands, but lay foundation for further establishment of a positive cycle.

1.2.4.4 Visit customers regularly

Regularly carry out planned follow-up services to customers, and visit customers by mail or in-site messages, so as to obtain customer feedback and suggestions for improvementon product quality and service. It is necessary to let customers have the impression that "our products and services are continuously improved and optimized under the guidance of customer-centric notion".

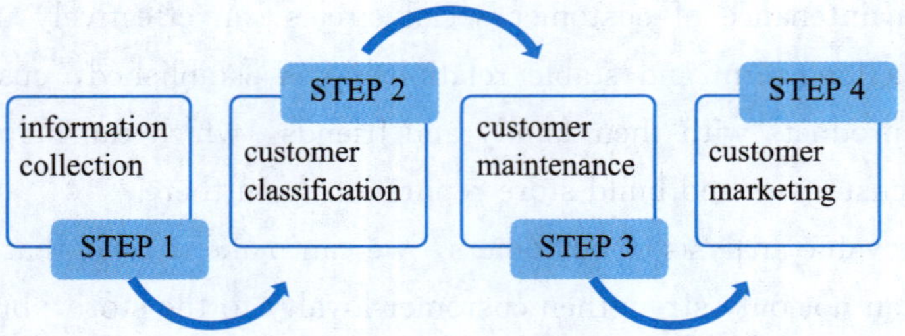

Figure 5-2 Process of Customer Relationship Management

1.3 Collect customer information

Customer relationship management includes four steps, namely: information collection, customer classification, customer maintenance and customer marketing. In this process, information collection is undoubtedly the first step in managing customers. In order to do a good job in information collection, first of all, it is necessary to clarify the path of collecting customer information. In general, the path to collect information is as follows:

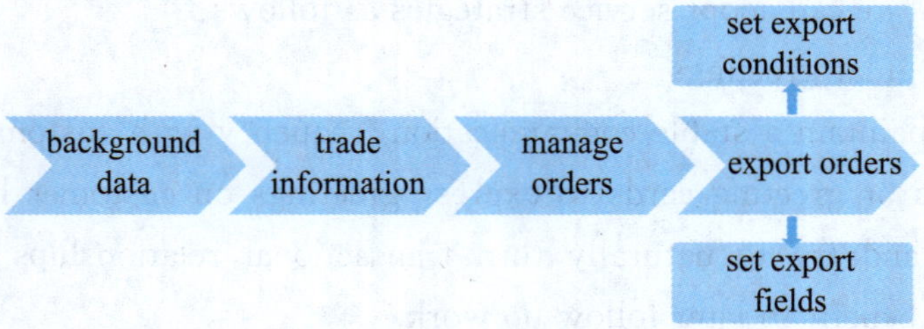

Figure 5-3 Process of Collecting Information

After the orders are exported in batches, we can use the Excel table to sort out the customer information, and filter the contents including user ID, email address, order amount, product information, delivery address, country, contact information, etc., to lay the foundation for further labeling management.

Table 5 - 1 Customer Information Sheet

User	E-mail	Order Detail	Address	Country	Contact	Review	Activity Levels

Based on the basic information of our customers, we can find potential regular customers and carry out targeted marketing. For example, focus on the evaluation status of both buyers and sellers, purchase frequency and purchasing habits to determine whether the customer has the willingness to wholesale, and whether he/she prefers high-priced or low-priced products. Of course, timing is also important when conducting a targeted marketing. In general, we can communicate with key customers through emails or in-site messages at the following time and date:

- When launching high-quality products or promoting new products;
- On special promotion days like Double Eleven, Black Friday and other discount seasons;
- On important festivals, such as Thanksgiving, Christmas, etc., when consumer demand grows rapidly;
- For buyers with fixed purchasing demands, right before the next purchasing.

In addition, when collecting information, we should not only organize explicit ones, but also dig and summarize the implicit information implied by customer data.

2. Customer Classification Methods and Coping Strategies

2.1 RFM model

Customer classification is to facilitate the management of buyers, treat customers in a differentiated way, and provide targeted services to customers. Among many classification methods, RFM model is one of the most widely used classification methods in addition to classifying customers by different attributes (social attributes, behavioral attributes, and value attributes). The name RFM is a combination of the first letters from three keywords:

R (Recency): The latest consumption, that is, the last time a customer made a purchase in the store. In theory, the more recently the customer makes the purchase, the deeper impression the buyer will have for the store. During this period, if we can provide corresponding guidance and services to customers, the possibility of getting responses is extremely high.

F（Frequency）：Consumption frequency，that is，the consumption times in unit time. The more a customer consumes，the higher satisfaction he/she will get. If the seller maintains high-quality services and products，a high level of stickiness will be seen among buyers，and their loyalty to the store will also increase.

M（Monetary）：Consumption amount，that is，ratio of the total consumption to the average consumption in unit time. When the store grows to a certain stage and the customer base is beyond the customer service carrying capacity，we should learn to use resources reasonably and focus on key customer groups. Since 80% of a store's profits often come from 20% of its customers，spending 80% of the effort on maintaining that 20% will yield a higher rate of return.

RFM is a simple and easy-to-use classification model，which can intuitively express the value status of customers by quantifying the three indicators of customers' recent purchase behavior，purchase frequency and consumption amount. For example，we can set the RFM to 3 to 5 stages：the R value refers to the opening time of the store，the characteristics of the product itself and the logistic cycle；the F value refers to the customer reviews and purchase frequency；the M value refers to the price of product.

Table 5-2 Customer Value Evaluation Framework

5	R≤90Days	F≥5times	1000USD≤M
4	90Days<R≤190Days	F=4times	500USD≤M≤1000USD
3	180Days<R≤360Days	F=3times	200USD≤M≤500USD
2	360Days<R≤720Days	F=2times	100USD≤M≤200USD
1	720Days and above	F=1time	M<100USD

Based on the RFM model framework，we can evaluate each customer's specific case.

Table 5-3 Customer Value Evaluation Form

customer	R	Rscore	F	Fscore	M	Mscore	RFMscore
Jack	80	5	1	1	22	1	7
Lucy	320	3	2	2	734	4	9
John	600	2	3	3	280	3	8
Peter	106	4	3	3	586	4	11
Cici	736	1	4	4	102	2	7

In this form，Jack's latest consumption is within 80 days，so the corresponding R score is 5；the consumption time is 1，so the F score is 1；the consumption amount is 22， and the M score is 1, in total, the customer's RFM score is 7 points. Through the RFM model, it is not difficult to find that a customer with highest transaction value is not necessarily the one with highest score; and the lowest score does not indicate the customer has the lowest transaction value. Therefore, customer value is not only a reflection of the transaction amount, but through the design and quantification of RFM model. We can screen out high-quality customers and prepare for precise marketing.

2.2 Other classification methods and solutions

According to the customer's consumption behavior, personality and specific psychology profile, we can carry out tagging management on the customer group, and use corresponding strategies to improve the quality of customer service.

2.2.1 Classification and strategies catering to customer personality

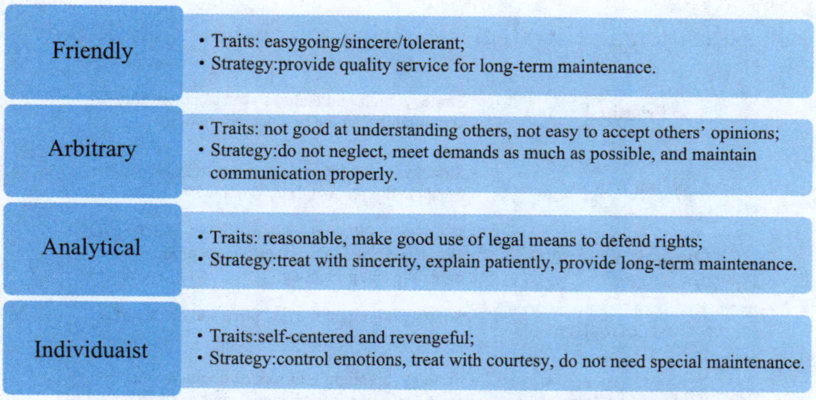

Figure 5-4 Customer Personality Types and Strategies

2.2.2 Classification and strategies catering to purchasing behavior

Figure 5-5 Customer Purchasing Behavior Types and Strategies

2.2.3 Classification and strategies of common questions from customers

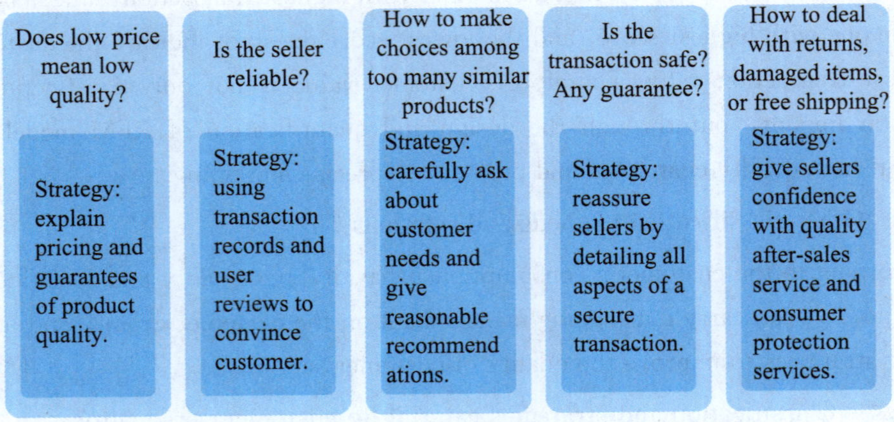

Figure 5-6 Common Questions from Customers and Strategies

2.2.4 Classification and strategies catering to consumer psychology

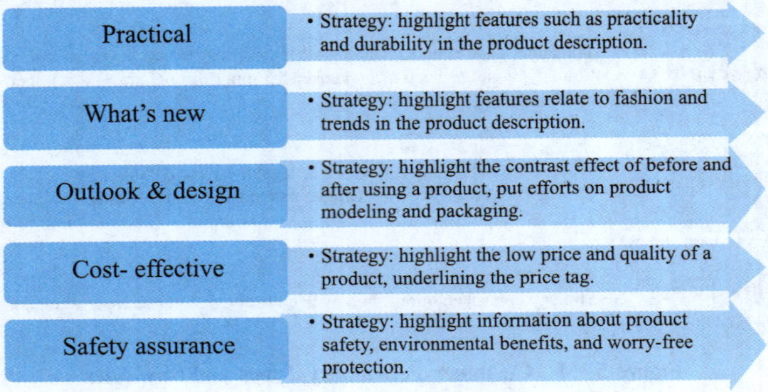

Figure 5-7 Classification of Consumer Psychology and Strategies

3. Customer Maintenance and Communication Skills

3.1 Customer maintenance skills

Satisfaction comes from every transaction. The continuous accumulation of satisfaction can not only increase customers' trust in the store, but also help the conversion of new and regular customers. Proper use of the following customer maintenance techniques can effectively improve their satisfaction.

3.1.1 Before receiving the goods

● Send messages to say thank you for each transaction. Any order placed by a customer is the beginning of building trust between two parties, and a simple "thank you" message is an indicator of that trust.

● Prepare give aways. It is recommended to choose stamps, pendants, greeting cards, paper-cuts and items that take up no space as give aways. A proper small gift can directly improve a customer's favorability of the store.

● Shipping Notice. Once a package is shipped, send a timely delivery notification to the customer, and always keep an eye on the logistic status. In case of abnormal situations such as flight congestion and delayed delivery, the customer should be notified in time and the delivery date should be extended accordingly.

3.1.2 After receiving the goods

● Comment on reward. After a customer confirms the receipt of a product, based on the product experiences and attentive service he/she has owned, in general, the buyer does not resist giving good comments on the shopping experience. At this point, sellers can give out coupons, discounts and other forms of promotions to actively urge customers give positive rates and reviews, while stimulate them to place orders again.

● Share on reward. Encourage and reward customers to share products or shopping experiences is a good opportunity for the store to join the customer's social circle.

● Exclusive day promotion. Consumers will soon be reluctant to receive information on regular promotions or announcements about new arrivals if the store sets no special marketing scheme. Therefore, setting up several exclusive days as special promotions for the customer may stimulate new purchases. For example, right after an order was completed (known as the "honeymoon period"), the store could present a "honeymoon gift" to the customer: "We are glad to find you were satisfied with our goods and give us five-star feedback, this means a lot to us and will keep us moving forward. Since now you are a VIP customer in our store, we have some special offers for you, please check out the following link to find out more." Similarly, targeted marketing activities like "30 days promotion", "100 days promotion" can also be conducted later on: "My Dear VIP Friend, today is the 100th day since we met, a $5 coupon has been prepared for you, enjoy shopping, my friend!" As a result, continuous promotion will attract customer's attention to the store, and the longer the promotion keeps, the more it will bring to the store.

● Relevant recommendation. Recommendation of relevant products based on what customers have already purchased may lead to more deals. Related products include vertical recommendation: for example, if a customer buys a wig, a special comb for wigs can be recommended; and horizontal recommendation: if a customer buys a straight wig, a curly wig can be recommended.

3.1.3 Maintenance frequency

One of the purposes of maintaining customers is to deepen the customer's impression of the store. Therefore, when we contact customers, we need to pay attention not only to the content of our messages, but also to the frequency of sending the message. Don't be in a hurry for quick success, we need to maintain a long-lasting relationship with customers. According to human memory cycle, we can seize 1, 2, 4, 7, and 15 as the proper timing for making the contact.

For example，when a customer places an order，we could send a "thank you" message and relevant product recommendations to the customer on the very first day; then send the logistic tracing notification and targeted coupons on the second day; inform the logistics information and comment on reward activity on the 4th day; inform sharing on reward activity and send a reminder to use coupons on the 7th day; update the logistics status and give holiday greetings to customers on the 15th day.

3.2 Customer communication skills

3.2.1 Professional services

3.2.1.1 Solve problems from a professional perspective

First of all，customer service personnel need to understand the importance of specialization，make efforts to improve the professional level of the work to help customers solve problems from a professional perspective. For example，when a complicated problem occurs，a customer specialist can clearly explain the real cause of the problem; or when it comes to terminologies，a customer service specialist can work down to earth to translate jargons into everyday languages to our customers; again，when negotiating solutions，a customer specialist can propose responsible and effective solutions according to specific circumstances，rather than putting things off or delaying processing.

In fact，it's not a bad thing for sellers to have customers questioning or complaining about problems they encounter. As long as the problem can be solved，the whole process can be to channel to effectively deepen the customer's sense of trust with the store，thereby forming customer stickiness. In other words，customer service personnel should take each problem-solving process as an opportunity to demonstrate their professional ability. Aided by professional toolkits and attitudes，problems will be solved properly and new customers will be ultimately turned into regular customers.

3.2.1.2 Provide reliable references

Due to long distance，multiple procedures，language and culture differences between the stores and customers，the incidence of cross-border shopping problems is much higher than that of domestic e-commerce. Therefore，whether in the face of customer inquiries or dealing with knotty problems，a customer service specialist should provide "visible and tangible" evidences as much as possible.

For products，we can use detailed pictures，detailed descriptions or short videos that can explain the details of the product as reliable references; on the logistic side，quantitative data such as parcel number，tracking URL，logistics updates are more intuitive. It should be noted that when customer service personnel provide evidence to customers，they should provide and clarify as much information as possible: complete logistics tracing information，logistics tracking websites in the buyer's country and other professional data in need.

3.2.1.3 Prepare diversified response

Customers can find numerous of high-quality products on CBEC platforms, as a result, problems may occur when they try to assemble a product or conduct post-maintenance of a product. Normally, manufactures will provide explanatory texts for customer service personnel to refer to, so when customers ask about technical problems, customer service personnel can search through texts for technical parameters, installation and application tips to respond customers with clear directions. However, when facing complex issues, text explanations may not necessarily solve the problem completely. Therefore, making "installation flowchart" or "video directions" could provide a more efficient way to respond customers and solve their problems.

3.2.2 Take the initiative

An excellent customer service specialist can not only handle angry customers, but also guide them to actively solve problems. Here are some tips to refer to:

3.2.2.1 Actively respond to customers

Customers may not familiar with complex international logistics in CBEC, or they cannot understand the user guide of a product. As a result, customers may show up with anxieties. In that case, the first thing a customer service specialist should do is to actively respond to customers and objectively analyze the problem from the customer's end. After the customer calms down, remember to assure the consumer that the problem can be and will be solved in no time.

3.2.2.2 Show gratitude

The idea of being grateful or giving thanks for good deals or customers is an obvious virtue in Western culture, and "Thanksgiving" is a typical representative. If a customer service specialist can always show a grateful attitude to customers, it will be beneficial to the smooth resolution of complaints and the creation of an impressive store image.

3.2.2.3 The last email

Emails, site messages and order comments are common channels for a customer service specialist to get in touch with a client. Based on business etiquette rules, normally the seller should send the last email when communicating with a buyer, and this last message has a certain positive effect on winning favor of a customer. In fact, the back-end system of the CBEC platform can count the average response time of site messages or order comments of a store. The shorter the average response time, the higher the efficiency, which also indicates the great services that a store can provide. Therefore, as a customer service specialist, sending the last email to customers is not only out of courtesy, but a reflection of quality service.

3.2.3 Responsibities

3.2.3.1 Be reasonable

When facing with dissatisfaction or complaints, a customer service specialist needs to find a sound and acceptable reason to respond to the customer, and this reason is preferably caused by a third party or force majeure. In fact, this rational explanation makes it easier for customers to accept the seller's proposed solution, which helps to resolve disputes efficiently.

3.2.3.2 Be responsible

Respond with rational explanation does not mean that a customer service specialist takes no responsibility. In order to better serve customers, a customer service specialist should take the efficiency of solving problems as a priority. In practical terms, reasonably attributing the blame to the third party and defining our position as "even if the fault is not ours, we are willing to solve the problems for our customer" can often ease the customer's anger and favorably reach a solution. In the long run, only by taking customers as our friends, helping them solve problems quickly and thoroughly with sincerity, can we win their trust over time.

Exercises

1. Multiple Choices

(1) Generally speaking, from what aspects can we classify customers of CBEC platforms? (　　)

A. From social attributes

B. From behavioral attributes

C. From value attributes

D. All of the above

(2) What is the meaning of customer relationship management? (　　)

A. CRM as in-depth analysis of customer information, it helps mining potential customer needs

B. CRM helps to improve customer satisfaction and customer stickiness

C. CRM helps to improve operational efficiency

D. All of the above

(3) The importance of actively maintain our regular customers lies in (　　).

A. Maintaining regular customers helps to increase the repurchase rate, optimize product and ensure product quality

B. Maintaining regular customers helps to increase the repurchase rate, optimize product and increase customer loyalty

C. Maintaining regular customers helps to build a brand with word of mouth, optimize product and ensure product quality

D. Maintaining regular customers helps to shorten the purchasing process, build a brand with word of mouth and ensure product quality

(4) What does RFM refer to? ( )

A. Rates/Friendly/Money B. Rates/Frequency/Money

C. Recency/Frequency/Monetary D. Recency/Friendly/Money

(5) As customer service specialists, we communicate with customers in a timely manner according to a relatively reasonable maintenance frequency. Which of the following frequencies is more appropriate when practicing customer maintenance? ( )

A. 1、2、4、7、9 B. 1、2、4、7、15

C. 1、3、5、7、9 D. 1、3、5、7、15

2. True or False

(1) A customer service specialist in CBEC only needs to communicate with customers in time. ( )

(2) A customer service specialist must take the initiative to bear mistakes no matter what the circumstances. ( )

(3) A customer service specialist needs to provide reliable evidence when communicating with customers. ( )

(4) A customer service specialist should save time and effort in serving regular customers, while concentrating to work on new customers. ( )

(5) When a customer service specialist successfully solve a problem, and the customer replied with a "thank you" message, normally, the customer service specialist do not need to reply to such information. ( )

Skills&Drills

1. Short Answer Questions

(1) Briefly describe the suitable timing for customer service personnel to conduct secondary marketing.

(2) Briefly describe the customer communication skills of a CBEC customer service specialist.

2. Case Study

During the shopping season of Christmas, when consumers are busy with big promotions, a group of online fraudsters are itch for action. A large number of Amazon users have posted on Facebook and Twitter that they have encountered false email scams, and many netizens have leaked important personal information.

People who received the scam emails were Amazon users located in UK, US, Australia and other regions. Some people were told that "the order could not be shipped", and "they could not access their Amazon account" . The only way to recover their account is by clicking the link in the email. It is said that the recipient is required to enter personal information like name, mobile phone number, address and bank card number to get the link. And right after entering personal information and clicking save, the page will automatically redirect to Amazon's official website, making people ignore the fact that they have been deceived.

Similarly, in other cases, consumer will receive an "order confirmation" email, claiming that the user's order has been confirmed, along with information such as order details and an estimated delivery date. If the user has not purchased the item, the order can be cancelled through the link in the email.

In addition to the above scams, there is another one known as "redeem gift cards": a user who posted on Twitter and @Amazon's official account said that he received an email and was told that he had received a gift card worth 110 euros. In order to activate the gift card, he needed to click on the link provided in the email. However, Amazon responded to the user that they had never sent such email.

With the continuous popularity of CBEC, consumers should be alert with "benefits", they received through unofficial channels when purchasing, in other words, they need to strengthen their precautions when their personal information are required.

Question: If a customer is facing similar problems and comes to the store to ask for help, as a qualified customer service specialist, how will you respond?

Reference answer

Mock Interview in Moral Education

A qualified CBEC customer service specialist needs to equipped with basic qualities such as empathy, efficiency and resilience, but if we want to further improve our professional skills, based on the goal of creating new customer shopping experience, we should actively master and practice another two key skills, namely, discernment and team spirit.

1. Discernment

The roots for customer service lies in "comprehensive and in-depth analysis of target products and target customers", which means, in order to achieve strategic success, we need to gain the foresight of the company's own environment and product characteristics, the foresight of competitor product information, the foresight of industry development trends, and the foresight of target customers (groups) needs. As the saying goes "knowing the enemy and knowing yourself", we must concentrate on cultivating analysis capabilities for different customer groups, and intensively enhance professional attainments of customer service. In fact, having a clear understanding of the industry and its influence on marketing is not only a reflection of the analysis ability of an excellent customer service specialist, but also a way for cross-border enterprises to win the industry opportunities. Only by adhering to the spirit of reform and innovation, can we deeply practice the values of "distinguishing truth from falsehood with 'vision' and serving customers with 'quality'".

2. Team Spirit

Customer service is an important part in the CBEC operation system. Customer service involves communication and coordination in all aspects such as warehouses, products and logistics. Therefore, good team spirit not only ensures a faster and more accurate response to customers, but also maintains a good relationship with cross-functional teams to get support and assistance when needed. As a result, great teamwork is also an essential quality of a good customer service specialist.

3. Mock Interview

3.1 Mini-interview

Suppose you have received an interview notice from a leading cross-border enterprise for the position of customer service personnel. In order to fully demonstrate your professionalism in the interview, please work in pairs to conduct a mock interview with your partner, choose 3 to 5 questions from the question listed below, and record each other's performance.

No.	Questions
1	Tell us about a time where a project did not go as planned. What can be done to avoid a similar problem in the future?
2	Have you ever needed to make an important decision quickly?
3	Tell us about a time you work successfully within a team.
4	Have you ever foreseen a problem before it happened? What did you do to prevent this from happening?
5	Imagine that you come to work to see that you have been sent 1,000 emails overnight. If you only have time to answer 200 of them, how would you decide which 200 emails to respond to?
6	A customer has come up to you with a problem while you are in the middle of talking to your manager about something very important. How would you react to this?
7	How do you keep yourself motivated when customers take their frustrations on you?
8	How do you measure success?
9	While in a meeting, your co-worker suggests a solution to a problem that you know will not work. Do you voice your concern to the team in the meeting?
10	What steps do you take when addressing a problem?

续表

No.	Questions
11	Describe a time when you noticed a problem at work and came up with a solution to fix it.
12	Tell us about a time when you set a lofty goal for yourself and achieved it. What steps did you take to make it happen?
13	If your manager made a mistake on an important document, how would you go about addressing it?
14	Is it better to increase prices to gain profit or lower prices to make customers happy?
15	Suppose you need to alert a customer because your product/service contains a major problem, how will you handle that task?

3.2 Evaluation and Review

After the mini-interview, we are now at a more critical stage of this practice: self-evaluation and peer evaluation. In fact, the process of answering the questions and evaluating performance afterwards is a perfect application of critical thinking. The more detailed and creative answers to the questions, the more we can discover about the personal features of a candidate, so as to conduct more objective evaluations. Generally speaking, evaluation can be carried out from the following aspects:

● Being logical. Critical thinkers do not let prejudice or stereotypes influence their decision. When answering questions, they are good at taking different situations into consideration and they tend to organize their answers logically. Therefore, a listener can easily grasp key points when listening to their presentations, and that's how we efficiently deliver information to others.

● Being convincing. Critical thinkers will not be influenced by subjective emotions. They are good at digging out key evidence or clues, making appropriate logical deductions based on facts other than making hasty conclusions. In fact, it is just because of the solid arguments that their views are generally convincing.

● Being innovative. Critical thinkers are also quite creative. If you hearing a "black or white" answer from an interviewer, it may show that the interviewer is not good at thinking outside the box. Apparently, creativity also comes from logic thinking, that's why people with critical thinking skills often come up with creative but logical solutions.

● Being complete. In fact, many critical thinking questions do not have the "right" or "wrong" answers. In order to test the interviewee's adaptability, language and inductive ability, questions are designed to figure out whether or not the candidate is able to give a thought-out answer backed by logical reasoning, complete structure and adequate content that makes sense. In this regard, the fact that we can justify ourselves in an interview is a good reflection of decent critical thinking skills.

参考文献

［1］Bennett，M. J. Becoming interculturally competent. In J. S. Wurzel（Ed.）Toward multiculturalism：A reader in multicultural education. Newton，MA：Intercultural Resource Corporation，2004.

［2］Bennett，M. Interactive Methods for Teaching about Cultural Differences. WISE Conference，North Carolina，USA. 2016.

［3］Cornum，R.，Matthews，M. D.，Seligman，M. E. P. Comprehensive Fitness：Building resilience in a challenging institutional context. American Psychologist，2011，66（1），4－9. doi：10. 1037/a0021420.

［4］Griffith，J.，West，C. Master Resilience Training and Its Relationship to Individual Well-Being and Stress Buffering among Army National Guard. Journal of Behavioral Health Services & Research，2013，40（2），140－155. doi：10. 1007/s11414－013－9320－8.

［5］Hyder，Z. J. Intercultural Competence：The Intersection of Intercultural Sensitivity and Self-Authorship. University of Tennessee Honors Thesis Projects，USA. 2015.

［6］Kim，Juram，Lim，Chiehyeon. Customer complaints monitoring with customer review data analytics：An integrated method of sentiment and statistical process control analyses. Advanced Engineering Informatics，2021（08），49. doi：10. 1016/j. aei. 2021. 101304.

［7］King，T. Development of Student Skills in Reflective Writing. University of Portsmouth，UK. 2002.

［8］Spreng，R. N.，McKinnon，M. C.，Mar，R. A.，& Levine，B. The Toronto Empathy Questionnaire：Scale development and initial validation of a factor-analytic solution to multiple empathy measures. Journal of Personality Assessment，2009，91（1）：62－71.

［9］Seligman，M. E. P. Building Resilience. Harvard Business Review，2011，89（4）：100.

［10］Shapiro，S. L. Rewire your mind：Discover the science ＋ practice of mindfulness. London：Aster. 2020.

［11］高莉莉．基于跨境电商的跨文化交际能力提升策略研究［J］．安徽电气工程职业技术学院学报，2018（2）.

［12］邓志新，赵秀娟，金珞欣，谭立静．跨境电商：理论操作与实务［M］．北京：人民邮电出版社，2018.

［13］韩雪．跨境电商客服［M］．北京：中国人民大学出版社，2018.

［14］柯丽敏，洪方仁．跨境电商理论与实务［M］．2 版．北京：中国海关出版社，2019.

[15] 刘宓庆．汉英对比与翻译（修订本）[M]．南昌：江西教育出版社，1992.

[16] 樊卫宾，窦菀．高中思政课学生自主辨析能力培养 [J]．思想政治课教学，2021 (5).

[17] 刘敏，高田歌．跨境电子商务沟通与客服 [M]．北京：电子工业出版社，2017.

[18] 速卖通培训中心．跨境电商客服：阿里巴巴速卖通宝典 [M]．北京：电子工业出版社，2015.

[19] 汪旭晖，赵博．跨境网购中消费者动态信任的构建——基于天猫国际、京东全球购和网易考拉的质性研究 [J]．营销科学学报，2019，15 (1).

[20] 易静，樊金琪，彭洋．跨境电子商务客户服务 [M]．北京：人民邮电出版社，2019.

[21] Edesk 网站：https://www. edesk. com.

[22] Helpscout 设计系统：https://www. helpscout. com.

[23] Hiver 网站：https://hiverhq. com.

[24] Hubspot 网站：https://blog. hubspot. com.

[25] 阿里巴巴国际站规则：https://rule. alibaba. com.

[26] 百度百科：https://baike. baidu. com.

[27] 百度文库：https://wenku. baidu. com.

[28] 哈佛商业评论网：https://hbr. org/2016/06/627.

[29] 行业会展网：http://www. 31expo. com.

[30] 家世比网站：http://www. homebi. com.

[31] 求是网：http://www. qstheory. cn.

[32] 知乎网：https://www. zhihu. com.

[33] 中国会展门户：http://www. cnena. com/.

[34] 雨果网：Http://www. cif news. com/ask/question/3721.

[35] AliExpress EU/EEA 卖家加入和运营评估规则 2021.

图书在版编目（CIP）数据

跨境电商客服 ：双语 / 张敏，茹宝主编 . -- 北京 ：
中国人民大学出版社，2023.1
新编 21 世纪高等职业教育精品教材. 电子商务类
ISBN 978-7-300-31071-8

Ⅰ. ①跨… Ⅱ. ①张… ②茹… Ⅲ. ①电子商务-商
业服务-双语教学-高等职业教材-教材 Ⅳ.
①F713.36

中国版本图书馆 CIP 数据核字（2022）第 185698 号

教育部首批国家级职业教育教师教学创新团队电子商务专业领域实践课题（跨境电子商务核心课程新形态教材和教学资源建设，项目编号：SJ2020110102）建设成果
国家级“跨境电子商务综合服务应用技术协同创新中心”建设成果
浙江金融职业学院电子商务与新消费研究院建设成果
中国特色高水平高职专业群（国际贸易实务）建设成果
浙江金融职业学院课程思政领航专业建设成果
新编 21 世纪高等职业教育精品教材・电子商务类

跨境电商客服（双语）

主 编 张 敏 茹 宝
副主编 杨 莹 刘东光 秦诗雨 卓佳妮 吕方伊

Kuajing Dianshang Kefu（Shuangyu）

出版发行	中国人民大学出版社		
社　　址	北京中关村大街 31 号	**邮政编码**	100080
电　　话	010－62511242（总编室）		010－62511770（质管部）
	010－82501766（邮购部）		010－62514148（门市部）
	010－62515195（发行公司）		010－62515275（盗版举报）
网　　址	http://www.crup.com.cn		
经　　销	新华书店		
印　　刷	中煤（北京）印务有限公司		
规　　格	185 mm×260 mm　16 开本	**版　　次**	2023 年 1 月第 1 版
印　　张	11.5 插页 1	**印　　次**	2024 年 8 月第 2 次印刷
字　　数	265 000	**定　　价**	35.00 元
